Plagiaris[m]
Learning

Written for High[...]
Internet and Stud[...]
model of plagiari[...]
a new way to co[...]
dealing with pla[...]

Sutherland-Sm[...]
which usefully in[...]
educational settin[...]
of plagiarism wit[...]
perceive, and res[...]
birth in Law to a[...]
cultural settings.[...]
discussing the co[...]
between institutio[...]
qualitative empiri[...] explain why it has emerged as a major issue. The book examines current teaching approaches in light of issues surrounding plagiarism, particularly Internet plagiarism. The model affords insight into ways in which teaching and learning approaches can be enhanced to cope with the ever-changing face of plagiarism. This book challenges Higher Education educators, managers and policy-makers to examine their own beliefs and practices in managing the phenomenon of plagiarism in academic writing.

Wendy Sutherland-Smith is a Senior Lecturer in the Faculty of Education at Monash University, Australia. She has been actively involved in researching issues of plagiarism in academic writing for the past decade, including her doctoral research thesis. She has recently spearheaded a year-long funded research project to gauge the effectiveness of commercial anti-plagiarism software in universities. Wendy is an active member of the international academic integrity community and her research interests span issues of cyberethics, social justice and ethics in education.

Plagiarism, the Internet and Student Learning

Improving Academic Integrity

Wendy Sutherland-Smith

Routledge
Taylor & Francis Group

NEW YORK AND LONDON

First published 2008
by Routledge
270 Madison Ave, New York, NY 10016

Simultaneously published in the UK
by Routledge
2 Park Square, Milton Park, Abingdon, Oxon OX14 4RN

Routledge is an imprint of the Taylor & Francis Group, an informa business

© 2008 Taylor and Francis

Typeset in Minion and Trade Gothic by
Florence Production Ltd, Stoodleigh, Devon
Printed and bound in the United States of America on acid-free paper by
Edward Brothers, Inc

Library of Congress Cataloging in Publication Data
Sutherland-Smith, Wendy.
    Plagiarism, the Internet, and student learning: improving academic
    integrity/Wendy Sutherland-Smith.
        p. cm.
    Includes bibliographical references and index.
    1. Plagiarism.   2. Internet research—Moral and ethical aspects.
    I. Title.
    PN167.S88 2008
    808–dc22   200704404

ISBN 10: 0–415–43292–8 (hbk)
ISBN 10: 0–415–43293–6 (pbk)
ISBN 10: 0–203–92837–7 (ebk)

ISBN 13: 978–0–415–43292–4 (hbk)
ISBN 13: 978–0–415–43293–1 (pbk)
ISBN 13: 978–0–203–92837–0 (ebk)

For Ilana Snyder—teacher, mentor and friend

Contents

Acknowledgments

It is ironic that this book, which challenges the notion of sole authorship, should begin by bearing my name only. There are so many people who have contributed to this work over the past seven years with ideas, assistance, encouragement and support that the notion of sole authorship is an absurdity. My thanks to the following:

I wish to acknowledge Mark Warschauer from the University of California, Irvine, who suggested I write this book and supported my efforts with practical advice. My thanks to Helen Pritt, formerly of Routledge, London, for her excellent advice and guidance during the proposal stage of this manuscript. I also wish to thank the extremely helpful editors at Routledge, New York—Sarah Burrows and, most particularly, Meg Savin. Without their insights and willingness to discuss and support my ideas, this book would not have progressed from proposal to publication.

I could not have begun this project, completed the data collection or analyzed the information without the support of the staff and students at South-Coast University. I am grateful to them all for sharing their perspectives and insights into plagiarism. A number of colleagues from Monash University have provided me with support during the completion of this book. My thanks to Margaret Somerville, Lesley Farrell, Ann Ryan, Scott Webster and Ilana Snyder for their ongoing enthusiasm and support. I am indebted to Terry O'Keeffe for her insights "from the chalkface" and to Heather Phillips for her invaluable assistance with manuscript preparation.

I also acknowledge the many people with whom I have discussed plagiarism over the years. Special thanks to Jude Carroll from Oxford

Brookes University, Sue Saltmarsh from Charles Sturt University, Janette Ryan and Sharon Gardner-Drummond from Monash University, Alaia Devey and Rodney Carr from Deakin University, Ishbel Galloway and Marti Sevier from Simon Fraser University and Diane Pecorari from Mälardalen University. Some of the ideas in Chapters 2 and 5 originally appeared in articles I published in *The Journal of Asia-Pacific Communication* (2005, 15(1), 15–30) and the *Journal of English for Academic Purposes* (2005, 4(1), 83–95), although this book fleshes out and expands some of those preliminary ideas.

Completing this work has been possible only because of the love and support of my family. I wish to acknowledge Bernard Smith and thank him for his patience and the thousands of cups of tea he has provided since I began preliminary work on plagiarism in 1999. My daughters, Kathryn and Sarah, have been incredibly understanding when meals have been burned and their appointments forgotten during the preparation of this work. Their unfailing support has made writing this book a worthwhile endeavor. Finally, special thanks to my father, Thomas Henry Douglas Sutherland, who lived the example that ethical teachers can and must lead education into the future as transformative intellectuals.

Prologue

It is a Monday afternoon and we sit around a large oval table in the Dean's meeting room at South-Coast University in Melbourne, Australia—six teachers, one university policy-writer and myself. I am wearing two hats— one as a teacher of 18 years' standing in both secondary and tertiary classrooms and the other is as an academic researcher. We are there because university management feels a crisis is looming over acts of plagiarism by its students. There is widespread concern voiced by academic staff, language support staff and international student liaison officers at the increasing number of students facing disciplinary procedures in various faculties for acts of plagiarism, collusion and cheating. International students—most of whom speak, read and write English as a second, third or foreign language (ESL/EFL)—are the highest proportion of students appearing before the University Disciplinary Board. The question is, why is this the case? Is it that international students get caught more frequently than local students for plagiarism? Do international students actually plagiarize more than locally based students, or are they unfamiliar with our academic writing conventions? Are there other factors at play in the mix?

As a teacher for over 18 years, I have been troubled about some of my students appearing before the various disciplinary committees. As a member of different disciplinary committees for the past five years, I am anxious about the effect of committee approaches, which are usually punitive in nature, on students' learning. Many of the students at plagiarism hearings appear devastated by the experience—before the "outcome" is even reached. Most maintain they were not aware they were breaching academic protocols. One of my many worries is that despite receiving penalties, many students do not seem to be able to "fix" the problem of plagiarism in their writing, as often they reappear before the committee in other subjects or in later years of study. Again, the following questions arise. Do penalties work? Are they simply ignored or not able to be enforced? A much more telling question is, what are the effects of punitive measures on the learning and teaching relationship?

Despite my fears, there are also other students appearing before the University Disciplinary Committee who readily admit that they have plagiarized whole assignments over many years, but have never been caught before. Some students in this situation claim that it as an indictment on the quality of education that they have successfully plagiarized and cheated their way through undergraduate courses and have avoided detection and punishment. It strikes me that there is little of educative value in either experience: one devastating to the student as a negative learning experience and the other missing the point of "intellectual engagement" required in any form of study. These issues have plagued me as a teacher for many years, so I proposed that the university form a "Plagiarism Working Party," as part of my ongoing research investigating the phenomenon of plagiarism in tertiary classrooms. Our task is to probe the complexities of the problem—particularly as it relates to Internet plagiarism—and to try to tease out the underlying issues. Why, for example, when students know there are penalties do they keep on plagiarizing? What can we, as teachers, do to help students realize that plagiarism undermines the kind of intellectual activity we value? Can we actually stop the problem, if it's as rife as the media suggests? The Working Party decided to investigate how plagiarism is perceived by students and staff, in light of their experiences and the overriding university policy, in order to consider how we might improve teaching and learning. But I wanted to do more than just that. Plagiarism is not just an Australian, English, American or Western issue—it's a global and ongoing matter of academic integrity. I wanted to probe the pathways students and teachers take in arriving at cases of plagiarism, and investigate ways in which to bridge the gap between plagiarism policy and plagiarism in practice.

This book is about the very essence of plagiarism and our experiences and concerns as teachers. It draws on perceptions of plagiarism in academic writing in countries such as Australia, Canada, China, New Zealand, the United Kingdom and the United States of America. The chapters that follow detail the experiences, reflections and concepts of plagiarism of classroom teachers and language support staff who deal with plagiarism in their students' work. The voices of the 186 students from 18 different countries for whom ESL or EFL are captured as international students relate their experiences of plagiarism when studying in a "Western" academic institution. The policies that construct the ways in which plagiarism is dealt with in our educational institutions are also discussed. The patchwork of perspectives presented in this book will resonate with many teachers, students and policy-makers involved in dealing with plagiarism in academic writing.

Plagiarism is a complex notion—and deceptively so. Although it appears easy to define the term and allocate a range of penalties for the act—that approach ignores the layered reality of the issue. Plagiarism carries negative connotations of dishonesty or cheating. Often people against whom allegations of plagiarism are made find themselves under public scrutiny—whether in university or college settings or in the broader community. Where plagiarism is reported, public debate and emotions can, and most often do, run high. Recently, two authors in England's High Court sued the author of the international best-selling novel *The Da Vinci Code*, Dan Brown, for plagiarism. They argued that the central idea of a conspiracy theory surrounding the alleged relationship between Christ and Mary Magdalene and the child of their union was plagiarized from their 1982 book *Holy Blood, Holy Grail*. Although *Holy Blood, Holy Grail* authors Michael Baigent and Richard Leigh lost their appeal to the English High Court, the case attracted international press coverage, public debate and speculation.[1] Heated public opinion about the case was voiced in the media in places as far away from London as Australia and New Zealand. But why is there such anger and outrage over allegations of plagiarism? What is it about the act of plagiarism that causes such angst? In short, why do people who are not immediately involved in allegations get so upset and feel it is their right to publicly decry plagiarists?

Part of the answer to this reaction lies in the historical development of Western notions of what it means to be an author—and the rights attached to authorship. How did plagiarism arise to assume such a controversial place in the life of teachers and students in the twenty-first century? The historical development of plagiarism from its roots in the English courts provides a clear foundation for understanding why plagiarism policies in our schools, colleges and universities are written as they are. Understanding the inherent connection between the discourse of plagiarism and its birth in the law enables teachers to deconstruct some of the management issues surrounding plagiarism. There is a clear link between legal notions of what it means to plagiarize—as captured in legal discourse, and the way in which plagiarism is regulated and meaning constructed in our university and college policies and practices. These policies often specify the ways in which plagiarism is to be handled in our institutions and in doing so, regulate the teaching and learning relationship between teachers and their students. This can cause great friction between the dictates of policy and the reality of practice in our classrooms.

To help frame our thinking about plagiarism, an innovative model of plagiarism based on the empirical research outlined above is presented in Chapter 1. The model—the plagiarism continuum—suggests lenses through which issues of plagiarism and classroom practice can be explored both by teachers and policy-makers. In the model, I have combined the views of teachers and students with cross-disciplinary understandings of plagiarism from law, literary theory and cultural studies as a new way in which to think about and act on issues of plagiarism. It is called the plagiarism continuum for two reasons: first, because plagiarism is a concept moving along a continuum of thinking—people and institutions perceive plagiarism in various ways. Second, it is a continuum because plagiarism does not remain static. To be more specific, individual students and teachers have mixed ideas about what constitutes plagiarism. This is also true for university administrators, policy-makers and members of various disciplinary committees or academic progress committees hearing allegations of student plagiarism. Therefore, any model of plagiarism must be open-ended to suggest that there will be changes and movements in understanding plagiarism as a phenomenon. Also, perceptions of plagiarism shift over time and space. The concerns about plagiarism that existed in the fifteenth century are not necessarily the same concerns that emerge in the "technoliterate"[2] world of hyperspace in the twenty-first century. Plagiarism also changes as writing evolves—from the fifteenth-century legal protection of quill and ink text as property, to current wrangling over hypertext and Internet intellectual property.

This book is of interest and value to teachers first and foremost. These teachers operate in a variety of educational settings and the teachers' voices in this book will represent those involved in teaching international students in mainstream university courses, bridging or transition programs and college preparation courses. The chapters discussing both the perspectives of teachers and students about plagiarism address questions often raised in teaching international students, but the situations described by teachers are pertinent to first language speakers of English as well as ESL and EFL students. The book is also of great interest to educators and administrators involved in the design of plagiarism policy and its implementation. Administrators and policy-makers alike will benefit from reading not only the voices of teachers and students from the classroom, but also their specific concerns about the divide between policy and practice. The plagiarism continuum model is designed to help all these groups reflect on and negotiate the complexities of plagiarism in our educational institutions.

Plan of the Book

Chapter 1 sets the scene and provides an overview of key issues surrounding plagiarism. Some of the key issues as well as teachers' responses are outlined in this chapter to give a sense of the concerns that teachers face in their daily interactions with students where issues of plagiarism arise. The difficulties for policy-makers are also a focus of the chapter and are interwoven in the discussion about responses at the university level to allegations of plagiarism. The plagiarism continuum—a conceptual model for thinking about responses to plagiarism—is introduced in the first chapter. This model is grounded in a three-pronged theoretical framework from the fields of critical legal theory, literary theory and cross-cultural studies. The concepts of transformational and transmissive teaching approaches are drawn from work by Henry Giroux (1993, 1996) and Stephen Sterling (2001). The model is also based on the practical concerns of 48 staff and 186 students who were part of a three-year study that also frames this book. The plagiarism continuum is a model that is of practical use for teachers, policy-makers and administrators dealing with the complex issue of plagiarism in academic work.

Chapter 2 gives an explanation of the historical development of plagiarism to assist teachers and students understand why plagiarism has become such a topical issue in higher education. Unpacking the direct connection between plagiarism and its legal roots in the English courts at the time of the English poet William Wordsworth provides a clear foundation for understanding the birth of plagiarism. The chapter also examines concepts of plagiarism from France, Germany, Australia and the United States to help readers appreciate the tensions that are inherent in different understandings of plagiarism. The law has been pivotal in shaping our understandings of plagiarism and has been a crucial force in molding ways in which educational institutions have defined plagiarism and set out procedures for its management. Critical legal theory also provides a way to examine the difficulties for the law in maintaining a traditional approach where Internet plagiarism and issues of authorship in cyberspace are concerned.

Chapter 3 illustrates the ways in which legal notions of plagiarism are borne out in practice—through the embodiment of legal principles, definitions and procedures in university plagiarism policies around the world. The chapter begins by detailing the myriad of ways in which plagiarism is managed by universities in Australia, Canada, China, New

Zealand, the United Kingdom and the United States of America. However, the policies from these different institutions fail to agree on one major area: whether the student intended to plagiarize or not. For some universities and colleges, it is essential to try to find out whether the act of plagiarism was deliberate or not, as some will only punish intentional acts of plagiarism. For other institutions, it does not matter—if plagiarism is detected in the work, the student is automatically penalized. The deconstruction of these policies into the essential six elements of plagiarism[3] forms a clear link with the earlier chapters and provides teachers and policy-makers with a means to critically examine their own institution's procedures and policies.

The focus of Chapter 4 is to offer alternative constructs of plagiarism. The combination of literary theory and cross-cultural studies can be mapped across a spectrum of responses to plagiarism. Indeed, the plagiarism continuum in Chapter 1, captures the theoretical and practical difficulties teachers face in applying traditional notions of plagiarism in the diverse student populations of our classrooms in the twenty-first century. An important aspect of classroom practice is how teachers cope with multiple understandings of plagiarism. In addition, literary theory challenges the very concepts of authorship and the roles of readers and writers, which has a bearing on teaching and learning approaches in classrooms. A detailed account both of the theory and practice of cross-cultural influences in academic writing forms the basis of this chapter and offers alternative lenses through which to view and respond to plagiarism.

Chapter 5 focuses on the challenges that Internet plagiarism brings for teachers, students and institutions. The Internet has re-articulated the role and meaning of authorship in a number of complex ways—textuality itself is confronted in the hypertext environment of the World Wide Web. That being the case, the notion of authorship is also questioned in cyberspace, which can play out in the ways in which students choose to use electronic sources in their academic work. Students and teachers reflect on their perceptions of Internet plagiarism in this chapter and raise many provocative issues that are fleshed out here. Questions fundamental to our work, but that appear to often be swept away in the daily routines of teaching and administration, are addressed as technology and text merge. Issues such as Internet writing services providing custom-made essays for purchase and a fear of a reduction in the emphasis of academic integrity in our seats of learning are some of the broader trends examined.

Chapter 6 details the ways in which teachers understand how plagiarism operates. In this chapter teachers discuss at length their experiences of plagiarism. They expand on their notions of intentionality in plagiarism, copying as a means of student learning, "patchwriting,"[4] and their ideas about cultural and linguistic factors as major influences on the extent of plagiarism in students' academic writing. Approaches to teaching and learning are also discussed in this chapter and characteristics of both transmissive and transformative classroom practices are outlined. This chapter provides a clear picture of the frustrations, angst, success and concern of teachers in dealing with the complex and often fraught issue of plagiarism. The chapter concludes with a summary of the issues the professional teacher faces in applying traditional concepts of authorship in classrooms of the twenty-first century.

In Chapter 7 the voices of students are heard—in particular, international students, for whom English is not a first language. These students have traditionally been caught in the centre of media attention about plagiarism and also cheating—but what issues face international students in our university and college classrooms? Importantly, what are our university and college systems and structures doing to assist them in their academic endeavors? This chapter portrays plagiarism through the eyes of international students taking a first-year undergraduate university writing course. Not only are the students' various understandings of plagiarism outlined, but also their own views on former learning and teaching approaches as well as cultural and technological influences on their writing practices. These views are enormously helpful to teachers and policy-makers who can build more effective practices based on a better understanding of the issues of plagiarism from students' perspectives.

Chapter 8 discusses some ongoing issues of plagiarism for teachers, policy-makers and universities. Approaches that teachers and institutions have taken to address issues of plagiarism are presented under three broad headings: technological solutions; procedural solutions; and holistic solutions. The chapter also provides an overview of ways in which the plagiarism continuum can assist teachers and institutions willing to engage in a critical examination of current policy and practice, in dealing with plagiarism and issues of academic integrity.

CHAPTER 1

The Plagiarism Continuum

But how could they do that to *me*... I'm their teacher and I thought they liked and respected me! How could they plagiarize work and hand it in—do they think I'm so dumb I won't know it's blatant plagiarism?

(Ana, teacher at South-Coast University)

As we sit around the oval table in the Board Room, having introduced ourselves and our reasons for agreeing to meet on the issue of plagiarism, Kate speaks. She is a very experienced teacher who works in the Faculty of Law. She tells us that she has been teaching for over 12 years at various institutions around Australia and is completing her doctoral thesis. She teaches a large cohort of first-year students—of whom 98 percent are international students. Kate says she takes her teaching responsibilities very seriously and has attended a number of workshops for staff focusing on understanding culturally different approaches to learning in the classroom, including expectations of the teacher–student relationship. She says a central aim of these workshops is to help staff improve communication for students where English is a second or other language. She has also attended the professional development seminars on PowerPoint presentations and effective teaching strategies offered by the university for ongoing staff. As

Kate speaks, I nod in response. I have observed Kate teach—in both lecture and tutorial situations—and her teaching approach is clear and material is explored thoroughly. She allows plenty of time for questions during lectures and also at the end of the lecture. She is friendly and approachable in manner but also clearly knowledgeable about her topic area. She appears caring and also builds clear and specific guidelines into her classes so that students understand how and when they should contact or meet with her to discuss any issues they may have with the coursework. Kate then says:

> Well I think plagiarism is a major concern for this university and us as staff members. I definitely think it's increasing—certainly there's more of it around now than when I started here seven years ago. I don't know about the rest of you but I am really worried about the responsibility on us to police the thing. My cohort has over 260 students and I just haven't got the time to check absolutely everything! Nor do I think that's necessarily my job—I'm an academic not a police officer! I am worried about the ramifications if cases of plagiarism get past me, though. I don't think the university provides enough support for staff if they really want us to take the whole plagiarism issue seriously.

Greg, a senior lecturer in the Faculty of Health and Behavioral Sciences, jumps into the discussion. He says:

> I couldn't agree more, Kate. I've sent numerous cases to Disciplinary Committee in my 12 years here and students keep getting off! I wonder what the point is, when you spend hours checking and finding the sources from which students have stolen the work and photocopying it, documenting it and then the university processes simply don't support you. I can't understand why the Committee is so lenient with these cheats! I was about to forget about it altogether when our faculty subscribed to this anti-plagiarism software service and it's great! Now I'm about to send a whole new batch to Disciplinary Committee with the techno-logical tool finding the plagiarism—I mean whole WHO reports copied in and not acknowledged—it's blatant! Let's see what their response is now that an independent technologically-savvy means of tracking and finding plagiarism is able to be used.

Greg sits back with folded arms in a semi-defiant manner. He is clearly throwing down the gauntlet to Sanji, one of the plagiarism policy-writers who is also a representative on the University Disciplinary Committee. Sanji is at this meeting to voice the concerns from the policy arm of the university. Greg is a well-respected teacher and has won numerous university and State awards for teaching excellence. I have observed one of his lectures and found it stimulating and interesting. He uses video snippets to illustrate points about health issues in cases of nursing trauma and uses practical tasks where students have access via video-link to some of the leading nursing practitioners in the area of trauma nursing in the country. The sorts of educational experience Greg provides for his students require enormous effort on his part to organize and his expectations of the quality of student responses in their work is correspondingly high. Greg sets a great deal of reading for students to complete outside class time and his assessment tasks are both practical and challenging. He takes his subject area very seriously and lets his students know that he expects a similar level of dedication from them. He has told me in our prior conversations that he spends a great deal of time marking assignments and checking referencing and sourcing of material because he "can't stand laziness and sloppy work handed in." Some of his students have said to me that he is a demanding teacher but very fair and that his classes are some of the most innovative in the Faculty of Nursing and Health Sciences.

Sanji, a senior administrator and one of the plagiarism policy-writing team at the university, responds:

> I'm not prepared to speak about Disciplinary Committee process in this forum but in terms of plagiarism, I really don't see what the problem is. The policy is very clear about what plagiarism is, how we define it and what is acceptable. I was part of the rethinking process when the policy was changed in 2004 and I consider it to be quite comprehensive. Our policy goes into detail about the definition of plagiarism as well as collusion and cheating and links to the penalties prescribed for offenders. How can students claim they don't know these things? The policy is printed in every subject guide in every unit taught in every faculty at this university. There's really no excuse to claim ignorance at all.

Sanji and I have spoken at length about the policy at South-Coast University. He was one of the key figures orchestrating the wholescale revision of the university plagiarism policy in 2004 and explains that the revised policy is modeled on what was considered to be a "best practice" model taken from a range of university policies around Australia and New Zealand. He explains that the new policy is expanded and takes account of the advent of technology so that areas such as computer programming are also mentioned as "things" or "objects" that can be plagiarized. Sanji also points out that the advent and use of anti-plagiarism software is also taken into account in the revised policy. He is clearly nonplussed that there is an issue, as he maintains that the policy is printed everywhere for students to read and it is really quite straightforward, in his opinion.

Georgiou, a senior lecturer in the Faculty of Science and Technology, exclaims:

> Absolutely! The policy is clear and therefore if students plagiarize—they have to be doing so deliberately. The penalties are there and it's their responsibility to understand these basic academic conventions. That's not our job as tertiary academics—we're not running a crèche here. The responsibility to write in an academic manner that complies with standards lies with the students. I'm not sure why they think they can deceive us in this way . . . I mean to say . . . they have very little comprehension of the field of literature and the current research compared to us as academics.

Georgiou's last institution adopted a zero-tolerance policy that he strongly advocates should apply to all higher education institutions. In his opinion, anything less is merely encouraging students to try to find a way to "cheat the system."

Ana, a new lecturer in the university sector, although she has been a teacher in secondary schools for eight years, speaks. She says:

> Well I find the whole thing just frustrating! I try hard but I can't believe that after I discuss plagiarism in class, I give them exercises and samples to work through that they still do it! I just don't know what to do any more. They just don't seem to get it no matter how hard I try! I sometimes wonder whether it's even worth the trouble you know. I mean to say . . . we have the policy up on the website, it's in all the subject guides, I go through it in class and also get the tutors to do the same and I always encourage students to come and ask me if they're unsure but none ever do. Then they submit plagiarized assignments and I can't believe they do that to me. It's all just too frustrating—what more am I meant to do?

The frustration and annoyance in Ana's voice is apparent. She clearly feels that she is doing all she can but fears she is "missing the mark." Her plaintive "what more can I do?" was uttered with her hands open in a gesture of asking for help and her eyes turned upwards as if seeking some inspiration from above. I have also observed Ana work in lectures and tutorials and found her to be lively and engaging—bringing a great deal of energy to her classes. Despite her lack of experience in the university sector, her secondary school experience enables her to respond to student queries by teasing out some of the issues that may be underlying some of their responses. Ana puts a great deal of effort into making her classes innovative and interesting for students and she keeps an electronic journal of each subject she teaches, in which she writes notes to herself at the end of class. Sometimes, if busy, she records her reflections on the teaching experience into a small Dictaphone and then types this up later. She informed me she is using her reflections and critical evaluation of her teaching experience in a Masters of Education unit she is undertaking part-time. Ana appears to be dedicated and patient with students and explains the intricacies of university referencing and citation systems as well as the practicalities of summarizing and integrating original sources into the text. She teaches an introductory writing unit to both international and local students in the Faculty of Education, who may feel they need extra experience in writing in an Australian university context.

Inger, also a relatively new lecturer in the Faculty of Arts, adds:

> I am also concerned. I teach a basic first year writing subject in the Humanities faculty and I think the students who are coming to us from overseas just don't have the grounding before they start. My chief concern is that these kids are not going to get enough assistance in the 13 weeks of this unit and then will be thrown to the wolves in other units. Thirteen weeks is not enough time to really understand plagiarism and be able to overcome it. Some students have a life-time of just copying textbooks to get over!

Inger has spoken to me about her worries over students not having enough time to "digest" (as she puts it) the ideas she tries to get them to grapple with. She says that learning to write in the academically acceptable way is a skill that takes many years to perfect, if at all. She says the expectations that the university and other staff members have, that one introductory unit or a 13-week intensive study course can turn out a student who is capable of meeting rigorous academic standards, is unrealistic. In saying this, she draws on her teaching experience in the area of ESL/EFL gained from 15 years in various countries around the world. She says that although students no doubt improve and many begin to understand what they are striving to achieve, the time needed to actually put that into daily practice is much longer than one semester in one subject. She has intimated in our previous conversations that many students are disillusioned, frightened and some experience a profound sense of failure that they cannot produce work that gets the high marks that they received previously in their home countries.

She says many students experience a deep sense of shame and are too embarrassed to seek additional help. Inger says that the problem of plagiarism is a great deal more complex and affects more than just students' perceptions of what plagiarism in academic writing actually means.

Although I have not seen Inger teach, I have taught my own classes in the room next door to her class. The students generally appear to be engaged in the class and leave chatting about work. Some students remain behind each week and prefer to ask her questions individually rather than in the whole class context. I have heard guest speakers, video presentations and role plays enacted in her class, and Inger adopts a variety of teaching strategies whereby students enter into a process of sharing understandings.

I ask CheeLing, the only teacher who has not spoken, whether she would care to add any comment at this stage. CheeLing is a senior lecturer in the Faculty of Business and Economics who completed her undergraduate studies at Beijing University and then completed Masters in Business Administration in Australia as a full-time postgraduate student. She is currently undertaking her doctoral studies part-time in Management theory. CheeLing cautiously responds:

> I understand the concerns of many people here and I share them. However, I wonder how many of you can appreciate that students who operate in a second or third language just sometimes don't have the right words in English at their fingertips. So, they resort to what I did in my undergraduate days—I copied the words from a book. In China, copying was rewarded at that time because the information was correct, although it is changing now to be more like here, I think. The action of copying is not intended to be insulting or disrespectful to teachers in any way—it is just a strategy to cope. Some of these international students come from places where copying from textbooks and even teachers' notes was standard practice at school and it got them high marks. They may be told here not to do it, but they don't know what else to do because they don't have enough correct words to say it themselves. How many of you speak two or three other languages or have ever had to write a long essay about complex theories in another language? It is just incredibly difficult if you don't have enough words to do it. I think the problem is far more complex than just a question of following or not following the policy. There are cultural things that are at the heart of this issue and they need to be acknowledged openly here and by the university, if it is, as the university claims in the vision statement, a truly internationally focused environment for international students.

CheeLing speaks quietly but in quite a determined manner. Her stance is challenged by some staff members in a general discussion about language entrance requirements for courses, and students' responsibilities in knowing that they have to communicate adequately in English as the medium of instruction in the university. The conversation becomes more heated as people begin to discuss where the responsibility for decisions about plagiarism lay as well as the effects of individual teacher's actions.

As can be seen from the brief discussion captured in the snapshot above—there is considerable diversity of staff opinion about some of the general issues that plagiarism raises. Plagiarism and the responses of people to it affect us all—not only in our daily interaction with colleagues but also in our relationships with students. As illustrated in this scenario, drawn from my interaction with university staff, people respond in many and varied ways to acts of plagiarism—both at individual and institutional levels. Similar experiences are well documented in the literature and provide a broader base from which to flesh out some of the underlying issues in reader responses to written acts of plagiarism.

Teachers such as Sherri Whiteman in the USA (Whiteman and Gordon, 2001) have written about their reactions to instances of plagiarism in their students' work. She recalls her despair to instances of Internet plagiarism in her students' writing, and admits her response as a teacher-reader was based on the "idealistic attitude of a newer teacher" because she had expected that her students wished to produce their own work. In this sense, her experience is similar to that of Ana. Some of the frustration and concern is because of her inexperience in the tertiary sector, but more so because there is a sense of "where to from here?"; Whiteman reluctantly writes that her ideals have "given way to reality" as she feels undermined and lacks confidence that her students will make a genuine effort to produce work that is not plagiarized. Steve Gardiner is another teacher who reacts strongly to plagiarism, but feels it is a personal attack on his degree of professionalism and his knowledge of the field. He writes: "How could they do this? I raged. Do they think I'm stupid . . . I felt victimized . . . I was too angry to continue grading" (2001, p.173). Steve goes on to describe his feelings of anger and frustration that some students appear to be trying to deceive him into thinking the work is their own. He ends his article quite bitterly saying that he is sad to think that students will resort to such means to ensure good grades and has lost his faith in the general student population to act honorably. Similarly, college teacher Kay Johnston (1991) describes her initial reaction to discovering plagiarism as fury and disbelief. "How could *they* do this to me?" she asks (original emphasis, p.285). Kay and Steve's reactions are similar to that of many teachers who have engaged in the plagiarism debate—in addition to the anger and frustration, an overwhelming sense of hopelessness in the fight to maintain academic integrity and get students to appreciate the educational worth of submitting their own work. Indeed, such responses may represent what Robert Briggs (2003) terms a "moralizing approach to plagiarism" because students blatantly disregard any respect for the status or knowledge and expertise of the teacher. Students who plagiarize may be seen by some teachers as challenging a relationship in which the teacher is seen as less authoritative by the novice student-writer. Such is the case when Georgiou says that he's not sure why students think they can "deceive" staff, particularly as they are in the position of novice student-writer in relation to the expert teacher-reader.

In the examples above, teachers may reflect upon the ways in which they have constructed textual meanings and intention in student writing and identify an emotional response. This is a tendency labeled as "moral panic" by British researchers Sue Clegg and Abbi Flint (2006).[1] Well-known American academic, Rebecca Moore Howard, claims this is often the case because an academic "will respond with emotion because he or she will feel personally affronted, his or her intelligence insulted, [or] his or her values degraded" when confronting text that appears to have been plagiarized (1999, p.165). This is clearly the case with Ana, Georgiou, Kay and Steve where they feel that there is some deliberate attempt on the part of the student to make them feel or look foolish by undermining their professional integrity through plagiarizing work with which informed teachers would be familiar. Augustus Kolich,[2] in a much-quoted article, agrees. He says:

> After all, plagiarism challenges each of our reputations as effective teachers. We may publicly acknowledge that plagiarism is hard to identify and difficult to combat, but we rarely confess to how much we fear it and hate it . . . We must fend off the threat as best we can, and we usually do so in one of two ways. Either we righteously punish offenders with the lightning revenge of instant failure, or we simply ignore incidents of plagiarism—especially if they may be difficult to prove.
>
> (1983, p.142)

Although written in 1983, Kolich's words still merit our examination. Teachers need to be increasingly aware of the way in which they respond to plagiarism and why they respond in these ways. Is the reaction to a case of plagiarism one of fear or loathing of the act, as Kolich suggests? Or is it as Ana and Steve describe—a sense of hopelessness in a situation in which teachers feel they have little control or perhaps institutional support? Examination of reasons for responses of the kind outlined by Kolich is one key to reflexive practice and may prove to be an avenue to tackle some of the underlying issues of teacher responses to plagiarism.

Teacher-Reader as Active Meaning-Maker

Teachers' responses to plagiarism are manifestations of their roles as interpreters of textual meaning. In reading the written work of students, teachers make judgments based on their individual interpretations of textual meaning about a range of issues—one of which is plagiarism. The process is one of active construction of textual meaning by the teacher-reader of the student-writer's texts. A decision that a text is plagiarized is made because essential meanings have been attributed to the product by the teacher-reader, not necessarily the student-writer. Probing the teacher's role as reader and interpreter of textual meaning is appropriate and may assist us to reflect upon ways in which we can take positive action in issues of plagiarism.

The need to examine the role of the teacher-reader in attributing textual meaning (sometimes called teacher reflexivity) is crucial according to many in the profession. Some teachers suggest that plagiarism lies not in the text itself, nor in the writer, but in the reader's reception of the writing. It is important to consider the role of the reader in the interpretation of the text when plagiarism is alleged to have occurred. Teachers react differently to instances of plagiarism in their students' writing, as illustrated at the start of this chapter, and echoed in the experiences of teachers around the globe.[3] In reading a student-writer's work, if the teacher decides plagiarism has occurred, then meaning has been assigned to the text by the teacher-reader. This supports Roland Barthes' (1977) theory that it is readers rather than writers who construct both textual meaning and authorial intention. In making the claim that readers impute plagiarism to writers, not that writers necessarily intend to plagiarize, Barthes radically questions the role of the author. Rather than perceiving authors as the individual creators of unique "works," he argues that writers only have the power to mix already existing cultural forms and knowledge: to reassemble or re-deploy text where "text" is understood to be socially produced. Writers cannot use writing to express themselves, he says, but as writers we only "draw upon that immense dictionary of language and culture which is always already written" (1977, p.66). Therefore, it is the language and not the author that is the repository of meaning. In his famous 1968 essay *The Death of the Author* he separates the text from the author. He argues that the term "author" is, in fact, an impediment to the ways in which the textual environment works. He claims that although the position and status of being an author is a powerful one, it is the language that speaks, through text, not the author.

He notes that, "words and forms can belong to *no-one*," which raises the issue of ownership and attribution of text (original emphasis, 1977, p.293). What Barthes is saying is that although the author is an important conduit for communication to take place, the true power lies in the language used in the text and the reader's interpretation of that language. In looking at the "reader–writer" relationship in this way, it is the reader who has the power in the relationship more than the writer. He proposes that the author, or as he prefers to term it, the "author-God" (p.146), is a relationship of power between consumers of text—the readers—and the text itself. This is an important and helpful viewpoint for teachers to reflect upon as teachers are the ones who read our students' texts and make judgments based upon such reading. These judgments include decisions on whether plagiarism has occurred or not. Barthes is making us aware that we, as teachers, are in positions of power, because we are textual consumers and we must examine not only the text but also our roles as teacher-readers when we make allegations of plagiarism.

If we apply Barthes' theory to help us understand the variety of responses the staff gave in the opening of this chapter, there is an overwhelming sense that textual meaning is constructed by the teacher-reader. It is the teacher who decides that the work is plagiarized, based upon their individual reading and interpretation of the text. However, a student-writer's intended meaning is not necessarily part of that construction. Kay's reaction of "How dare they!" is quite common, where teachers attribute students with an intention to deceive them. Conversely, CheeLing's statement that "copying is not intended to be insulting or disrespectful to teachers in any way—it is just a strategy to cope" indicates she believes that for some students, there is no intention to deceive at all, copying is merely a technique for academic survival. Construction of intention by the teacher-reader is of crucial importance here. Did the student intend to plagiarize or not? The issue of intention is a pivotal point around which notions of plagiarism revolve. Imputing intention in writing is also one of the most challenged concepts in theory and forms the basis of the plagiarism continuum described later in this chapter.

Intention in Plagiarism

Literary theorists such as Annette Patterson (1995) argue that intention is decided by the reader—but the point at which that occurs is upon the release of the writing into the public arena. These claims rest on the ideas, drawn from the law, that once a text is written and released from the writer (or author) it exists "independently of the author and of his declared intention" (p.140). This idea is based upon the outcome in Prynne's case[4]

(1633) in which William Prynne was charged with seditious libel in England's Star Chamber Court when he published a work denouncing all theatrical performances. The Star Chamber judges declared that although the writer, Prynne, may not have intended any ill harm to the monarchy in his text denouncing theatre, the readers of the text interpreted those words as seditious.[5] The judiciary decided that the interpretation of textual meaning belonged to the reader. Although Prynne argued that his words had been incorrectly interpreted, the judges declared that once a work was released into the public domain, the work could be interpreted in any way the reader wished. This challenge to authorial intention was founded in the concept that "the construction of another's meaning lay with the reader" (Hirsch, 1976, p.244).

If this is applied to student-writers, once the work is written it is free from the students' control and open to teachers as readers to interpret. The student-writers must clearly state their intentions and presumably this applies to plagiarism as well. In the context of university and college students—many teachers require students taking their subjects to include some statement or declaration about the authenticity of their work, stating that the work submitted is their own and not acquired or unacknowledged from other sources. Some universities mandate the practice in public Honor Code signing ceremonies, in which students publicly commit to submitting their own work and not plagiarizing or cheating in their studies.[6] In requiring students to declare that work is their own, either in a public ceremony or on a document submitted as part of the assessment process, ensures an interpretation of "public declaration of intention" as stipulated in Prynne's case. Often such declarations have been relied upon as material evidence where plagiarism has been alleged by staff members in university or faculty Disciplinary Committee hearings. This means that despite the student's declaration that the work is their own, through signing such documents, their teachers decide that students intended to plagiarize some or all of the work. The decision that plagiarism is present has been made by the teacher, despite the student's declaration to the contrary.

Other literary theorists, such as Alastair Fowler (1976), however, caution against adopting views suggesting that the reader alone is responsible for constructing meaning and intention in a work. He discusses the variety and extent of literary intention and surmises that most debate surrounds the notion of semantic intention. This kind of intention, he claims, is linked to the meaning attached to particular words and is used to "distinguish meaning held to be true or valid" (p.245). He says:

> This practice seems not without significance for its bearing on authorial privilege . . . A reader has always to *construct* the words

and the work, starting from marks on paper (or sound-waves in air). He does this by interpreting them, according to codes more or less fully shared with their encoder, as indications of the vocabulary choices intended. These choices, in turn, he interprets as signal of intended grammatical (or rhetorical metrical numerological, etc.) forms; and so on up the artifactual pyramid. At the top, as it were, above even the intended themes, the work's unity waits to be reconstructed . . . What we try to construct is the original work, in the sense of the intention realized by the author . . . Our critical questions are Did the author intend this? And minimally, Can he have meant that?

> (emphasis in the original, pp.250–251)

The point Fowler makes is that readers construct meaning by utilizing the guiding signals provided by the writer in order to ascertain the truth of meaning—the correct or most logical interpretation of the text. However, this interpretation of intention—that there exists a "truth" in meaning that a reader can arrive at through reading—does not appear to take into account the full extent of the life experiences of readers. His breakdown of the "artifactual pyramid" is quite clinical and does not seem to allow for what Annette Patterson describes as the "shift away from formalism towards the history and theory of culture" (1995, p.146). Many classroom professionals argue that culture is one of the most important considerations teachers should take into account when ascribing "truth" to textual meaning. ESL and EFL classrooms have provided the setting for a great deal of work on cultural aspects of academic writing and plagiarism—particularly with regard to plagiarism and intention.

Cross-Cultural Notions of Intention

The Board Room clearly illustrated that teachers' attitudes to plagiarism range across a spectrum of intention. At one end, for example, there are teachers like Georgiou who believe that there should be no tolerance of a breach of plagiarism policy. At the other end are teachers like CheeLing who maintain that there are a complex number of factors that muddy the waters surrounding the issue of plagiarism. The spectrum of views of teachers are captured in the plagiarism continuum illustrated later in this chapter. Teachers such as Georgiou and Sanji from the scenario, Glenn Deckert in Hong Kong and Augustus Kolich in the United States consider that if plagiarism is found in students' work, then it is there deliberately. The basic argument is that students know not to breach academic codes of conduct by committing acts of plagiarism. Moving towards the other end of the spectrum there are other teachers such as Jude Carroll in the United Kingdom, Rebecca Moore Howard in the United States, Stephen Marshall and Maryanne Garry in New Zealand, Shelley Yeo in Australia and Shelley Angelil-Carter in South Africa who argue that the situation is not that easy. Inadvertent and accidental plagiarism also occurs and it is not a deliberate act. Other teachers argue that where plagiarism is intentional, then it moves into the realm of cheating and deserves the most serious forms of punishment available. However, they assert that if plagiarism is unintentional the students require some form of additional educational support to assist them—rather than punishment. Many teachers feel that cultural considerations and lack of skilled academic writing techniques are more useful places to start addressing issues of plagiarism. There are yet other teachers at a point further along the spectrum who consider that there can never be any plagiarism in academic writing, because the notion of plagiarism does not exist. This is based on the notion that "original thought" is not possible, therefore the concept of "authorship" is inherently flawed and there cannot be any transgressions against the non-existent persona of the "author" (Levin, 2006). Many teachers support the view that plagiarism can be both intentional and unintentional and agree that intention is the key element in their decisions about plagiarism.

Plagiarism as Cheating

If we examine how plagiarism has been defined in the literature, an early examination of plagiarism as it was construed in college and university policy documentation found that definitions ranged from common dictionary meanings or single words that all signified some sort of immoral intent—lying, cheating, stealing, dishonesty and deception.[7] What emerges from these attempts to define plagiarism is that it falls under the umbrella of "academic cheating," which commonly is seen as an academic misconduct offense and deserving of punishment. Indeed, some researchers and teachers consider plagiarism to be closely aligned to cheating in its darkest form.[8]

Teachers who categorize plagiarism as cheating often regard plagiarism as an act of intellectual rape. Proponents of this view state that plagiarism in academic writing is "intellectual murder most foul" and a "clear and present danger to intellectual liberty" (Mirsky, 2002). Some argue that civilization itself will be "eclipsed" if literary originality is not preserved in writing (Navarazov, 1993, p.40), supporting the idea that authors own their works and that proprietary relationship must be preserved. American educator Augustus Kolich contends, "the worm plagiarism spoils the fruit of intellectual inquiry and reason, and starves the seeds of originality that fosters such inquiry" (1983, p.145). He argues that plagiarism is morally reprehensible but says it can only be prevented when teachers encourage a sense of intellectual curiosity and discovery in their students. Therefore, although he regards plagiarism as a heinous offense and repugnant to ideas of academic integrity—he advocates the idea that teachers should work to encourage their students to intellectually engage with ideas.

Other educators, such as Edna Loveless, claim that plagiarism is "the cardinal sin of academe" (1994, p.10) and Ellen Laird regards plagiarism as an "academic felony." She warns teachers that Internet plagiarism in particular is a burgeoning problem because although it "costs student-thieves neither time nor money, will cost us all" if it continues unchecked (2001, p.59). Alice Drum says "plagiarism is a disease that plagues college instructors everywhere," adding that plagiarism is "as much a pedagogical offense as a legal one" (1986, pp.241, 243). Similarly, in a South African study conducted by Shelley Angelil-Carter, plagiarism is described as "the scourge of academic life" (2000, p.68). In commenting on allegations of plagiarism in the United States, Sharon Walsh categorizes plagiarism as "the worst academic sin" and one that "undermines the intellectual activities of a university" (2002, p.12). New Zealand researcher, Judy Le Heron (2001), characterizes plagiarism as a "synonym for cheating and learning dishonesty" in reporting her six-year study of plagiarism in an information systems course at a New Zealand university. Across the Tasman Sea in Australia, David Pyvis in reporting on a high-profile case at Curtin University in Western Australia proclaims plagiarism an "anathema" and contends that where university plagiarism policy and procedures are inconsistent, communication breakdown can result and an "ethical vacuum" for students and staff emerge (2002, pp.33–34).

As we can see from this brief overview of some teacher and researcher perceptions of plagiarism from around the world, the language used to describe plagiarism in academic writing is couched in terms varying from moral reprehensibility to criminal activity. Words such as "cardinal sin," "scourge" and "danger to . . . liberty" embody the ideas of moral wrong. Yet other teachers align plagiarism with criminal behavior and describe it in terms of "intellectual murder," "felony," "dishonesty," "cheating" and label the students as "thieves." For these teachers, plagiarism is conceptualized as an action of intentional and calculated theft—as reflected in many of the plagiarism policies of the institutions that are outlined in Chapter 3. It is also important to recognize that some teachers see plagiarism as a form of cheating, whereas others do not. Some claim that plagiarism is an offense and categorize it alongside actions such as cheating on examinations. Another group of teachers are hesitant to make this claim. They see only some forms of plagiarism as akin to cheating—offenses such as buying a paper from the Internet, or engaging and paying another person to write an assignment for submission. These situations clearly have an element of deliberate and calculated action and most teachers support the idea that cheating should be punished (see Chapter 3 for a full description of the "elements" of plagiarism).

In contrast, there are teachers who argue that plagiarism is wrong and is akin to cheating but that the intention of the student is irrelevant. Australian teachers John Godfrey and Russell Waugh (2002) argue that plagiarism is a form of cheating because it is intentional by definition. They claim that students who plagiarize know what they are doing is wrong, therefore they are engaged in inappropriate academic behavior that warrants punishment. Glenn Deckert[9] agrees and argues that whether plagiarism is unintentional or not is irrelevant because the action of copying is unacceptable. In discussing his Hong Kong students' "habit of copying unidentified strings of words into writing that is supposed to be their own" he says that "such writing is unacceptable in genuine academic exchange and the problem it represents deserves and demands complex professional response" (1993b, p.94). English teacher-researchers Peter Larkham and Susan Manns argue that plagiarism is largely a case of cheating but they claim that there are "degrees of plagiarism" and that both plagiarism and cheating are a matter of breach of trust and ethics (2002, p.346). They conducted a small-scale stratified sample study of plagiarism in nine higher education institutions in England, and concluded that it was problematic to actually gauge intention because sometimes plagiarism is merely poor scholarship and at other times there is clearly deliberate action taken in order to gain unfair advantage over students who complete all work themselves. They concluded that "an unethical student is likely to be an unethical practitioner" (p.348), which is a point that has been picked up by more recent studies. In 2001, Sarah Nonis and Cathy Swift conducted a survey of 1,051 students who were undertaking business studies across six universities in the southern and Midwestern areas of the United States. Their research found that students who believed acts of misconduct were acceptable in the academic environment believed dishonest behaviors were also acceptable in the work environment. They argued that increased scrutiny of business practices in the professional marketplace means that tertiary educational providers, such as colleges and universities, must demonstrate that they promote high standards of academic integrity and ensure that students who plagiarize or cheat are not rewarded with university degrees. It is clear that by identifying academics as gatekeepers for ensuring ethical practices by graduates entering the professions in both the United Kingdom and United States, the onus is placed on teachers, and institutional processes are seen to bear the onus of responsibility to detect and deter student plagiarism.

However, many teachers also distinguish between these deliberate actions falling at the intentional end of the plagiarism continuum with other actions that are accidental or unintentional in nature. Where students forget or are sloppy in their citations or referencing, such as first-year undergraduate students who may be unfamiliar with referencing codes in our academic institutions—some staff consider these actions as unintentional plagiarism. Often these instances are not reported. Unintentional plagiarism poses real difficulties for teachers, as they must decide whether plagiarism that has been detected in the student's work was intentional or not.

Unintentional Plagiarism

Unintentional plagiarism is generally manifested where students do not have any intention to deceive the teacher. In such circumstances teachers consider that students merely use incorrect citation or referencing practices, such as lack of quotation marks indicating direct speech, poor or non-existent bibliographies and incorrect or no reference lists. Christopher Hawley (1984) claims that many students present "unacceptable documentation" to teachers from "sloppy paraphrasing to verbatim transcription with no crediting of sources" (p.35). Others describe it as a "slip in scholarship" (Leatherman, 1999, p.22) or a "lapse rather than a crime" (Gray, 2002, p.102). Some teachers faced with cases of unintentional plagiarism are reluctant to allege academic misconduct when it may be more appropriate to focus on citation strategies. Paul Richardson (2001) argues that plagiarism is not necessarily easily classified as "cheating" and that staff, at times, find it difficult to assess the situation and act equitably. He describes plagiarism as a "spectre" (p.5) for students and staff because "writing in the academy is infused with notions of originality, creativity, authorship, intellectual inquiry and Western writing practices. For students, the problems of avoiding plagiarism are often more complicated than academic staff acknowledge" (p.3). These sentiments are supported by British researcher and teacher in the area of plagiarism, Jude Carroll.[10] Carroll's work examines the myriad of factors that may impact upon students' plagiarizing, including: poor time management; inadequate language preparation for the demands of tertiary courses; poor understandings of the processes involved in transforming information into knowledge; as well as student choices to follow certain paths, including cheating or plagiarism. She supports the view that plagiarism is a multi-faceted phenomenon. Alastair Pennycook from Australia considers it impossible to characterize plagiarism as "a simple black-and-white issue" (1996, p.201). In describing the writing practices of students in Hong Kong, he observes, "it is certainly important to distinguish between good and bad plagiarism, that is between those who reuse parts of texts very well and those who seemed to randomly borrow" (p.226). He considers that not all acts of plagiarism are filled with the intention to plagiarize and asserts "it is important to understand the cultural and historical specificity of notions of ownership and authorship and to explore the implications of these concepts as being increasingly promoted as international norms" (p.203). He encourages us, as teachers, to take a broader cultural view of academic writing and its conventions.

Teachers such as Peter Shaw use the notion of intention as the crux to decide whether plagiarism exists or not. Where a student uses the work of another person with an intention to deceive the marker as to its original source, this is seen as equivalent to plagiarism. However, if a student uses the work of another but without an intention to deceive the marker— perhaps the source is used naïvely, mistakenly or sloppily, then this is not equivalent to plagiarism. Taking this view, the decision that a student's action is one of plagiarism requires the student to use the information intentionally, in a manner to deceive. Anything less than a clear intention to plagiarize should be considered as an action less than plagiarism. Fellow British teacher, Christopher Hawley (1984, p.38), agrees:

> Plagiarism is not carried on exclusively by evil students whose sole intent is to defraud the unsuspecting professor. Much unacceptable documentation in fact, may come more from simple ignorance rather than deceit.

Hawley conducted a campus survey about plagiarism with 425 under-graduates and found that 12 percent said they had asked someone to write a paper for them; 14.6 percent said they had submitted work that had been written by another student; and 5.6 percent said that they submitted work that they had purchased from a research service. More frightening to us as educators were his findings that 25 percent of all students surveyed agreed with one or more of the survey questions that plagiarism is an acceptable academic practice. This tends to link with the concerns expressed earlier that students who are unaware of the ethical dilemmas in plagiarizing or cheating during their school studies, may consider such actions as legitimate both in the tertiary and workplace settings.

In an examination of novice ESL/EFL writers' use of academic sources, North American researcher Rebecca Moore Howard (1995) concludes that students can intentionally or unintentionally plagiarize. She considers intentional plagiarism to include actions such as downloading a paper from the Internet and submitting it for assessment under a different name. This she categorizes as cheating. Cases of unintentional plagiarism are, she claims, where students are simply ignorant of accepted citation conventions or, as novice academic writers, are clumsily engaging in a process of learning to use academic genres. Further, she asserts that even where students intentionally plagiarize, the motivation for this action needs to be explored, as it is not only the intention to plagiarize that teachers need to address but also the action of plagiarism itself:

> In reading students' prose, we need first to know whether the writer intended to plagiarize. If the plagiarism was intentional, we then need to know motivations: Was it for personal gain at the expense of others? In order to challenge the concept of plagiarism itself? To weave new patterns from the fabrics of others? And if the plagiarism was not intentional, we still need to know motivations: Was it engendered by an ignorance of citation conventions? By a monologic encounter with unfamiliar words and concepts?
>
> (Howard, 1995, p.797)

When the teacher decides the text is deliberately plagiarized rather than inadvertently plagiarized, the teacher (as reader) presumes knowledge of the writer's intention. It can be argued that reader's construction of textual meaning in instances of plagiarism may hinge on their interpretation of authorial intent. Many teachers acknowledge that intention is the decisive element in making a decision on whether plagiarism in student academic writing has occurred or not. A number of teachers distinguish between "plagiarism" as an act of academic misconduct and the unintentional and "accidental" lack of referencing (Warschauer, 2004) or "imitation" (to use Shaw's 1982 term) also perceived as "sloppy referencing" (after Hawley, 1984, p.35) found in some students' work. An advocate of formally recognizing such a distinction is Howard (1995, 1999, 2000, 2002) who coined the term "patchwriting" to cover unintentional forms of copying texts.

Unintentional Copying of Text: Patchwriting

Rebecca Moore Howard argues that students use a textual strategy she terms "patchwriting" in their academic writing learning process. Patchwriting involves "copying from a source text and then deleting some words, altering grammatical structures or plugging in one-for-one synonym-substitutes" (Howard, 1999, p.xvii). She argues that although direct copying of text is involved, this does not amount to plagiarism because it is a strategy in the ongoing process of learning to write in a new academic discourse. She maintains that patchwriting reflects the student's desire to write effectively. More recently, she has said that patchwriting can occur because a student does not have "the linguistic resources" to explore texts using her own words effectively (2004). However, she explains that the most common occurrence of plagiarism is because students are required to engage at a "deep" level with unfamiliar texts. She says, "for our undergraduate students, nearly every class is an encounter with whole new fields of discourse. Little wonder that they might struggle for ways to insert themselves into that discourse, searching for language other than that of the text" (Howard, 2004, p.2).

Classroom teachers applying her idea that students learn academic writing through a process of acquisition—"patchwriting"—support her view that students are evolving as academic writers. These teachers assert that students should not be punished by having their textual work constructed as plagiarism. Canadian teachers Ishbel Galloway and Marti Sevier (2003) describe their 60 Chinese students as "textual borrowers" and state that patchwriting strategies are "necessary in the students' writing development." They explain that their students recognize there is a need to develop their own sense of voice within the text. Galloway and Sevier state that students struggle to achieve the balance between reliance on textual sources and their emerging powers of analysis. This often results in sections of patchwritten text. They conclude that such efforts to become proficient in academic writing genres should not be put in the same category as plagiarism and treated as academic misconduct. Danielle De Voss and Annette Rosati[11] support this proposition as they suggest that "students aren't necessarily evil or unthinking, but instead they're learning to negotiate and do research in new spaces" (2002, p.197). They explain that students are learning to negotiate the new spaces of the academic discourse communities they seek to enter, so that punishing students possessing underdeveloped academic writing skills is inappropriate. Patchwriting is seen as a means of developing from apprentice to skilled writer, rather than as an issue of deliberate flouting of academic integrity guidelines.

Indeed, if unintentional plagiarism is a situation where students are unaware they are crossing borders of academic integrity, the question for us as teachers is whether we should or could "teach" notions of academic integrity? Many American institutions have created "Honor Codes" to instill a sense of honesty and trust in their student populations. Indeed, the Center of Academic Integrity (CAI) was created at Duke University in North Carolina—and is now operating at Clemson University in South Carolina—to promote the importance of academic integrity to students and staff. The Center, created in 1992, is a consortium of over 220 universities and colleges both in the United States and worldwide, with a primary aim to advise students about the importance of acting fairly, respectfully and responsibly in their academic assessment practices. Their Center defines academic integrity as:

> a commitment, even in the face of adversity, to five fundamental values: honesty, trust, fairness, respect, and responsibility. From these values flow principles of behavior that enable academic communities to translate ideals to action.
>
> (2007)

In this role, the CAI identifies and promotes the values of integrity by requiring students to sign a pledge—in some institutions this is a public witnessing—that they will not cheat or plagiarize. World-renowned US researcher Don McCabe has been involved in researching issues of academic integrity for many years. He asserts that where Honor Codes work best in the United States, students have been involved in the overall process. He says there is often "student participation in campus judicial or hearing bodies that review alleged infringements of the Honor Code" but that students should have even greater input and be involved at all stages. He argues that students should also "have a voice on task forces or committees charged with informing other students about the purpose and philosophy of the code and they should play a major role in its development and implementation" (2004, p.10). He believes that where Honor Codes are effectively in place, with student support and involvement through all stages of allegations of misconduct, then levels of cheating are lower than institutions without Honor Codes (McCabe and Bowers, 1994). Robert Evans from Wales also calls for notions of academic integrity to feature in dealing with plagiarism. Evans completed a two-year evaluation study of Turnitin's anti-plagiarism software in 2006 (see Chapter 5), and commented that "if academics are to have time to teach, then the integrity of students remains essential" (2006, p.96) and that "trust and student honesty thus remain central to a successful academic system" (p.87). Although it has been shown by research that students respond to being involved in a community sense of fairness for all— embodying notions of academic integrity—it is still a difficult task for teachers and administrators to imbue some sense of honesty in students.

Where then, does this leave us? In puzzling over the issue of plagiarism as a teacher in secondary schools and universities for many years, it has become clear that one of the focal points in the debate is the issue of intention. Did a student intend to plagiarize or not? How can we, as teachers, ascertain a student's intention? Should the penalties directly relate to the student's intention or are there other factors to take into account? By utilizing cross-disciplinary theoretical lenses from critical legal theory, literary theory and cross-cultural studies, I have devised a model called the plagiarism continuum that may help us reframe our approach to plagiarism—both in terms of conceptual awareness and also in terms of teaching approach.

A Conceptual Model of Plagiarism: The Plagiarism Continuum

The model draws on major theoretical perspectives from the disciplinary areas of Law, Literary Theory and Cross-cultural studies (see Chapters 2 and 3). It also aligns with many current university plagiarism policies (see Chapter 3). The model draws on the practical aspects of Stephen Sterling's (2001) sustainable education ideas as well as Henry Giroux's (1993, 1996)[12] notion of transformative teaching. The model is, therefore, an intertwining of theoretical perceptions of plagiarism with teaching practices. The perceptions of plagiarism are drawn from tertiary teachers, students and policies. The practices are based on actions that teachers and institutions take, as well as the theoretical framework described above. The model is presented as a spectrum that is open-ended, as plagiarism is a concept that changes across textual space and historical time. The continuum is explored in relation to both students' and teachers' experiences and understanding of plagiarism in classrooms, including virtual classrooms and the practices employed in addressing the issue. This model is a useful way in which to explore why there are different understandings of plagiarism held by students, teachers and administrators and how they relate to each other. The spectrum of intention forms the basic horizontal axis and delineates the teaching approaches from the different perspectives of plagiarism, as shown in Figure 1.1.

Figure 1.1 is the diagrammatic representation of the plagiarism continuum. The diagram's overall design illustrates the point that the notion of plagiarism is not bounded, but alters depending upon individual and institutional definitions. The horizontal double-headed arrow is the foundation of the continuum, suggesting that plagiarism moves beyond the parameters of this book, as it evolves into the future. Ways in which plagiarism may be manifest in technologically mediated realms of education will be of continued study and interest. The plagiarism continuum stretches between the contentious criteria of "intentional plagiarism" and "unintentional plagiarism" as supported by the data from students, teachers and policy-makers, as well as previous work on plagiarism. The axis of intention allows teachers and policy-makers to see where they sit in relation to responses to plagiarism; authorial intention, in this model, is decided by the reader—not the writer. It is the teacher-as-reader who ascribes meaning to the textual product of the student-writer as indicated in both in theory

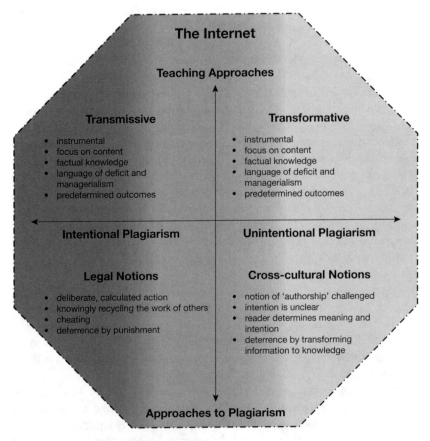

Figure 1.1 The plagiarism continuum.

(see Chapters 2–4) and research findings on practices (see Chapters 5–8). Intention is the crux of punishment in most plagiarism policies—where if the student is thought to have unintentionally plagiarized, the penalty is often less severe than that meted out for intentional acts of plagiarism. Intention is also at the heart of debate in literary studies and composition studies about reader and writer relationships and ways in which meaning is negotiated and established. Thus, the contested notion of intention is the delineating dimension for the continuum as represented by its importance as the foundation of the horizontal axis of the model.

On the left of the plagiarism continuum is the legal notion of plagiarism as an intentional act. Intentional plagiarism includes actions such as: a student taking the essay of another student and copying out parts of it or a student downloading sections of Internet sources with no references for the reader. These are clearly deliberate actions by the student, and often are designed to deceive the teacher, although occasionally there are situations where students may be unaware that these actions are not sanctioned.

On the far left of the arrow is the end of the continuum based in the law, called legal notions of plagiarism. At this end, plagiarism encompasses "knowing" acts of appropriation often seen as the deliberate, calculated and intentional action of a person to appropriate the work of others without due acknowledgment. This point of the continuum shows that plagiarism is usually punished and, often, words such as "offender," "penalty," "stealing," "misconduct" and "misappropriation" are used to describe both the person and the action. These words are from criminal law. The continuous arrow to the far left indicates that plagiarism may extend to new means of deliberate appropriation of texts—some that have not yet been technologically realized. This may, for example, include sophisticated forms of digital piracy, forgery, theft or cloning of works.

Legal notions of plagiarism also encompass actions of "cheating." Although I argue that "cheating" should be deliberately distinguished from plagiarism, at times, I agree with Russell Hunt (2004) that these areas merge and blur. My research indicates that most academics, students and some policies conceive that "cheating" involves actions that demonstrate there is no desire to engage at all with the subject or unit being studied. Actions such as buying a custom-written assignment and submitting it (sometimes called cyber-pseudepigraphy[13]), taking cheat notes into an exam, using a camera-phone to send an exam or test paper to another student or stealing work from another student's memory stick and submitting it as one's own constitute acts of cheating. When a student cheats, the student's actions are centered around an intention to deceive the teacher or assessor of the work and gain an unfair advantage over other students. I consider that this is different from an action of recycling an assignment—where the student has, at least, engaged with some of the work in the subject, even if it is just to know that the assessment task is the same as a previous one. "Cheating" has been included at the legal notions end of the model because many policies treat cheating and plagiarism as the same offense or misdemeanor.

On the top quarter of the continuum, above legal notions of plagiarism, is a teaching approach often used by teachers in both my study and previous research. I have used Giroux's (1993) notions of a "transmissive" approach to teaching and listed some of the core characteristics observed in this study above the "intentional" end of the spectrum—this approach is adopted by many teachers working in subject areas where the course is content-driven and content-assessed. In a transmissive approach to teaching, the units of study have been devised in such a way that students demonstrating a grasp of factual knowledge are highly valued. Quite an instrumental approach is taken to the learning and teaching relationship, where the teacher provides some basic information to be absorbed and the student is then tested in order to gauge the extent to which that information can be reproduced or applied. Course and unit guides provided by teachers in this study indicate that there are often pre-determined outcomes, usually in the form of examinations where "testing" for correct answers on principles and factual recall are rewarded. In a transmissive approach, often teachers are concerned to "get through" a vast amount of factual material; consequently lectures are laden with slides containing factual material or data that students scramble frantically to copy down. In order to maintain departmental grade averages, often these teachers adopt a transmissive approach to their work. By this I mean that much of the work is teacher-driven, teacher-centered and focused on students copying down notes in lectures. Although the aim of tutorials is that students answer questions and apply information to new fact or problem situations, this rarely occurs. Most often, students wait for ready-reckoner style answers to be provided, either in tutorials or "revision" periods before examinations are scheduled. There is little scope to permit students to discover their own meanings from material provided. Many of the teachers adopting such an approach also consider that plagiarism is an affront to academic integrity in any form and regard any infraction as punishable. Some of these teachers approach plagiarism by following the plagiarism policy to the letter. Many of these teachers do not consult students about allegations of plagiarism, other than to inform them that formal process will be followed through the appropriate disciplinary body. Often the teachers' rationale for doing so is that they have informed students about plagiarism; the information is also available in study materials, unit guides, university websites and faculty handbooks, so it is the student's responsibility to ensure that plagiarism is not in their work. The model suggests that there is a relationship between approaches to the teaching and learning relationship and ways in which teachers perceive plagiarism to occur.

Moving to the right along the continuum, cross-cultural studies, literary theory and composition study's concepts of plagiarism appear. Here there is a blurring of boundaries between intentional and unintentional plagiarism. This section of the continuum supports views that students "patchwrite" and mimic accepted academic norms of writing as they engage in the process of learning academic writing genres and conventions. Both patchwriting without citation (often described as "sloppy work") in both the literature and by participant teachers—and patchwriting with citation (where the citation is incomplete or incorrect)—appear at this point on the continuum. The far right-hand point of the continuum indicates the extension of the idea from some critical literacy theorists that there is no such thing as plagiarism because the concept of an "original author" is not necessarily viable. This is often referred to as the notion that plagiarism is a *chimera* (something that is a fanciful conception) because there are no original ideas remaining—all we are doing is manipulating a set of symbols. Here the swift current of virtual reality texts and infotainment race ever further away from traditional ideas of authorship and ownership of texts as stipulated in the law.

At the "unintentional" end of the spectrum, teachers are far less likely to consider plagiarism has been established. Teachers speak about plurality of texts, cross-cultural notions of authorship and teaching approaches based on inter-subjective learning and deconstruction of knowledge. Some teachers argue that plagiarism is determined by the teacher-as-reader and therefore the student-writer must be consulted about their intentions before any process can be implemented. These teachers speak with students to work through students' understandings of the content of the piece of assessment before determining what action should be taken. Although some teachers still impose a penalty, there is often a great deal of work done to ensure that something of educative value comes out of the experience for the student. A primary aim is to work towards educating students to develop an individual sense of authorial voice in their writing. I call this a "transformative" approach to teaching, following Giroux (1993), as the focus is on students being able to transform information into knowledge, through their own constructions of meaning. This is in contrast to the "transmissive" approach to teaching in which the focus is on content. In classes, transformative teachers are observed to operate with an emphasis on open-ended inquiry into an area of study as well as a strong student-driven approach. Here students negotiate responsibility for preparation of sections of the course and drive both discussion and assessment feedback. Teachers adopt a role of facilitation in a joint learning–teaching relationship, rather than a traditional teacher-centered role. I observed that teachers using transformative approaches in teaching set up democratic classrooms in which seminars and general sharing of lessons occurred. Rarely were traditional formats of lectures and tutorials used. Assessment criteria and formats were also negotiated with students to greater and lesser extents, in a bid to engage students in understanding how and why work would be assessed.

The color grading on the continuum reflects the theory from the disciplines, as described above, previous research findings and my own research data focusing on student and staff views about plagiarism in academic writing. The "legal notions" of plagiarism at the far left of the continuum are darkly shaded as this reflects research findings that most teachers react angrily and emotionally when they detect plagiarism in their students' work. Many of these members of staff consider the act of plagiarism as a deliberate affront to their professionalism and the intellectual integrity of their courses. This has sometimes been referred to as the "moral panic" stance (Clegg and Flint, 2006). Commonly teachers' responses have been comments such as "What do they think I'm *stupid* or something? Don't they think I've read that book or know the major works *in my own field?*." This reaction is often followed by a response of punishment by teacher—whether as an individual or institutional response. In addition to staff reactions, the dark color reflects the way in which plagiarism is often defined in the policy of the institution, including the processes by which the "offenders" will be punished. The dark color also reflects the reactions of many students, particularly international students, to allegations of plagiarism. University counselors and college advisors report that many students react with dark despair where plagiarism allegations are proven and punishments delivered. The dark coloring represents a myriad of complex responses by institutions, teachers and students.

Along the mid-section of the continuum are various mixed reactions of academic staff that tend to support the literature from both "literary or composition studies" and "cross-cultural studies." The continuum moves from ideas of plagiarism as an intentional action—represented by the "legal notions" end of the spectrum, through ideas that students often mimic or copy ideas and words in an apprenticeship model of learning a new academic discourse. Rebecca Moore Howard's (1995) notion of "patchwriting" is often used to describe this learning curve, as are Bakhtin's theories on hybridization of texts. Cross-cultural studies add the dimension of cultural relativism and critical pedagogy to views, and these are explored in detail in Chapter 4. There is an overlap in literary and cross-cultural theories of authorship, which also indicates that these two theoretical bases share common concerns about legal notions of authorship. At the far right-hand side of the continuum is the lightest shading—indicating that there are some academics who believe current notions of plagiarism are inappropriate in the twenty-first century, because there is no such thing as a clearly defined "author," particularly for Internet driven online classes.[14]

The dotted space surrounding the continuum and the words "The Internet" represent the Internet as a textual space. It is dotted for two reasons: first, the Internet is unbounded because it represents the uncertainty with which notions of authorship will apply to the Internet in the future. Legal, literary, composition studies and cross-cultural notions of authorship are contested in cyberspace. Second, the space remains open because the Internet changes and shapes textual practices in ways that are unable to be predicted and foreseen today. Who would have thought in Wordsworth's time that e-books would exist, or that a work once written could be altered by the reader rather than the writer? Internet information can be deliberately appropriated through intentional cutting and pasting of text, as claimed by many of the staff and some students. Other respondents argue that patchwriting occurs when information is downloaded and reworked by students but the information is insufficiently paraphrased, summarized or cited. The Internet embraces all variations of the concept of plagiarism. Neither legal views of plagiarism embodied in intellectual property laws attempting to control hyperspace nor cross-cultural views of plagiarism (that Internet information is in the public domain and does not require citation) have claimed dominance in the textual space of the World Wide Web.

Thus, the continuum ranges across concepts of intentional plagiarism, where there are yet to be enacted areas of cheating and intentional deception, to unintentional plagiarism—capturing the idea that there is no such thing as plagiarism at all. It also ranges across transmissive and transformative approaches to the teaching and learning relationship. The Internet embraces all perspectives of plagiarism as well as various teaching approaches and will continue to push both conceptualization and practice in technology-mediated classrooms.

How Can the Model Help Teachers and Policy-Makers?

The model offers a way forward for teachers in their thinking about plagiarism—in light of their own teaching practices. For example, if plagiarism was detected, how does the teacher react? Angrily? Intensely sad? Confused? These reactions by the reader will help teachers understand a great deal about the ways in which their practices operate in plagiarism detection and the resultant action. Do teachers counsel students individually if plagiarism is found or is there no opportunity in the learning environment to do so? If not, what is the educative value in pointing out plagiarized work to students? Are students punished and sent on their way to try and work out how to overcome the problem, or is there some ongoing advice and practical writing support offered for students for whom plagiarism is an issue? In using the model as a means of conceptualizing plagiarism, teachers can reflect upon their own reactions to plagiarized work and decide what pedagogical practices will enhance their classroom approaches to issues of plagiarism.

Policy-makers will find the model useful to reflect on policy within their own institutions. The different interpretations of policy from students and teachers provides policy-makers with insights into the dilemmas that occur in policy interpretation. Incorporating these perceptions when reframing policies will be of benefit to all who work with the issue of plagiarism.

Summary: Intention and Plagiarism—The Nexus

Plagiarism as a concept is complex and fraught with difficulties as teachers try to grapple to decide whether plagiarism is deliberate or not. However, plagiarism is regarded as an academic offense under most university regulations around the world. The link between the concept of plagiarism as an offense and the punishments imposed arguably places plagiarism in the realm of academic criminal behavior—the stealing of the words or kidnapping ideas of another. If plagiarism is categorized under the university penalty system as a quasi-criminal offense, then an important element of the offense is the intention of the perpetrator. The element of intention is important, as "taking" the words of another must be deliberate or intentional for the offense of plagiarism to occur. Many academics have debated whether plagiarism, by its very definition, is an intentional action, with some concluding that plagiarism alters the very act of individual learning. One view is that a plagiarist, rather than creating a work of her own, merely appropriates ideas and words of others, and, in so doing, discards the established ethical principles of higher education in general. Many equate this form of plagiarism as cheating. Another view is that where the appropriation is unintentional, there is no act of plagiarism, merely a lack of attention to citation conventions; and this is not any kind of academic offense at all. The next chapter examines how plagiarism historically arose and makes clear the connection between plagiarism and the all-important concept of intention.

CHAPTER 2

The Birth of Plagiarism

> Copyright doctrine tends to assume the importance of authorship as a privileged category of human enterprise, rather than to examine where this notion arose or how it has been influenced by the law.
> (Martha Woodmansee and Peter Jaszi, 1995, p.455)

Whereas the previous chapter outlined some of the broad concerns teachers and policy-makers hold about plagiarism and detailed a model for teachers to use in reflecting on their teaching practices, this chapter briefly details the historical origins of plagiarism. It is important to understand the birth of plagiarism because the way in which plagiarism has been applied in educational settings such as schools, colleges and universities in many countries around the globe is closely aligned to its historical roots in English and international law. The origins of plagiarism and the differences in the competing ideas about originality in writing, intention to plagiarize and the very concept of what it means to be an "author" are covered in this chapter. The debate that continues to rage, particularly in cyberspace, about concepts of authorship and ownership of text is derived from the early legal cases involving the "Romantic" notion of authorship. Understanding the tensions that exist around the very concepts that form the phenomenon of plagiarism is essential if it is to be addressed by teachers and administrators alike.

Where Does Plagiarism Come From?

The term "plagiarism" is derived from the Latin term for plundering. In fact, the idea that kidnapping the words of others, as a child is kidnapped from a parent, is appropriate to explain the way in which plagiarism is defined. There was general acceptance in eighteenth-century England of the concept that words could be kidnapped or misappropriated by someone with legal recrimination. The basis of this acceptance, in the Statute of Anne of 1710, was also embodied in the laws of former British colonies such as Australia, Canada, Hong Kong, India, New Zealand and the United States. The birth of the idea that a person could "own" words and exercise ownership or authorial rights over their creation was unleashed in various copyright laws around the world. Plagiarism is closely aligned with legal rights of copyright and pursued in courts today.

The Origins of Plagiarism in Writing

Before Gutenberg's printing press in 1450 revolutionized the way in which the general public had access to written works, control of literary texts remained with the Church. The literate members of the Church maintained control over the spread of information as only they and the members of the educated elite could read and write. The Church maintained control over the ways in which the pre-literate general population understood the world, as the Church controlled and delivered the oral explanations of religious doctrine. This meant that the general public had no access to information to make up their own minds about matters, as not only were there no publications for the masses, but they did not know how to read. They were in a completely subservient position to the educated few. However, several factors combined to shift the power of the Church and its dominant position as controller of information.

One factor was undoubtedly the invention of the printing press by Gutenberg around 1450. With the ability to manufacture large volumes of literary works for the general public to consume, publishing houses were able to engage in mass publication. Such a move would be fruitless, however, if the general public were still pre-literate. As education became more widely available and accepted by the rising middle classes, and the general population became increasingly literate, demand for reading material rose. In addition, the lapse of certain legislation, such as the Licensing Act in 1675, meant that there was an explosion of publications for the general public to read and a choice about what information the readers chose to believe. In 1704 London had nine newspapers but by 1709 the number of newspapers had risen to 19—thereby providing different perspectives of newsworthy events. The increasingly literate public could, for the first time in their literate history, choose whether they wanted to follow oral or written forms of information. It was not just general news that was consumed by the eager public. There was also an increase in demand for academic works written for general public consumption. To satisfy the clamoring from the general public to know more about what was happening in science, medicine, the arts and discoveries from the New World, the Royal Society of London published a monthly journal titled *Philosophical Transactions*. In conjunction with increased public demand for the supply of literature to satisfy an increasingly curious citizenship, an ideal was born that people were individuals with rights. The more informed population began to embrace concepts of possessive individualism over traditional means of public control by the Church and State. Possessive individualism was the perfect conduit to support ideas of authorial rights.

Possessive Individualism and Copyright

"Possessive individualism" is the belief that individuals are entitled to protect themselves and the products of their labors. Under this idea, the individual has the right to decide how his physical body and the product of his labor will be used. This idea then extended to ways in which his mind and the product of his intellect could be used and owned. By the early sixteenth century, possessive individualism had spread to capture the thoughts and ideas of an individual person. The notion of individual possession as a right took hold, and in 1710 the thoughts and ideas of a person were legally categorized as "property." This meant that where an individual person created new "works" in writing or speech, they belonged to him[1] as tangible property. At the same time, however, the law stipulated that the "work" must be "original" and add to or extend existing "knowledge" or information. Therefore the combined effects of the invention of the printing press bringing print text to the masses, the demand for books by an increasing readership and the spread of the ideology of the individual promoted the notion of the author as an individual creator of text. Wherever individual authors created a "work" from their own thoughts, legal protection in the form of proprietary rights was sought. The protection afforded to authors came under a branch of intellectual property law known as copyright, which exists in our legal and social systems today. It must be pointed out that this legal protection only existed after printing and reading came to be popular forms of gathering information. As Elizabeth Eisenstein[2] says, "The terms plagiarism and copyright did not exist for the minstrel. It was only after printing that they began to hold significance for the author" (1983, p.15). She means that for minstrels, the clergy and other purveyors of oral information, the emerging world of print and reading signified a decline in their role as traditional messengers of stories, news and important happenings. This is important, as with the decline in the supremacy of oral traditions in favor of the dramatic rise of print as a reliable form of receiving information, authors sought legal protection over their products. Authorship as a legal concept began to be debated.

The Birth of "Authorship": England

In 1518, England adopted the early sixteenth-century system of printing privileges. Printing privileges previously existed in the nation-state of Venice and a number of other European States. The system involved certain stationers having the right to print a particular work. Ideas of legal copyright began when a group of London publishers, angered that a Scottish publisher was putting together a compilation of poetry, met to find ways to fight what they conceived to be a direct attack on their literary property. By taking this action, the stationers sowed the seeds of thinking about written text—whether appearing as poetry, plays, stories or other forms of writing—as a form of "property" that could be owned. At this point in time in the sixteenth century, such ownership of written texts rested with publishing houses that bought or commissioned written works, rather than with individual authors. Ownership then, as now, was often legally challenged in the court system, but rights could only be enforced if Parliamentary laws, known as Acts, permitted such enforcement rights. There is considerable debate as to why legal protection of copyright arose in this period.

British historian John Feather[3] (1994) argues that the State needed censorship and control over trade, particularly in the form of written texts. The demand for books by an increasingly literate readership exceeded the censorship abilities of the government of the day. He says that the State managed to maintain and increase control over publishing houses and provide a degree of indirect censorship, by creating a parliamentary control over authorship. Copyright law was born. Similarly, American Marlon B. Ross[4] argues that the emergence of legal rights of control over written work was linked to the changing patterns of social control exercised by the king and government of the time. He claims that the State developed the law of copyright so that it could control and censor what, how and when works were printed. The purpose was to use the printed works as an instrument of control over citizens, therefore "the monarchic state developed the licensing system to control the authority that is transmitted through the medium of print" (Ross, 1994, p.242).

Australian Professors of Law, Sam Ricketson and Megan Creswell (2001), agree. They argue that the Crown's interest in printing moved from the realm of trade to that of censorship in a bid to control the wider circulation of undesirable ideas, particularly in matters of religion. The greater availability of the written word meant it was easier to spread and promote new ideas that challenged the status quo, so legislation became a political tool. American Professor of Law, Peter Jaszi,[5] supports the idea that copyright law was used to support political ends, but he sees the birth of legislative control over printed material in a different light. He argues that the emergence of legal protection for authors was spawned by established London-based publishers and booksellers, who claimed that the legislation was a way to fight the increasing economic competition in print publishing. He concludes that "authorship remained a malleable concept, generally deployed on behalf of publishers rather than writers" (1994, p.32). In other words, commercial priorities promoted by publishers, rather than State concerns about declining adherence to traditional ideas, were driving the push towards legal copyright. It is important to note, however, that both printing houses and individuals lobbied for authors to be recognized as proprietary owners of literary works.

In the mid sixteenth century, poets such as William Wordsworth were petitioning for individual writers to be granted authorial rights, rather than investing booksellers with proprietary rights over literary works. It must be noted that no government laws had been passed at this time to award individual authors the right to protect their individual creations. However, by the late sixteenth century the idea emerged that a written text was a unique individual creation—unlike any preceding it. This view was nurtured and strongly promoted by poets and authors alike as, at this time, writers produced works under a traditional system of patronage. Patronage meant that a wealthy patron would engage a writer to produce a work. However, the writer did not possess ownership rights over the text once it had been produced and disseminated. All these ongoing rights passed to the patron. The courts witnessed a series of cases where writers and poets sought to redress this disparity. Literary figures argued that each author was an individual genius who created an original work. This literary work, which was a labor of intellect, warranted legal protection in the form of proprietary rights. This English sixteenth-century concept of "author" is now commonly referred to as the "Romantic" notion of authorship.

At this time, authors increased pressure to wrest legal control over their creations from their publishers. Such action caused tension with the

Stationers' Guild, which had always sought to regulate the production of books in its various publishing-house members. The Guild began to seek copyright protection over the textual works printed in addition to the regulatory control it enjoyed. As Mark Rose[6] explains:

> A gap was beginning to develop between the institution of stationers' copyright, which was based upon a traditional conception of society as a community bound by ties of fidelity and service, and the emergent ideology of possessive individualism.
>
> (1993, p.15)

When the Court of the Star Chamber was abolished in 1641, the Stationers' Guild suddenly lost its primary instrument of authority and monopoly. This meant that anything could be printed by anyone able to access a printing press. Although the Stationers' Guild in 1643 petitioned Parliament pleading for recognition of what it said were the ancient rights to control copies for its members, it failed to reinstate regulation and proprietary rights. The importance of this stand lies in the fact that the Stationers' Guild considered property rights over literary works extended to both publication and regulation. As the seventeenth century closed, a general ideological change in the ways in which the general populace seemed to be thinking about individual rights to claim authorship over their literary creations had begun. Rights of individuals to own their work, rather than just their ink-penned manuscripts or goods produced by hand, had gained community support. The combined pressure of authors and the Stationers' Guild pressed the legislature for legal proprietary rights of authors over their creations to be publicly affirmed. Legal protection for individuals was also in accord with the general public's rising belief that individuals should have such rights and be able to pursue them through the courts. Legal protection for individuals occurred in England's Statute of Anne of 1710, which legalized an author's claim of proprietary rights over his literary work. The author was seen as the "father" or "begetter" of the work and the text itself was the "child." With the recognition of authorial rights was the birth of copyright law and with it, the notion of plagiarism.

The reason that the Statute of Anne of 1710 was passed by the government was because a legal tussle arose between two groups of booksellers in Scotland and England over the property rights to certain books. This booksellers' battle was undoubtedly commercial in nature, even though the Statute itself was based more around concepts of honor and reputation rather than any sense of economic property. The Statute was based on the concept of paternal ownership, which was embodied in the nature of society at the time. For example, the idea of passing property from father to son was understood by the people and firmly entrenched in laws that already existed in relation to property. Another way of interpreting the idea of authors' rights to own their works also existed in the traditional master to servant relationship, which was evident in earlier legislation of the sixteenth century. By seeing the literary work, for example a book, as a kind of landed estate and the author as the master of the estate, helps us to understand the relationship between the property and the master through those eighteenth-century notions. This is important, as the slowness of the law to recognize individual rights to ownership of early forms of intellectual property, has had an effect on the ways in which literary works were published. Although the Statute of Anne recognized that there was a relationship between the author and the work, it is not until the Copyright Act of 1814 that the author is legally protected as the creator and therefore the owner of literary works as property.

Although the English Statute of Anne (1710) did not protect authors per se, it is important because it legally recognized the idea of literary property, or authorial ownership over texts. This Act opened the door for authors to claim acknowledgment as the proprietary owners of their "literary works" and gave authors legal standing to go to court to enforce their rights. The first case in England was *Burnet* v. *Chetwood* in 1720.[7] In the decision of this case, it was clear that the judges intended to treat literary property as any other kind of property, therefore the author had to possess the property claimed for proprietary rights to be upheld. This requirement becomes problematic where the author sells the "work" for publication, as the legal argument is that there is no ownership of the property by the author, as the work is common to all by virtue of publication. Sale of property also implies that ownership has passed to another party. This meant that the author's ideas were placed in the public realm to be used as the public saw fit. Such interpretation by the courts led to dissatisfaction from litigants, as proprietary rights in the literary work ceased to exist upon publication. A flurry of cases followed Burnet's case but the landmark legal decision was when the great English poet Alexander Pope sued Edmund Curll in (1741).[8] This is recognized as the first English case where the new term "copyright" appeared. In *Pope* v. *Curll* (1741), the Lord Chancellor, Lord Hardwicke, made a distinction between writing and social exchange, determining writing a text as "a solitary and self sufficient act of creation." This decision, granting the poet Alexander Pope ownership rights as the sole creator of his poetic works, provided the foundation for others to sue people breaching copyright in the English courts. Pope's case did more than that—it also provided the moral framework for the idea that the author was a "solitary genius, writing in isolation" (De Voss and Rosati, 2002, p.200) and needed protection under law. English society was now beginning to embrace ideas of individuality and the concept that individual authors should be protected by legislation. However, the work had to be "original."

The Concept of "Original" Work

In Pope's case, the English Court of the King's Bench decided that the concept of originality was a key element in their decision as to whether Pope could sue Curll successfully or not. The court had to consider what the term "originality" meant. The court searched for the first appearance of the requirement for originality, which it found recorded in the English Printing Register in 1584. According to the Register, printing a work was conditional upon the work being "original." An author's work could be printed as long as it was not "collected out of anie book already extante in printe in English."[9] Therefore, the idea of originality meant that the work could not already exist in print form. After Pope's case, the element of originality was essential to a legal claim of authorship, but it was not until the 1790s that broader social and philosophical shifts in conceptions of authorship emerged.

The idea that originality of thought was valued and worthy of protection by the courts was popularly held towards the end of the 1790s. The writings of the philosopher John Locke were evidence of the change towards a philosophical stance of supporting private ownership of not only material goods but also intellectual goods. According to Locke, private property is created when individuals take matter from its natural state and by the force of his own labor, a person produces some new creation—a personal product is created by the sweat of an individual's brow, so to speak. This Lockean principle, which is written about in his work, *Treatises on Government*, captures Locke's idea that every individual has property within himself—the notion that bringing individual labor to bear on something that was not of great value before is the gift of each individual. This principle was easily incorporated into the legal discourse of originality. The act of an author using individual labor to create an original authorial work, which gave rise to the individual author's rights to the work as property, rather than the State or publishing house owning the work, became popular with leading literary figures such as Wordsworth and Pope. The leading English poets intimated that the writing process of authors "ought to be solitary, or individual and introduce a new element into the intellectual universe" (Woodmansee, 1994, p.27).

The legal protection afforded to individual authors—providing the work was "original"—emerged as the dominant form of social thinking in the late eighteenth century. Edward Young, the English essayist and writer, is credited with formalizing the notion of originality in his 1759 essay titled

Conjectures. He wrote that authors should have legal protection over the creative spark that represented their original genius and which was used to produce an "original" work. In so doing, Young successfully bound the work's concept of originality with the individuality of the author. As the work was of value, so too was the "original genius" of the author, who was entitled to protect and retain rights to the intellectual property of the work. American Professor of English and Law, Martha Woodmansee (1994), states, "Copyright law has been informed by the aims of the self-declaring original genius—which has in turn been empowered by this body of law" (p.771). It was the "original" work that needed the protection of law and the author of that original work had the right to "own" the work and dispose of it as he saw fit. Mark Rose (1993, p.121) adds:

> What Young has done is to introduce the notion of original genius into the traditional discourse of authorship, thereby producing a representation in which the originality of the work, and conse-quently its value, becomes dependent on the individuality of the author.

These social ideals were further supported by the courts. Justice Aston, when deciding the 1769 case of *Millar* v. *Taylor*,[10] said, "I confess I do not know, nor can I comprehend any property more emphatically a man's own, nay, more incapable of being mistaken, than his literary works." The judge added, "I think an author's property is in his works and the copyright is fully and sufficiently established because it is admitted to be property in his own hands and that he has the original right of first publishing them."[11] Justice Aston was clearly attributing property rights to authors over their creations and providing them with the right to dispose of their "works" as they saw fit. This marks an important change in the rights of individuals, as prior to these legal decisions, the right of disposal rested with the traditional owners—the publishers or Stationers' Guild.

Following these court decisions, in the late eighteenth century, authors were in a much stronger position to demand greater ownership protection over their work. In England, the 1710 Statute of Anne legislation gave some protection to authors over their literary works and was extended under the new 1814 Copyright Act. This legislation acknowledged that authors could exercise some publication rights over their works. It also allowed the original work to remain the literary property of the author even after death.

This brief history of the emergence of copyright law and plagiarism in England demonstrates some of the essential elements that are still prized in the twenty-first century in terms of what is regarded as a copyrightable work. The elements of originality and the author's creative genius being embodied in the work are still referred to as the "Romantic notion" of authorship. This is because this particular view romanticizes the idea that the author is the sole creator or "originator" of the text that is a product of the solitary genius of the writer. This perspective, of course, completely ignores the many influences from sources outside the writer—the social, cultural, economic and political environments will all influence the way in which a text is crafted, as well as a myriad of personal factors that influence the "author" in the writing process.

However, the Romantic view of the author was not only embodied in English law in the 1814 Copyright Act, but this legislation provided the basis of copyright law in the independent nation of the United States, as well as in Australia and other British colonies. The copyright laws of these nations were built on the Romantic ideals of the original work and the sole creator. However, while England and her Empire embraced one view of what it meant to have rights as an author, across the English Channel in some European countries very different ideas of the rights of individual authors existed in Europe.

Legal Notions of Authorship

Some Western European nations had also established protection for authors over their literary works in the sixteenth through to the eighteenth centuries. However, unlike the English laws where authors possessed property rights over their works, the Europeans based their legal views on the premise that an author had moral rather than economic or property rights over works.

France

In France in the early sixteenth century, the idea of *droit morale*, or moral rights, was extended to authors seeking to protect their literary works. *Droit morale* was the idea that while authors did not own their texts in a sense of property rights, it was improper for anyone to reprint or use the work without the author's permission. In contrast to the English law's proprietary or economic model, European moral rights' philosophers did not consider the economic rights of an author to be paramount. They believed that protection of the soul of the creative work was more significant than pure economic considerations. The French legal system's stance to affirm moral rights includes: the right of disclosure (*droit de divulgation*), the right of recall over the work because of a change of opinion (*droit de retrait ou de repentir*), the right to claim authorship as the "father" or begetter of the work (*droit á la paternité*) and the right to integrity of the work (*droit au respect de l'oeuvre*). This is known as the moral rights view of authorship.[12] Three of these rights, the right to disclosure by the author, the right of recall because of change of opinion, and the right of integrity, are not found anywhere in the English ideas of authorship at all. However, the French legal right proclaiming the author as the "begetter" of the work—in French, the word "*paternité*" is used—corresponds with the English notion that the author was the "father" and the work was the "child." The right of integrity is founded purely on moral views of the way in which the product of authorial labor may be used. Although early cases on the right of integrity do not exist in English translation, an example of this French concept of authorship is found in the 1962 case of *Fersing* v. *Buffet*[13] heard in the Paris Court of Appeal.

THE FRENCH MORAL "RIGHT OF INTEGRITY"

In this case, the defendant was the famous French artist Bernard Buffet. Buffet painted designs on all sides of a refrigerator. The refrigerator owner proposed to dismantle the object and sell the individual panels as separate works of art. Buffet was able to stop the owner from acting in this manner, as he successfully argued to the Paris Court of Appeal that it was a violation of his moral artistic right of integrity.[14] Buffet's central argument was that he as the creator gave part of his inner being to the production of his artwork, and therefore, morally, he should be allowed to influence the way in which the artwork would be displayed or used. He successfully argued that his "right of integrity" was impinged upon and, morally, it should be protected by the law. French academic, Ysolde Gendreau, states that the notion of individual authorship is the desire of the author in acting to protect the "personal bond" he has created with his work (1999, p.19). However, the moral rights view does not allow authors to claim literary property rights over words. In other words, it is not possible for an author to claim ownership over words, as it is in English law, as the moral rights position argues that words cannot be owned by one person—they belong to the whole community. The moral rights view does, however, protect the author's moral right to be given credit and acknowledgment for his work— the right of disclosure. A French author has the right under Article L 121–1 of the French Intellectual Property Code to decide whether or not he will disclose his work to the public. The extent of legal protection is limited to, as Jerome Passa reports, "the author's right to demand that his name be mentioned on copies of his work" (1999, p.73). This is because the moral rights of the author are limited to claiming credit only as the producer of the work because the author has drawn words and text from the public domain. The author has the right to be acknowledged in having done as much, but no more. The contrasting English view, also existing in Australia, Canada, New Zealand, the United States and many other former colonies and territories of the British Empire, awards actual "ownership" or tangible property rights over the words used by the author. The position of legal rights for authors was also different in Germany.

Germany

In Germany the debate over what constituted an author's rights to claim property rights over work was at its height from 1773–1794. The German law differed from that of the English and the French in that it focused on the question of legality of reproduction of books. The German lawmakers used Johann Fichte's concept of "form," which was crucial in establishing the philosophical grounds for German writers' claim to ownership of their work. Fichte distinguished between the material and the immaterial aspects of a book in determining the elements of a "literary work." He then divided the immaterial aspects into content and form; the content of the book— the ideas—could not be considered property. This is the argument that ideas exist in the public arena and therefore, similar to the application of public domain to words, German law proclaimed that ideas could not be owned by individual authors. Fichte did allow that the form of the book, that is, the specific way in which the ideas were presented, remained the author's property forever. This is because authors chose certain ways to express their ideas and that form warranted protection. As Fichte wrote, "each writer has his own thought processes, his own way of forming concepts and connecting them."[15] It is clear that in the late 1790s in Germany, authors could assert proprietary claims over the form or layout of their work, but could not own the ideas or content written in the text itself. This view is in stark contrast to the position in England where authors had full property rights over their creations—including text and content.

Contrasting the Legal Protection in Western Europe and England

European law of the eighteenth century was the foundation for the protection of authors' moral rights, whereas the English system was based on protection of the economic and property rights of authors. The reasons for such differences are unclear. The English focus on protecting economic property rights of authors may have emerged from the battle between authors and publishers over the monopoly over publication by the Stationers' Guild. The changing philosophy of society to favor individual rights may also have stimulated the need to introduce the legislation. Economic lobbying by publishers or political desires to regulate the masses through censorship control are also possible reasons to explain the changes in law. Nor are the reasons for legal protection of authorship in early eighteenth-century France and Germany clear.

Acknowledging the fact that different ideas of authorial rights emerged in England and its colonies, compared to some Western European countries, is essential to be able to gain an understanding of different ideas about what it means to attribute words to certain authors in today's world. These legal foundations imbue the societies in which they exist with a sense of what is appropriate for legal protection. The next section sketches the situation in two former colonies of Britain—the United States of America and Australia.

Legal Notions of Authorship

The United States

The United States of America essentially adopted the basic elements of the eighteenth-century system in England. This means that the legislation in the United States embraced the idea of individual authors creating an original work in isolation—as described in *Pope* v. *Curll* and *Millar* v. *Taylor*. Importantly, under United States copyright law, the writer is at the centre of authorship protection. When examining the United States Copyright Act of 1976, John Logie points out, "US copyright is about sustaining the conditions of creativity that enable an individual to craft out of thin air, and intense devouring labor" the original, authorial work (1998, p.132). The key factors in determining whether an individual who is creating or crafting a literary work out of "thin air" can seek legal protection under the law is whether the text is original or not. The way in which originality have been interpreted in America is essentially the same as the early English judiciary—the "Romantic" notion of authorship. Additionally, the United States laws have adopted the English Lockean view that the fruits of individual labor deserve legal protection. Not surprisingly, the Romantic view that the "sole" creator of the "work" produced it as solitary genius and in isolation because he could craft it out of "thin air" is inherent in the legal protection afforded American authors.

What distinguishes the United States law from English and European law, however, is the economic benefit provision. Under United States law, prescribing an element of "public good" in Section 101 of the Copyright Act 1976 for copying work without authorial approval is permitted in certain circumstances. In specific situations, where it is of public benefit that a work is able to be copied without prior approval or attribution, such action is lawful. This means that in America placing "public good" as a secondary consideration to economic benefit is in contrast to the European model, where protection of public rights is the primary aim of the legislation. The United States "public good" provisions include the idea that an author's work can be copied where it is necessary for the public good. This is called the legal doctrine of "fair use." The doctrine of fair use began in 1841 in the United States, but was not fully incorporated into the legislation until 1976. The "fair use" provisions indicate that US law attempts to balance public need for access to information—similar to the French "public domain" ideal—with the English system of individual property rights for authors.[16] Boston Professor of Law, Alfred Yen considers that the US legislation diverged from the English model because "early Americans did not view copyright as a purely economic instrument. Instead, they referred explicitly to copyright's support in both economics and natural law" (1994, p.164). "Fair use" provisions allow individuals or institutions to copy another author's work, an amount up to 10 percent of the whole, for certain purposes, such as education and training. Martha Woodmansee explains that, "as interpreted by the courts, such 'fair uses' have traditionally included criticism, news reporting, reading and scholarship" (Woodmansee and Jaszi, 1995, p.774).

Therefore, in the United States, there is legal protection for the author under copyright law dating back to 1841. The US laws for authors to claim protection over their works falls somewhere between the French moral rights approach and the English proprietary approach. However, a balance between "public good" and "individual" proprietary rights must be maintained. Another former British colony, Australia, has followed the US example in terms of its approach to authors' rights over their works.

Australia

Australia, as a colony of England, inherited the English system of law and its principles of application. Romantic views of authorship tied to property rights of the author over the literary work were accepted as part of the legal codes of the Australian colonies. Authors were granted rights to their literary works provided the author could successfully prove the "work" was original under the English cases of *Pope* v. *Curll* and *Millar* v. *Taylor*. When changes were made to copyright legislation in England, including changes to the Copyright Act of 1814, they were absorbed into Australian colonial laws. All English amendments were also incorporated in the Australian legal system until Australia became a nation in 1900. Even after Australia attained nationhood on January 1, 1900, English laws were primarily adopted by the fledgling nation, including the English Copyright Act of 1912 and the amendments that followed until 1968.

In 1968 the national Australian Parliament (Attorney-General's Department, 1968) passed the Copyright Act (1968) Commonwealth, which was the first unifying legislation to operate throughout the Australian States and territories. This meant that for the first time in the nation's history, copyright law operated uniformly throughout all states and territories. The purpose of the 1968 Australian Copyright Act was to protect the original "work" from unauthorized use or adaptation. This represents a significant departure from the English law's stance of protecting the work as the property of the author. The 1968 Australian legislation broke with the colonial tradition of following the mother country and instead followed the US approach by adopting the US economic benefit test of "fair use." This test presumes that public access to information is free from copyright restraints where the economic test of "fair use" is satisfied. "Fair use" exceptions apply to educational institutions, and section 40 of the 1968 Copyright Act lists a range of activities that are considered to be in the public interest for freely available access to information. For example, educational institutions such as schools and universities were able to continue their tradition of reading and performing "literary, dramatic, musical or artistic work"[17] providing the purpose was for research or study. In adopting the US approach, the Australian legislature has attempted to balance the author's rights to economic benefit with reasonable fair use and public access to the work. In addition, the national government of Australia recognized the need to protect the "moral rights" of authors to their works in 2000.[18] This law acknowledges the "moral rights" of authors to include rights to attribution of authorship, which aligns the Australian legislation more closely to the French notion of being granted creative rather than economic ownership. The Copyright Amendment (Moral Rights) Act also sets out provisions for false attribution, which makes it an offense to falsely claim authorship over a literary work or alter text from the original without the author's permission. This again points to the government's attempt to balance the previously purely economic and proprietary position regarding authors' rights over their works, with the European idea of moral rights of attribution. Such a move by the government means that Australia not only complies with international legal obligations, but re-establishes the natural law obligations founded in the early English Courts of Equity in English court decisions such as *Millar* v. *Taylor*. Interestingly, these moral rights provisions, in which false claims over authorship are treated as an offense, bear a striking similarity to the way in which plagiarism policies are often framed in educational institutions. (The framing of plagiarism under policy is discussed in Chapter 3.)

International Obligations to Recognize Authorship

The Berne Convention

The rapid growth in use of technology has been one force that has helped shape Marshall McLuhan's "global village."[19] These "digital neighborhoods"—to use Nicholas Negroponte's (1996) phrase—have become signatories to international accords and treaties. Membership of international committees is seen as increasingly necessary for survival in the global political and economic arena. Along with the benefits of belonging to a powerful international body comes the obligation for member nations to comply with agreed rules: nation-states' national laws must comply with international conventions. Copyright is one such area of law and the law of copyright has strongly influenced the way in which plagiarism has been applied in various settings.

The Berne Convention for the Protection of Literary and Artistic Works is the oldest international agreement designed to protect creators of literary and artistic works and was implemented in 1886 for member nations. It has been successively revised in 1896 (Paris), 1908 (Berlin), 1914 (Berne), 1928 (Rome), 1948 (Brussels), 1967 (Stockholm), 1971 (Paris) and 1979 (Berne Union). Although the international copyright law itself has no direct authority, which is called *jurisdiction* over the national laws of member nations, member states are expected to incorporate and implement key areas set out in the Berne Convention. When the United States joined the 119 member nations in 1980, Berne became the dominant world convention dealing with international copyright.

At the 1971 meeting in Paris, the Berne Convention added computer programs "whether in source or object code" to the growing list of "works" to be protected with international law. This is interesting, illustrating the growing need at an international level to recognize technological advances in software design, programming innovations and the like as a form of intellectual property. As such, the "authors" of these "works" could expect protection under international law. Previous agreements to establish international accord on the protection for technology were given by member nations under the TRIPs (Trade-Related Aspects of Intellectual Property) Agreement.[20] The effectiveness of TRIPs is that it combines the international community's agreed regulations on copyright with the ability to enforce compliance through application of trade sanctions against any nation-state that breaches the agreement. The TRIPs agreement is administered by the World Trade Organization (WTO) with advice from the World Intellectual Property Organization (WIPO).

The World Intellectual Property Organization (WIPO)

The World Intellectual Property Organization (WIPO) updates the Berne Convention to reflect changes in world copyright needs, including the effects of digital technology. These changes affect all 119 signatory nations. The current Copyright Treaties 1996 state:

> The purpose of the two treaties is to update and supplement the major existing WIPO treaties on copyright and related rights, primarily in order to respond to developments in technology and in the marketplace. Since the Berne and Rome Conventions were adopted or lastly revised more than a quarter century ago, new types of works, new markets, and new methods of use and dissemination have evolved. Among other things, both the WIPO Copyright Treaty 2002 and WIPO Performances and Phonograms Treaty 2002, address the challenges posed by today's digital technologies, in particular the dissemination of protected material over digital networks such as the Internet. For this reason, they have sometimes been referred to as the "Internet treaties."
>
> (WIPO, 2002)

According to the Assistant Director-General of WIPO, these "Internet treaties" seek to protect as far as possible, the rights of authors in their literary and artistic works. Under the Internet treaties, "literary works" are defined as writings and computer programs, original databases, musical works, audiovisual works, works of fine art and photographs. This international copyright law forms part of international law that signatory nations are bound to honor. The WIPO Internet treaties form part of that obligation. Many member nations, such as Australia, Canada, China, New Zealand, the United Kingdom and the United States, for example, have incorporated the Internet treaties provisions into domestic law, for example the Australian Copyright Amendment (Digital Agenda) Act of 2000. Initiatives such as these indicate that international influences on traditional areas of the nation-state's jurisdiction and power are highly effective. Membership of such international conventions has had an enormous effect on the shape and development of national laws. A global approach to notions of copyright will inevitably set boundaries and influence national copyright initiatives. The cost of international membership to bodies such as the United Nations and its subordinate councils, such as WIPO, is that individual nations must comply with the international formulation of global regulation on copyright. If not, international economic sanctions may be imposed by the global community under the auspices of the Berne Convention.

The effect of the Internet treaties means that there is legal recognition that authors have legal rights to more than just written words. For example, in the Australian High Court—the highest court in Australia—the *Computer Edge Pty Ltd* v. *Apple Computer Inc*[21] in 1986 posed a dilemma for the judges in the legal interpretation of the purpose of a computer program. Although the human readable form (language) of the program resembles a literary work, which would satisfy the legislation's criteria, the purpose of the program was to control a computer's execution of the task after the "work" was converted into a machine-readable form (language or code) and stored in the computer's memory. This meant that it was not a "literary work" but a function of control by the program. The court ruled that the term "computer program" was also a "literary work." Although the Australian Federal Parliament passed additional laws to restrict the definition of "computer program" in 1999 and 2000,[22] the legislation has moved closer to the definition in section 101 of the US Copyright Act of 1976.[23] The Australian Federal Parliament stated that the intention of these new laws was to enable a uniform application of the law by the courts and to provide a practical enforcement regime for copyright owners. There is still debate about the new laws, which have been criticized on the grounds that they are too restrictive and technology specific, which means that they will not cover all types of machines that are capable of being programmed or that use other computer languages. However, only future legal cases will show how effective the laws are to protect digital authorship.

The effects of decisions such as these mean that the concept of a "work" over which an "author" has control is rapidly changing in line with information communication technologies. No longer are the pen and ink writings of artists such as William Wordsworth the canon of "literary work" under the law. Literary works include plays, concerts, film texts, computer-generated images and a range of multimodal texts. As the concepts of "literary works" change, so will the claims as to authorship and ownership. The fields in which plagiarism can occur will also broaden, and teachers in the twenty-first century have a much broader notion of "work" to judge as original or not. For example, teachers in areas such as fine arts must now decide whether students who produce computer-generated works of choreography have plagiarized steps and music as well as graphics and simulations. These will all prove not only challenging to teachers and plagiarism policy-writers but also to the law, as it tries to regulate expanding textual spaces.

Summary of the Historical Development of Plagiarism

As this chapter has illustrated, legal protection for works written by authors has arisen in many Western countries from the development of legal notions of copyright. These legal frameworks of copyright law and its offshoot, plagiarism, have grown from the social and cultural views of what it means to be an author and the essential ingredients of a literary (or other) work. The views of authorship held in various countries gives us insight into ways in which expectations of the relationship between a writer and the work are founded. Where authorial rights are ignored or not properly acknowledged claims of plagiarism can arise, as is seen in the case of *The Da Vinci Code.*

Global international forces are part of the changing complexity of copyright laws governing authorship, ownership and moral rights of authors to their literary works. "Works" no longer cover merely literary works, but incorporate music, choreography, computer programs, computer software and a myriad of authorial production. Although the law seeks to protect authors' rights to their authorial works under copyright law, one of the concerns authors have is that some people use their works without giving credit, paying economic dues or seeking copyright permission. Some nations consider that false claims over authorial works are punishable as a moral offense.[24] Using copyrighted and non-copyrighted work without attribution or acknowledgment is known in educational settings as plagiarism. Many tertiary institutions have drafted plagiarism policies to reflect the legal nature of a copyright offense. Understanding the differences between legal concepts of "property" and moral ideas of authorship assists us as teachers, administrators and students to appreciate why there is such variation in plagiarism policies and the interpretations of plagiarism around the globe. A second reason to examine the way in which copyright law has branched into areas such as plagiarism is to notice how it changes to meet the growth of new technologies. The point here is to see how rapid the changes are becoming. For example, when Australia first adopted the 1814 copyright laws of England, the laws remained relatively unaltered until the 1968 national unifying legislation. Since 1986, there have been three major amendments and additions to the original copyright law. Two major amendments were approved within the space of one year. My point here is to indicate that although the law remained unchanged for 154 years, the advent of technologies has necessitated that governments respond not only more rapidly but also more frequently to the escalating area of digital copyright, cybercheating and online plagiarism. This is important in the later discussion of Internet plagiarism and anti-plagiarism software in Chapter 5.

The key point for us, as educators, is that the law has been one primary instrument framing our understandings of what plagiarism is and how it should be dealt with. It is critical to reflect on the framework that shapes our thinking about plagiarism—Western legal discourse. If we acknowledge this molding of our ideas of what it means to be an author, how authorship is structured and the relationship between the writer and text, it is possible to see that these constructions are only one world view of the notion of plagiarism. The next chapter deconstructs the discourse of plagiarism policies from around the globe and discusses six "elements" ascribed as the essence of plagiarism. In doing so, I argue that the role of Western legal discourse has been the primary tool used to fashion plagiarism policies in our institutions. The law has also framed our ways of managing plagiarism in educational settings—usually following the punitive path that is reminiscent of criminal law penalties. It is these policies and processes that to date, have guided our practices as teachers.

CHAPTER 3

The Six Elements of Plagiarism

With few exceptions, the policies examined appeared to assume a universal view of plagiarism as an academic crime. Inadvertent plagiarism was rarely acknowledged, and even then it is attributed as much to carelessness as to lack of citation skills. Universities that respond to plagiarism with an attempt to educate students are few; punishment is the norm.

(Diane Pecorari, 2001, p.18)

As the last chapter pointed out, because plagiarism was born in legal notions of copyright, it is of practical importance for us as teachers to understand how this affects our professional judgments. The embodiment of legal concepts of what authorship entails and therefore what it means to plagiarize from authors is defined in the plagiarism policies of our institutions. This chapter outlines the fundamental similarities and differences in plagiarism policies from universities and colleges of advanced education in Australia, Canada, China, New Zealand, the United Kingdom and the United States of America. By examining these plagiarism policies, varying ways in which tertiary colleges and universities define plagiarism are evident. The fact that one clear definition of plagiarism has not been globally adopted supports the view that plagiarism is complex, contextual and open to interpretation. This provides one way of understanding how confusing it is for students, particularly those from other countries, to come to terms with differing perceptions of plagiarism. After discussing the definition of plagiarism in the first part of the chapter, the second part of this chapter discusses these policies in light of the six elements of plagiarism.

Plagiarism: The Complexities of Definition

It is not surprising that there is no universal definition of plagiarism to satisfy all situations. This is because the meanings people give to plagiarism depend on various interpretive contexts. Indeed, the term "plagiarism" itself is contested as it is not only a cultural and economic word but embodies intensely personal notions of intellectual politics as well. Despite the indeterminate nature of plagiarism, classroom teachers and their students still have to work with concepts of plagiarism in a way that permits some degree of determination and knowledge. Many teachers, including myself, have sought assistance in obtaining clearer understanding of what plagiarism is deemed to be, from various dictionary definitions. Common definitions of plagiarism are to:

1 take and use another person's thoughts, writings, inventions as one's own

(Australian Concise Oxford Dictionary)

2 take and use (the thoughts, writings, inventions etc.) of another person as one's own. (2) pass off the thoughts etc. of another person as one's own [L. plagiarius, kidnapper]

(Concise Oxford Dictionary)

3 appropriate or use (ideas, passages, etc.) from (another work or author). From Latin plagiarus plundered, from plagium kidnapping

(Collins Dictionary of the English Language)

4 steal and pass off (the ideas or words of another) as one's own: use another's production without crediting the source; to commit literary theft: present as new and original an idea or product derived from an existing source.

(Webster's Online Dictionary)

The common thread running through these definitions is that plagiarism is a form of fraud. The fraudulent action is embodied in the taking and using of the words of someone else and passing them off as if they were one's own. The use of the word "take" in both the *Australian Concise Oxford Dictionary* and the *Concise Oxford Dictionary* definitions suggest an intentional action is needed for plagiarism to exist. The American *Webster's Online Dictionary* suggests even more strongly that intention is necessary, as the words "steal" and "pass off" are used in the definition of plagiarism, which certainly imply intention on the part of the plagiarist. The *Collins Dictionary* definition uses the words "appropriate or use," which are less clear in terms of intention. However, although the word "appropriate" does have connotations of some degree of intention, as people usually "appropriate" goods or objects with a clear idea about what they are doing, the word "use" can apply to both intentional and unintentional acts, as you can unintentionally use someone's work if you did not know it belonged to another person. It seems, therefore, that some dictionaries define plagiarism as an intentional act whereas other dictionaries have it as both an intentional and unintentional act. The question of intention is not only apparent in the dictionary definitions, but is linked to the way in which the law views authorial rights.

The Nexus Between Plagiarism and the Law

Although plagiarism itself is not defined in the law, it is tied to both civil and criminal legal notions. In civil law, plagiarism is related to the legal concept of a breach of the moral rights of authors. In countries that specifically legislate for moral rights, such as France[1] and Australia, authors are able to have their "literary work" protected from infringement. In the Australian Copyright Amendment (Moral Rights) legislation, for example, the moral rights of the author are defined as:

- a right of attribution of authorship; or
- a right not to have authorship falsely attributed; or
- a right of integrity.[2]

This means that authors can expect legal protection of their literary works so that others may not take the whole or even parts of their work and attribute them to a different authorial source. Additionally, authors expect that if their work is used by another, it will be correctly "attributed." Attribution is required for: "reproduction, publishing, performing, transmitting or adapting the literary work."[3] This means that if a person uses or adapts the literary work of another without correct attribution, it is in contravention of the Act and punishable under law. The moral rights provisions also indicate that false claims to authorship (such as claiming a work to be yours when, in fact, it was produced by another) are also punishable under the legislation. This is also true of the French legislation. Penalties are also prescribed in the Act, as the harm is seen to be of economic loss in nature. This means that under civil law, where work is plagiarized, it is seen as an offense against the moral rights of authors.

The moral rights of authors are not only covered by the civil law in some countries, but the very definition of plagiarism is also linked historically to criminal law. Thomas Mallon in his 1989 work entitled, *Stolen Words: Forays into the Origins and Ravages of Plagiarism*, explains that a "plagiary had been one who kidnapped a child or slave" (p.6). He supposes then that plagiarism, which comes from the Latin term plagium, is akin to theft. He says a plagiarist is "a thief in literature; one who steals the thoughts or writings of another" (p.11). This idea that an act of plagiarism is kidnapping the words of others can also be seen as being similar to the action of kidnapping a child from a parent. This is shown clearly in the connections drawn by Mallon between plagiarism and theft or kidnapping of works under the English Statute of Anne of 1710, which was enacted with the belief that the author was the "father" or "begetter" of the work and the text itself was the "child." So both the early English legal perceptions of plagiarism and the dictionary definitions share an understanding that plagiarism involves words being kidnapped or misappropriated by one party. The English law formed the basis of the criminal codes in countries such as Australia, Canada, New Zealand and the United States of America. In fact, the words "kidnapped," "misappropriated," "stolen" and "theft" are all terms described in the criminal law codes of these countries.[4] The action of "theft" is broadly defined in these criminal codes as a kind of dishonest act of appropriating the legal property belonging to another person, with a clear intention of doing so in order to retain the property. If plagiarism is seen in terms of "misappropriation," do these legal connotations apply in university or college regulations governing plagiarism? Is plagiarism regarded as a criminal action in the university or college context? What is the effect of plagiarism in our higher seats of learning?

Plagiarism in Universities and Colleges

Plagiarism, if exposed in the university or college environment, is often damaging in terms of the public perception of the standards of academic excellence. The very integrity of the institution is called into question and reputations suffer. Often media reports contribute to images of educational institutions condoning plagiarism by inactively pursuing plagiarists. Journalists imply a "dumbing down" of standards in education and general deterioration of academic rigor and integrity (Hunt, 2003; Yaman, 2003).

The 2003 case of the University of Newcastle, New South Wales, Australia, illustrates the seriousness of plagiarism's links to the perceptions of falling standards in educational integrity. In this case, a lecturer, Ian Firns, failed a number of students' final assignments for plagiarism as he had found whole sections of text downloaded from the Internet. The students were studying a Masters of Business Administration course through the University of Newcastle's offshore campus in Malaysia. Mr Firns maintained "intellectual thievery" occurred and he failed the assignments after locating the websites and reporting the 15 students to the university. In a series of events led by senior management personnel, another lecturer, who was unaware of the previous grading, was asked to re-grade the papers, which he passed, and the students were awarded their degrees. Mr Firns then took legal action against the university and went to the media. The incident received national coverage in print and electronic media for many months. There were news reports of public dismay, and polls taken revealed there was a drop in the level of public faith, not only in the University of Newcastle, but in universities in general. The incident assumed such a national profile that the New South Wales government called an independent inquiry into the case in 2004. The Independent Commission Against Corruption (ICAC) released its report on the university's "handling of plagiarism allegations" in June 2005.[5] The commission found that the then Head of the Graduate School, Dr Paul Ryder, and the Deputy Head of School, Dr Robert Rugimbana, had engaged in corrupt conduct by failing to apply the university plagiarism policy and failing to properly investigate the original allegations of plagiarism by Mr Firns. Furthermore, the commission found that the failure to institute a proper investigation of plagiarism was rooted in the "illegitimate" motives of trying to avoid damage to the university's offshore program in Malaysia. The commission also found that the then Vice-Chancellor, Professor Roger Holmes, and the then Deputy Vice-Chancellor, Professor Brian English, had seriously failed in their duties under the university's code of conduct to inform the Academic Senate, University Council or the Senior Executive Group of the situation. The commission set out a series of recommendations about changes to policy and procedure that needed to be implemented at the University of Newcastle to avoid similar situations arising in the future.[6]

The effect was felt around the nation and Vice-Chancellors from other universities were reported in the press as saying that such scandals involving plagiarism "undermines all values of scholarship and is the death of a scholarly institution" (Davis, 2003a). The then Australian Education Minister, Dr Brendan Nelson, also stated, "A contaminated product, even if it's only a small part of a total export, does great damage to reputation in the market . . . our entire reputation as a country is diminished" (Davis, 2003b). Public confidence in the University of Newcastle was undermined and the institution was pressured to overhaul its plagiarism policy and procedures, under the glare of public scrutiny. The effects of the incident are not known, but the university did not release its student intake numbers the following year. Plagiarism by students is not the only negative publicity for universities and colleges. Where staff, particularly at senior levels, have been found to have engaged in plagiarism—public confidence in the academic integrity of tertiary institutions of learning erodes even further.

In 2002 the former Vice-Chancellor of Monash University, noted international academic Professor David Robinson, was accused of plagiarism in books published from 1979 to 1983. Although eventually admitting he did not acknowledge his sources adequately, he said it was due to the pressure to publish. He resigned eventually as Vice-Chancellor because he said "he was causing damage to the university"—a sentiment echoed by the President of the student body and other Monash academics. Despite receiving a substantial severance package, his punishment was the ultimate "academic death penalty" (Howard, 1995, p.788)—a publicly reported loss of his position at a reputable university and the subsequent damage to his professional reputation in academic spheres. Australian universities are not alone in experiencing public outcries and scrutiny where allegations of plagiarism are made.

In South Africa, Vice-Chancellor Mbulelo Mzamane, formerly from the University of Fort Hare, was accused of plagiarism when he wrote a short story that used paragraphs copied from a 1995 Pulitzer prize-winning novel. He admitted to the charges but was not sacked at that time. In the United States in early 2001, Professor Mary Zey, then a tenured professor at Texas' Agricultural and Mechanical (A&M) University, was charged with plagiarism of the work of two of her colleagues. Although initial moves by the University Provost, Ronald Douglas, to sack her were withdrawn, she was put on notice and her employment terminated in 2002. In December 2006, Shantou University, in southern Guangdong province in China, sacked one of its professors, Hu Xingrong, after allegations were substantiated that he had plagiarized the work of a doctoral student in media studies from another university. Although Chan Yuen-Ying, the director at the Cheung Kong Institute at Shantou University, where Hu was teaching said she had no difficulty in making the decision because she wanted to implement international standards of academic integrity, her decision was highly criticized within the province. Despite the protestations of some of the accused, universal condemnation of plagiarists and those tarred with the brush of plagiarism is the outcome of these reports. Often punishment is swift and severe.

Plagiarism arouses emotional responses from members of the public and academics alike. This confirms that plagiarism is seen as an action that affronts the very nature of academic integrity in universities and other educational environments. This is due, in part, to the fact that universities and tertiary institutions of advanced education are viewed as places where knowledge production is the life-blood of the higher education environment. People expect ethical standards to apply to that which is hailed to be an advance in knowledge or a new discovery. Trust in the system as well as individual people is shaken when plagiarism is found to have occurred and commonly, responses have been punitive. Unlike most penalties under criminal law, which are imposed for a set period, expulsion from a university on the grounds of plagiarism may be life-long—truly an academic death penalty. As American Professor of Law, Peter Jaszi (1994, p.9), points out:

> The stakes are high in disciplinary actions against students [and staff] accused of intramural offenses against authorship. Indeed, our institutions underline the seriousness of these proceedings by giving them the form, as well as some of the content, of legal actions for violations of copyright law.

Universities and tertiary institutions harness acceptable practices of knowledge production and set boundaries over knowledge workers through policy.

Plagiarism in Policy

Universities and colleges regulate the ways in which plagiarism will be dealt with in their individual environments through their plagiarism policies or Honor Codes. These documents are usually provided to both students and staff and there are expectations that everyone involved in the academic life of the institution will have read the policies or codes and abide by them. So what do these policies say and how well are they able to be implemented? A cross-section of key parts of policies from universities in Australia, Canada, England, China, the United States and New Zealand are discussed in order to illustrate the common elements of the policies as well as the distinct differences in the ways in which different institutions view plagiarism and how it should be handled.

Monash University, Australia

Monash University, in Melbourne, offers detailed information about plagiarism under academic regulation 4.1 of the Discipline Statute. The university states that intention is the key to a decision about plagiarism. Intentional plagiarism is defined as cheating and unintentional plagiarism is defined as "academic misdemeanor." There are also other forms of cheating and collusion described in the regulations. The regulation states:

> Plagiarism means to take and use another person's ideas and or manner of expressing them and to pass them off as one's own by failing to give appropriate acknowledgement. This includes material from any source, staff, students or the Internet—published and unpublished works.
>
> In the process of dealing with cases of suspected cheating, it is important to distinguish between intentional plagiarism (non examinable cheating), copying of work with intent to gain an unfair advantage and unintentional plagiarism copying of work without due acknowledgement. Plagiarism may be considered unintentional, and therefore a misdemeanour, where the student has simply quoted other sources without due acknowledgement. Where the staff member determines that the plagiarism was unintentional they are required to counsel and warn the student of further transgressions.
>
> (Monash University, 2007)

The regulations then specify penalties and procedures for implementation of the policy. This policy is interesting in that intention is the linchpin of the decision as to whether cheating has occurred or not. If a teacher decides that plagiarism has been intentional, then it is a prescribed offense of theft and cheating. If the teacher decides the student did not intend to plagiarize the work, merely made errors in writing, then it is a case of academic misdemeanor, although penalties may still be applied in this case. The responsibility of proving intention lies with the academic staff—initially the teacher and then the subject or unit co-ordinator or "Chief Examiner" as stated in the regulations.

Simon Fraser University, Canada

The policy at Simon Fraser University states:

> Plagiarism is a form of academic dishonesty in which an individual submits or presents the work of another person as his or her own ... Plagiarism also exists when there is inadequate recognition given to the author for phrases, sentences, or ideas of the author incorporated into an essay.
>
> (Simon Fraser University, 2002)

The policy at Simon Fraser University is representative of how most teachers envisage plagiarism policies to be framed. Plagiarism is seen as a form of intellectual dishonesty by an individual. Interestingly, this policy appears to limit the misconduct to essay forms of writing and specifically outlines that it is groupings of words, such as phrases or sentences, that constitute a breach of policy. This is in stark contrast to Monash University, which spells out different ways in which plagiarism can be embodied, such as illicit use of computer programs, inappropriate group work as well as through individual misconduct. Monash University does not limit the activities to essays, as appears to be the case at Simon Fraser University.

A different approach to plagiarism is taken in the United Kingdom by Birmingham University, which denotes the degree of plagiarism as a deciding factor in whether the action is punishable or not.

Birmingham University, England

Birmingham University's regulation 4.7.10 covers plagiarism. The University expects the different schools to deal with plagiarism and sets out a detailed process under which this will be done. The School of Humanities at the university gives very detailed information about how cases of plagiarism are both decided and also penalized. The school acknowledges that plagiarism is a matter of judgment by academics but students are responsible for their own standards of academic integrity. The school is at pains to point out that the issue of intention to deceive is difficult, so that where certain elements are found in work submitted by students, the school will assume the student intended them to be there. The school does not accept the idea of "accidental plagiarism," which is where students reference a work at the start of a paragraph and assume that the reader will realize that the rest of the paragraph is taken from the same work. Birmingham University's School of Humanities has decided that the quantity of plagiarism in the assessment piece is the most important piece of information for judging the seriousness of the offense. So, the school has a graded scale of penalties depending on the level of study and the degree of seriousness of the offense. The school says plagiarism is judged as:

Serious plagiarism if:

sustained or repeated lifting of text (verbatim) from a source or sources not correctly attributed; "sustained or repeated" means more than 10% of the text, i.e. more than 250 words in a 2,500 word essay. These 250 words would not necessarily be continuous. For example, four separate 5-line instances would be equally serious.

sustained or repeated instances of unreferenced paraphrase from a clearly recognisable source or sources (i.e. the plagiarism is not a verbatim copy of the source, but the changes to the source are rewordings which disguise the fact that the source is being plagiarized); "sustained or repeated" has the same meaning as above.

no source text is demonstrably copied or paraphrased, but it is clear that at least 75% of the ideas and arguments in the essay are taken unchanged and unanalysed from a recognisable source or sources.

Moderate plagiarism if:

significant lifting of text (verbatim) from a source or sources not correctly attributed; "significant" means more than 5% but less than 10% of the essay, i.e. between 125 and 250 words in a 2,500 word essay. Significant instances of unreferenced paraphrase from a clearly recognisable source or sources (i.e. the student text is not a verbatim copy of the source, but the changes to the source are rewordings which seek to disguise the fact that the source is being plagiarized); "significant" has the same meaning as above.

no source text is demonstrably copied or paraphrased, but it is clear that at least 50% of the ideas and arguments in the essay are taken unchanged and unanalysed from a recognisable source or sources.

Slight plagiarism if:

lifting of text (verbatim) from a source or sources not correctly attributed and amounting to less than 5% of the text, i.e. up to 125 words in a 2,500 word essay. Instances of unreferenced paraphrase from a clearly recognisable source or sources (i.e. the student text is not a verbatim copy of the source, but the changes to the source are rewordings which disguise the fact that the source is being plagiarized) up to 5% of the text. No source text is demonstrably copied or paraphrased, but it is clear that at least 25% of the ideas and arguments in the essay are taken unchanged and unanalysed from a recognisable source or sources.

Birmingham University's School of Humanities distinguishes between plagiarism and other academic infringements that do not amount to plagiarism. The School maintains this is an important distinction because plagiarism is a disciplinary offense, which is penalized by a special scale of penalties and then recorded. The policy assists teachers to decide how serious the case of plagiarism is by quantifying the amount of plagiarism in the student's work: "serious" is calculated as 10 percent of the complete work; "moderate" is calculated as between 5 and 10 percent and "slight" is where less than 5 percent of the total work has been plagiarized. In this situation, teachers clearly have to calculate the amount of plagiarism that appears over the whole of the student's work in order to decide how serious the case of plagiarism will be. Once that calculation is complete, the penalty for the offense will automatically follow the formula.

Tsinghua University, China

Tsinghua University was one of the first Chinese universities to adopt international standards when in 2004 it advised students that it was better to use their own words than simply to repeat expert opinion. However, that appears to be the extent of the regulation. Peking University also has taken steps to make students and staff aware of the issue of plagiarism. One policy states:

> Academic Dishonesty
>
> There will be none. Under this heading are included plagiarism, the use of work done by others, or examination irregularities. Please consult SIS/PKU staff if you have any questions, particularly about what constitutes plagiarism.

One of the greatest problems with plagiarism in China appears to be that there is no national consensus about how to approach plagiarism within the university sector. Many Chinese academics agree that there is an issue with plagiarism and advocate that it must be dealt with nationally. For example, Professor He Weifang from Peking University considers Chinese academics must view plagiarism as academic corruption and fight to preserve academic ethics. He, along with 100 academics from around the nation, has called for national supervision mechanisms to be put in place to stamp out plagiarism. Professor Weifang says that "academic corruption" refers to institutions making use of their resources to gain improper income or power. He says that academic misconduct is slightly different and is often an individual action such as plagiarism, distorting experiment data and tampering with original work. One of the most pressing reasons, he claims, for plagiarism to exist within the Chinese academic community is the pressure to publish a great number of academic papers in order to obtain either permanency or promotion. Professor Weifang says that a colleague of his has been demoted because he only published two papers in key academic journals in one year. The situation for students is also problematic, with many students seeking excellence in marks to attend postgraduate courses overseas.

The Chinese Ministry of Education announced in March 2006 that it would set up a special 25-member commission to monitor academic fraud and plagiarism. The committee would be made up of academics from across the university sector and one of its roles would be to develop detailed rules on criteria and punishment for academic corruption and misconduct and investigate such cases. Education Minister Zhou Ji has urged researchers to comply with ethical guidelines or otherwise be "disciplined." The new commission will not handle specific cases of plagiarism, but will focus on prevention of academic scandals through case studies, public hearings and supervising the establishment of monitoring organizations in local colleges nationwide. Minister Zhou has mandated all universities and colleges to handle reports on academic fraud or plagiarism seriously.[7]

University of West Virginia, USA

The University of West Virginia states that there is an expectation that all students and staff will act honorably and honestly in their academic work and lives. The university divides acts of academic dishonesty into three areas: plagiarism, cheating and fraud. The plagiarism policy is defined in terms of proscribed acts and the policy states that if plagiarism is confirmed, then penalties will apply, regardless of intention. This has been referred to as the "zero tolerance" approach to plagiarism policy. The policy reads:

> Students are expected to understand that such practices constitute academic dishonesty regardless of motive. Those who deny deceitful intent, claim not to have known that the act constituted plagiarism, or maintain that what they did was inadvertent are nevertheless subject to penalties when plagiarism has been confirmed. Plagiarism includes, but is not limited to: submitting, without appropriate acknowledgement, a report, notebook, speech, outline, theme, thesis, dissertation, or other written, visual, or oral material that has been copied in whole or in part from the work of others, whether such source is published or not, including (but not limited to) another individual's academic composition, compilation, or other product, or commercially prepared paper.

West Virginia University then goes on to detail what activities constitute cheating and also fraud or misrepresentation of information. Under a zero tolerance policy, intention is irrelevant, as the case for plagiarism is proven upon establishing any plagiarism exists within a student's work. As the name of the policy suggests, plagiarism is not tolerated at all and serious consequences flow if it is detected.

The University of Auckland, New Zealand

The University of Auckland regulates plagiarism as follows:

> Plagiarism is the inclusion in your assignment of material copied or closely paraphrased from someone else's writings (including textbooks and assignments by other students) without an explicit indication of the source of the material.

Auckland University's policy further states that it "takes a serious view of plagiarism." The university regulations indicate that intention is irrelevant and it does not matter whether the student "was intending to cheat, it is clear that submitting someone else's work or ideas is not evidence of your own understanding of the material and cannot earn you marks." This is similar to the stance taken by West Virginia University and penalties apply once the charge of plagiarism has been substantiated.

South-Coast University, Australia

The Board Room in which the teachers introduced in Chapter 1 found themselves is based at South-Coast University.[8] South-Coast University has incorporated the ideas of moral rights of authors in its policy on plagiarism. The policy is found in university regulation 4.1, which is reprinted in the handbooks for staff and students and is also set out on the university website. Regulation 4.1 states:

> *Plagiarism* is the copying of another person's ideas or expressions without appropriate acknowledgment and presenting these ideas or forms of expression as your own. It includes not only written works such as books or journals but data or images that may be presented in tables, diagrams, designs, plans, photographs, film, music, formulae, Web sites and computer programs. Plagiarism also includes the use of (or passing off) the work of lecturers or other students as your own.
>
> The University regards plagiarism as an extremely serious academic offense. The penalties associated with plagiarism are severe and extend from cancelling all marks for the specific assessment item or for the entire unit through to exclusion from your course.

Like other tertiary institutions, South-Coast University treats the act of plagiarism as an offense, and prescribes penalties that are clearly meant to be punitive. South-Coast's regulations indicate that the university also views plagiarism in terms of protection of authorship and notions of ownership of "works." The explanation follows regulation 4.1 at sub-section (2):

> Regulation 4.1 (2) states: Students should also be aware that there are laws in place to protect the ideas and expressions (i.e. the intellectual property) of individuals and/or groups and their right to be attributed as the authors of their work. These are known as "copyright" and as "moral rights" and are included in the *Copyright Act.* Plagiarism offenses may also be breaches of the *Copyright Act* and students may be subject to penalties independent of the University's regulations and procedures. Unauthorised collaboration is a related form of cheating.

South-Coast's regulations indicate that the intellectual property of individual authors is viewed as moral rights. The university supports upholding those rights through sanctions against violators of authorship attribution. The penalties range from reprimand to "exclusion of the student from the University or from any part of it or from any courses and/or units either permanently or for such lesser period as the Vice-Chancellor or delegate may decide" under Part 3.4.3 of the regulations. Some academics consider that regarding plagiarism as a legal sub-set of copyright law leads to the mistaken assumption that "plagiarism regulations cannot be changed unless copyright changes first" (Howard, 1999, p.97). At South-Coast University, the intertwining of plagiarism with legal conceptions of copyright appears to have already taken place within the university regulations. Similar traits are seen to exist with West Virginia University's detailing of plagiarism and other offenses—where particularly legal concepts of fraud, misrepresentation and intentional deception are used. These terms are from criminal codes, as was explained earlier in this chapter, and the processes also appear to follow the criminal law's means of punishment.

Plagiarism Policies—The Issues

As can be seen from these examples of various policies from a variety of universities around the world, plagiarism is constituted differently among diverse institutions. No definition is the same as any other. Some universities, such as Birmingham, West Virginia and University of Auckland, decree that the student's intention is irrelevant—the action of copying text alone indicates plagiarism (although the amount of text copied is important in Birmingham's case). Other universities delineate between intentional plagiarism, which is categorized as cheating, and unintentional plagiarism, which is categorized as an academic misdemeanor of "failing to cite a source correctly." Universities such as Monash imply that plagiarism is an intentional offense by using the word "knowingly," while yet other institutions remain silent on the element of intention. Most universities and colleges have a range of penalties from warnings, reprimands, failure of the piece of assessment under review, failure of the unit or subject in which the plagiarism occurred, suspension from study for a period of time, monetary fine or expulsion from the university. Some universities and colleges have implemented a zero tolerance policy, meaning that if allegations of plagiarism are upheld against you, the penalty is automatic expulsion from the university. This makes it difficult for teachers to interpret plagiarism in the same ways, as can be seen from the Board Room discussion between teachers in Chapter 1. It is hard to imagine a situation in which academic members of staff are likely to coin similar definitions of plagiarism, let alone view it in the same way. This is because, as clearly demonstrated in this chapter, institutions differ markedly in what they consider plagiarism to mean in policy and processes, and penalties also demonstrate striking diversity. However, one way in which to move towards opening the discussion on some common ground is to examine these university definitions of plagiarism in line with the six essential elements of plagiarism.

The Six Elements of Plagiarism

As part of her doctoral thesis Diane Pecorari (2002) conducted an empirical study of the way in which plagiarism was defined by seventeen postgraduate students in the United Kingdom in the discipline areas of science, engineering, social science and humanities. She compared their textual responses to the generic definition of plagiarism she elicited from the study of plagiarism policies from universities in Australia, the United Kingdom and the United States. Fifty-three definitions of plagiarism were given, but six common elements could be elicited from these definitions, which she developed into a definitional model. The six elements of her definitional model of plagiarism are:

> an object (i.e. language, words, text)
> which has been taken (or borrowed, stolen etc.)
> from a particular source (books, journals, Internet)

by an agent (student, person, academic)
without (adequate) acknowledgement
and with or without intention to deceive.

(Pecorari, 2002, p.60)

Using this definitional model as a means to examine the policies of the six universities reproduced above represents a generative way in which to examine the way in which plagiarism is formulated in our own institutions. The definitional model also offers teachers and administrators the opportunity to compare their own institution's policy to the six elements. In fact, the six elements model provides a very useful starting point to discuss ways in which there are similarities and differences between policies and why this may be so.

Element 1: An Object (i.e. Language, Words, Text)

If we compare the six universities' policies from various parts of the English as first language speaking world, all six universities indicate that a range of "objects" are caught under element 1. These range from individual words through to phrases, sentences and larger sections of text. Some universities, such as South-Coast, capture "ideas" as well as text in the definition and yet other universities, such as West Virginia, specify "what" can be plagiarized as text from "written, visual, or oral material." West Virginia's plagiarism policy specifies that written and oral forms of text—as well as conceptual ideas—can be elements of plagiarism. What counts as an "object" of plagiarism depends upon each institution. It is clear that institutions having such a broad range of *what* can be plagiarized will propagate wide-ranging interpretations of the object or content of plagiarism.

Element 2: Which Has Been Taken (Borrowed, or Stolen)

All six universities specify the "object" has been in some way "taken." Words used to describe this act of appropriation include: take, use, copy, pass off, include, illicit collaboration, closely paraphrase, submit, present and falsely represent (in the case of collaboration). The range of appropriation is also broad and although not one of the universities uses the word "stolen" or "theft" to convey the idea of appropriation, the term "illicit" carries tones of criminal intent. The point here is that the "taking" of the "object" has been some form of illegal activity and certainly one of academic misconduct. For some universities, the very action of illicit taking is enough to enforce tough penalties. For other universities—the "taking" of the material must have been an intentional action.

Element 3: From a Particular Source

Universities indicate that plagiarism comes from a range of sources, such as: textbooks, journals, another student's work, lecture notes, tapes, audio-visual material, images, theses, unpublished works, working papers, seminar and conference papers, internal reports, works of creative art, websites, computer program data and assignments. The range of material is broad and not limited to print-text, as can be seen by the inclusion of spoken and audio-visual forms of text as well. Only one university in this sample, South-Coast, specifies websites as a source of textual appropriation in the broad array of sources listed. Many teachers are of the opinion that the Internet offers a considerable avenue of opportunity to take material in an illicit fashion. The issue of Internet plagiarism is covered in Chapter 7.

Element 4: By an Agent

In each case, the universities indicate that the agent of plagiarism is an "individual" or "student(s)." It is pertinent to note that in the academic misdemeanor policy, staff are not explicitly mentioned, although it is assumed that individual staff contracts of employment would document the procedure should plagiarism by an academic occur.

Element 5: Without (Adequate) Acknowledgment

Most university policies specify there is lack of acknowledgment or attribution to the source involved in plagiarism. Words used to indicate the degree of adequacy include: without appropriate acknowledgment, without an explicit indication, inadequate recognition and failing to give appropriate acknowledgment. Some policies, such as those at Monash and Simon Fraser universities, give detailed lists of the ways in which lack of acknowledgment may occur; for example, they specify texts, ideas, research or computer data. Other policies just state that insufficient or lack of acknowledgment constitutes plagiarism.

Element 6: And With or Without Intention to Deceive

The element of intention is strenuously debated in allegations of plagiarism. Some of the definitions reproduced above do not specify whether intention is required or not for an act of plagiarism to be established—as with South-Coast University. Other universities state that intention is irrelevant—if plagiarism is found to occur in a student's work, then it is, by default, an intentional act. This is the case for Birmingham University and the University of West Virginia. If their students engage in any of the listed actions they will, by virtue of their action, have plagiarized. These universities are applying what is known in legal parlance as a "strict liability" term to its definition of plagiarism. For a strict liability offense, the element of intention is regarded as irrelevant, as merely contravening the regulation is enough to establish that there is a case to answer. Yet other universities, such as Monash University and Simon Fraser University, use the words "knowingly" or "a form of academic dishonesty" to indicate there is an element of intention required to categorize the offense as one of plagiarism.

The element of intention is arguably the most subjective within the six-element model and also the most difficult to ascertain. Teachers' reactions to intention vary, as was seen in Chapter 1, and trying to establish whether plagiarism was an intentional act or not remains contentious both in theory and in practice. The previous chapter illustrated how intention is put into practice using a legal lens, but this represents a single-dimensional focus that does not take account of a variety of factors such as different cultural interpretations of textual sharing or ideas about what is appropriate to acknowledge and what is not. Naturally, there are other ways of interpreting "intention" in writing. What was the writer's intention when they were actually producing the text? How did the writer intend to acknowledge the ideas or words of others? These are important questions to ask before making a determination of plagiarism.

Summary

The aim of this chapter has been to present a detailed discussion of the relationship between definitions of plagiarism within university policies. The manner in which legal notions of authorship as outlined in Chapter 2 are embraced within the wording of university plagiarism policies are clearly evident. Most policies are framed in a way that suggests upon proof of plagiarism (evidence) a person (student) found to have acted improperly (misconduct) will be punished (penalty). The point at which there is most debate and disagreement is the point of ascertaining the intention of the party to the misconduct. This is similar to juries making decisions about the "guilt" or "innocence" of parties in a criminal case before a court of law, where the "intention" of the party is crucial. For example, if a person intended to kill—or cause serious harm to another person who died—it is classified as "murder." However, if a person did not intend to kill another, but in a series of events that were accidental or reckless or negligent, someone died—it is classified as "manslaughter." Although in both cases a person dies—the crimes are classified differently and have different penalties—and all this hinges upon a jury (Academic Progress or Disciplinary Committee) deciding the intention of the person alleged to have committed the offense (plagiarism). The definitional model outlined in this chapter provides a base from which teachers and policy-makers can scrutinize plagiarism policies in their own educational settings. Although no universal agreement on plagiarism appears to exist at a policy level, the greatest disparity occurs in the perception of a student's intention to plagiarize. However, legal notions of authorship are only one view of authorial rights and relationships between authors and their works. The way in which texts are constructed and the roles the writer and reader play are crucial in the plagiarism debate, as has been shown by matching policies against the six element model. Literary theory and cross-cultural studies offer multi-dimensional ways of exploring the notion of intention in writing and reading and provide an alternative way in which to view plagiarism.

The element of "intention" to act is a key in understanding not only the student-writer but also the teacher-reader's reactions to plagiarism. To date, intention has only been discussed in the way it is constructed by law. The next chapter examines literary notions of authorship, which challenge legal views and detail alternative ways of understanding literary intention.

CHAPTER 4

Plagiarism—A Global Issue

> The idea that language can be owned, cordoned off and protected
> from trespassers, bought and sold like parcels of real estate—whether
> by an autonomous and stable Romantic author/genius or by a
> multinational corporate author/surrogate who claims absolute right
> to control of dissemination and use—must be scrutinized by teachers
> of writing everywhere.
>
> (Andrea Lunsford and Susan West, 1996, p.390)

Plagiarism is a growing concern in the global educational arena and
there are concerns that it is increasing, particularly with access to digitized
information (Park, 2003, p.471). In the last few chapters we have looked
at concepts of plagiarism from a legal perspective and how this plays out
in plagiarism policies around the world. The six-element definitional
model is presented as one way in which teachers can examine the policies
of their own institutions and reflect upon the way in which plagiarism is
perceived in their own teaching and learning settings. In this chapter, other
lenses through which plagiarism can be perceived are explored—specifically through the eyes of literary and cross-cultural theorists, researchers
and teachers. The focus is on researchers and teachers in academic
writing classrooms where students for whom English as second or foreign

language (ESL/EFL) are located. The classrooms are situated in various places around the world, including Italy, Canada, China, Australia, New Zealand, the United Kingdom and the United States. The teachers range from very experienced to first-time teachers and they share their concerns and insights about plagiarism in academic writing. These teachers challenge some current ideas and practices around plagiarism management because many current approaches do not seem to be reducing plagiarism. They also call for a re-examination of university and college approaches to plagiarism, particularly where institutional policies reflect only one culturally and historically contingent view of authorship. Many teachers and classroom researchers adhere to the idea that texts are socially constructed and so they consider it is essential to gauge the extent to which other factors are involved in the creation of a text. Of course, individual approaches to teaching, modes of assessment used and the inherent construction and distribution of power in the classroom also shape notions of academic writing. All these factors contribute to mold students' approaches to learning.

The Construction of "Text" in Plagiarism—The Theory

In Chapter 2, the legal framing of the Romantic ideal of the author—as an individual who creates an original "work" through the sole pursuits of his labor—were outlined. Bakhtin (1986) and Barthes' (1977) challenge to textual construction was also foregrounded. In this chapter, ways in which texts are constructed or viewed by readers and writers are probed further. Here we delve into the relationship constructed between readers and writers, because where allegations of plagiarism in writing exist—there is usually at least one reader and also at least one writer. The reader, in reading and thinking about the writer's work, may decide that the writer did not come up with the words and/or ideas alone, that they were, in fact, misappropriated from someone else. The writer, in writing the work, may have intended to borrow the words of others without acknowledging the source, or not. It depends on how the language and the text under scrutiny are constructed. There is an inextricable link between the reader alleging plagiarism and the writer producing the work. In coming to understand this relationship, literary theory provides useful guidance for teachers in excavating the ground around reactions to plagiarism and the resultant action taken by teachers and policy-makers. There are a number of different schools of literary thought on language and textual construction, which are presented to illustrate the complexity of viewpoints about the relationship between reader and writer (author).

The Romantic Notion of the Author is Dead

One school of thought, which includes theorists such as Terry Eagleton (1983) and John Frow (2000), is that the Romantic notion of the author is dead. These theorists argue that allowing control or ownership over language, as in granting property or copyright and ownership rights, is complete nonsense—language cannot be bought and sold by individuals. They argue that in a post-structural world, the notion of the author as the sole creator of a work, over which she has control is not possible. They urge us to examine how writing occurs and what frames the written product. It is not typical that a person shuts herself away from the world, its political, cultural, social, environmental and economic forces, and remains in a solitary and sterile world to create her "masterpiece," which is written in final form with no input from any other source—human or technological. To have an image that this is the way that writing occurs is far removed from reality. They argue that writing is a negotiated, interrupted and often frustrating process and it occurs within a context—whether it is in school classrooms, workplaces, homes or mixtures of all these places. Written works are started, interrupted or stopped before being resumed again at a later date and it may take days, weeks, months or years before a final work is produced. Rarely is a final work produced without input from "sources"—whether these be human sources such as friends, colleagues, classmates, family or supervising bodies or, alternatively, input from technological sources such as Youtube, MySpace or electronic database information. This is true for many students who write assessment tasks over a period of time. In between the starting and stopping process, the writer has been influenced by a myriad of events, sounds, images, words and thoughts of others. The very language in which the writer has been immersed and also shared with others will influence the written product. The structure of language itself produces a textual reality and sometimes a boundary for both writer and reader. American academics Andrea Lunsford and Susan West (1996) urge us to resist the notion that ownership can apply to the way in which we view the written product of our students. For teachers making a decision as to whether plagiarism is present or not in a student's work, contemplating what it means to "author" a piece of work is also important. Teachers such as Brian Martin (1992) argue that if we construe plagiarism as one part of the general problem of cheating, we need to openly discuss how often we believe cheating and plagiarism occurs, and this is where one problem arises, because common agreement on authorship "in the fashion expected in a scholarly environment" is difficult to attain (p.3).

Professor of English, Harold Love (2002), further argues that supporting the idea that the written product is the end result of one literary author is "disintegrationist." He argues that the "myth of the Romantic author . . . the single author creating a text in solitariness" does not take account of all contexts, situations and events that happen before the writing even takes place. He details these acts that include necessary preliminary skills and exchanges, such as "language acquisition, education, experiences, conversation, reading of other authors" (p.33). He suggests that a literary creation is the result of a conglomeration of life experiences and that any form of writing is the result of a myriad of social, political and cultural factors —not the least of which is the influence that other people have over the writer and the text. He stresses that texts are born from social impetuses, interactions with others and behaviors, all of which a writer merely notes.

Such views are often supported by teachers of writing composition, who urge their students when writing essays to take account of all their experiences, reading of bodies of literature and reflection upon their own position in relation to various texts. Contemporary composition theorists, Danielle De Voss and Annette Rosati (2002), support his view. They argue that teachers should "dismiss the romantic, modernist notion of Author (writing in isolation, suffering, the tortured artist at *his* craft)," while acknowledging that the problem is that "most of us still focus on a polished, final product by an author whose name appears (alone) at the top of the first page" (De Voss and Rosati, 2002, authors' emphasis, p.194). Their views suggest strong dissonance with the Enlightenment era's Romantic view of the sole author as creator of the work. They suggest that it is important to examine contextual influences when interpreting textual meaning. This involves exploring the relationship between the author and reader as well as the discourse community and societal influences surrounding textual production. Canadian academic Russell Hunt (2004) pushes the point further when he argues that the "concept of originality in utterances runs counter to most language practice" (p.6). He points out that it is not only Bakhtin's theories that alert us to this fact, but the idea of original thought being expressed by students, particularly at undergraduate levels, is "bizarre, modern (and it's arguable, narrowly Western)" (Hunt, 2004, p.6).

These academics are asking us to examine the very heart of the notion of plagiarism—that the student-writer is misappropriating words that "belong" to another. It is at this point that the conflict emerges between the traditional Romantic view of the writer, as embodied in legal theory— that words and language are a form of property that can be "owned" by authors—and views of literary theorists. It is the concept that language can "belong to another" that is contested by this group of literary theorists, researchers and teachers.

Texts are Socially Produced

Mikhail Bakhtin (1986), Roland Barthes (1977) and Michel Foucault (1972) agree that the Romantic notion of the author is dead as it is no longer appropriate. However, they do not do so because they object to the notion of ownership of language, but because they argue that language is socially produced and exists within a social context. Their view is that in writing, the textual production is one way of representing knowledge and understanding of situations and events. As individuals, our experiences in society are shaped by which social groups we participate within and our own individual life experiences. Everything around us in the social world will influence the ways in which we produce language and how we make meaning from our life experiences. Language and meaning are—they argue—essentially social phenomena. Each individual will understand the same event differently. This then represents the very essence of individual subjectivity—and is unique for each one of us. That is to say, no two people will think that plagiarism is the same thing or perceive it in the same way. Many of the decisions we make, as teachers, depend on our individual perceptions of plagiarism, which are mediated by our membership within various social groupings. This also means that whether a person has a degree of privilege or is someone who is marginalized, those very factors will affect the individual's experiences and views of herself. For example, teachers in most nations around the world are required to undertake various forms of higher education studies before they are permitted to become registered teachers. Access to higher education in many countries can be difficult for economically disadvantaged people and the "user pays" system of education will affect the ability of some individuals to follow desired career paths. Therefore, many of the teachers in our schools have already had a degree of privilege—that of access to higher education—which can shape their attitudes, expectations and responses to the reading and writing activities of their students. Michel Foucault (1972) said the relationship between language, social institutions, subjectivity and power was complex and he called it the "discursive field."

Mikhail Bakhtin (1986) unpacks the relationship between language and social institutions further and argues that as all texts are socially produced, the key to understanding textual construction and interpretation is to examine social and cultural contexts. Theorists from the so-called Bakhtin Circle were among the first to suggest that language has to be considered in a social context and every utterance is potentially the site of a social struggle. They view each segment of discourse as alive with meaning and possessing multiple possibilities of interpretation, which are contested in the textual environment. Bakhtin's (1986) work, particularly associated with Russian Formalism, is vital in this discussion as he challenges the view that proprietary rights by authors extend over words and should be protected by law. He believes that language cannot be separated from ideology and that "ideology is not separable from its medium—language" (p.41). He argues that language is a social phenomenon and that words themselves are "active" in the oral exchange. For Bakhtin, words are alive and embodied with intention and meaning and he describes each word as having the "tastes of the context in which it has lived its socially charged life" (p.293). If we accept his theory, then how is it possible to own words? Indeed, how do authors claim legal protection over texts they have created if it is dubious that textual forms can be owned at all? Bakhtin asserts that words are active and living text is capable of multiple meanings, therefore construction and interpretation do not depend on the author but on the site of textual production. That is to say, the language itself, particularly where it is created, is of primary importance in its interpretation, and not the writer. This notion places the author in a far less dominant position in relation to her work than is supposed by the Romantic, legal understandings of how texts are constructed. Bakhtinian perspectives on authorship there-fore remove the author as the point of focus in an examination of textual meaning and redirect attention to the textual site and the power and discourse relationships that flow from it. Indeed, it opens up the question of the role of the reader and writer in interpretations of plagiarism and whether the author can exist at all.

Is There Such a Being as an "Author"?

Although Bakhtin raises awareness of the issues surrounding ownership of text, he does not imply the radical questioning of the role of the author that arises in the work of Roland Barthes (1977). Rather than perceiving authors as the individual creators of unique "works," Barthes argues that writers only have the power to mix already existing cultural forms and knowledge: to reassemble or redeploy "text" where text is understood to be socially produced. Writers cannot use writing to express themselves, says Barthes, only "to draw upon that immense dictionary of language and culture which is always already written" (1977, p.66). Therefore, it is the language and not the author that is the repository of meaning. In his famous 1968 essay *The Death of the Author*, he separates the text from the author and considers the term "author" to be an impediment to the workings of the textual environment. He claims that although the "sway of the Author remains powerful"[1] by the very status of being an author, it is the "language which speaks, not the author" through text (1977, p.143). Barthes notes that, "words and forms can belong to *no-one*" (p.293, emphasis in original), which raises the issue of ownership and attribution of text. This means that although the author is an important conduit for the communicative event to take place, the true power lies in the language used in the text. This stance proposes that the author, or as he prefers to term it, "Author-God" (p.146), is a relationship of power between consumers of text—the readers—and the text itself. This is important for teachers, as we are often the ones who read the student texts and decide at the first instance that plagiarism has occurred. Barthes is making us aware that we are in positions of power, not only as teachers but as textual consumers[2] and we must examine not only the text but also ourselves and our attitudes and responses to texts as readers, particularly in allegations of plagiarism.

Michel Foucault's *What Is an Author?* argues that the author is not dead, but is the means of production or "the principle of thrift in the proliferation of meaning" (p.159). Just as Barthes interprets the Enlightenment notion of the author as historically dependent upon concepts that the author was a single person who created original works of genius—Foucault considers that the author is "an ideological product" (1979, p.159). The relationship of the individual writer to the text can be explained by the Foucauldian notion of the author-function. Foucault (1979) says, "The coming into being of the notion of 'author' constitutes the privileged moment of individualization in the history of ideas, knowledge, literature, philosophy and the sciences" (p.141). He argues that the author does not embody the work, nor is the author an individual creator of wisdom. According to Foucault:

> We are used to thinking that the author is so different from all other men, and so transcendent with regard to all languages that, as soon as he speaks, meaning begins to proliferate. The truth is quite the contrary: the author is not an indefinite source of significations which fill a work; the author does not precede the works, he is a certain functional principle by which, in our culture, one limits, excludes, and chooses; in short, by which one impedes the free circulation, the free manipulation, the free composition, decomposition, and recomposition of fiction.
>
> (1979, p.159)

Although he disagrees with the idea of an individual writer of text being linked to the identity of the person producing the text, he does believe that the individual demonstrates a desire to protect the "work" created. The "work" is the product of the author and is then the subject of argument in terms of originality. He questions both how the author "became individualized in a culture like ours" and "when the moment authenticity and attribution began" (p.141). Foucault's identification of individual writers' desires to protect their work and ensure others acknowledge use of it leads us to a consideration of authorship and ownership of text. It is the very union of concepts of "author" and textual "attribution" that sanction an alliance between attribution (plagiarism) and ownership (copyright) of text. This union is often protected and promoted in university plagiarism regulations and disciplinary statutes, as argued in Chapter 3.

Reader Interpretation of Text = Decision as to Plagiarism

There are yet other theorists of the opinion that language itself is embodied with meaning that is only realized when the reader interprets the text. Therefore it is the role of the reader rather than the role of the author or writer that is critical to textual construction.[3] Writing and Rhetoric teacher and theorist, Rebecca Moore Howard, maintains an "incredulity toward the autonomous, originary author." In her view, the notion is challenged by "critical theory, bolstered by the new digitized information systems and by postmodern literary theory" (1999, p.76). She further points out that from an intertextual theorist's viewpoint "it is the reader, not the writer or the text, who instigates meaning" (2007, p.9). These statements capture a core element of literary theorists' argument over the roles of the author as creator of text and the reader as interpreter of text in light of plagiarism allegations. Generally, literary theorists challenge the notion that a sole author is an owner or proprietor of text. They also question the traditional role of the reader.[4]

If we applied these theoretical ideas to all students' production of written texts, but particularly ESL/EFL students, it may shed some light on the different ways in which these students perceive language operating in their own socially constructed circles. Of course, their own life experiences mean that our students will have different understandings of plagiarism from us, their teachers—as well as different understandings from each other. This adds to the complexity of the teaching task in ensuring that students are aware of the way in which plagiarism is constructed in each particular institution. As was clearly shown in Chapter 3, universities and colleges perceive plagiarism and its effects in different ways and frame their policies to reflect the ideals of the institution. It therefore falls upon the institution to ensure that students entering courses are aware of its concept of plagiarism and acknowledge that the students studying under its auspices may bring different experiences. Often the responsibility of deciding whether plagiarism has occurred or not is the task of the person reading the text—the teacher. Because the decision about plagiarism is made at the point of reading the text, it becomes necessary to probe the role of the reader (or teacher-reader) in this plagiarism decision-making process.

The Role of the Reader

If we adopt Roland Barthes' position, we support the view that the meaning of the text lies both with the language and the meanings construed by the reader of the text. The text itself is "a tissue of quotations drawn from the innumerable centers of culture" (1977, p.146). This means that the *reader* is the point where the multiplicity of textual images come together as "drawn from many cultures and entering into mutual relations of dialogue" (Barthes, 1977, p.148). The point here is that the reader's inherently individual sense of meaning brings different connotations to the life of the text. To credit one author with an ability to create meaning for the reader is problematic for Barthes, because it is a limitation on the text itself. He claims that text is constructed through the use of language and its context. It is given meaning by the reader, as interpreter of the text, not the writer, although society claims that the writer is the "author."

It is interesting to examine this proposition a little further in light of classroom experience. Using Barthes' idea that the readers construct the meaning of the text through their interpretations—some teacher-readers are angry at the appearance of plagiarism and others are worried. The readers are determining the multiplicity of textual meanings drawing on their own experiences, beliefs, cultural connotations and views, regardless of the writer-author's intentions. Raman Selden, Peter Widdowson and Peter Brooker support the view that the author is not the original source of textual meaning. They "reject the traditional view that the author is the origin of the text, the source of its meaning, and the only authority for interpretation" (1977, p.156). They propose the idea that by questioning the role of the writer with respect to the role of the reader, we can open the way for the reader to assume a more active role in order to make meaning. They suggest that readers can connect texts with a myriad of experiences in order to make meaning and ignore the author's intention completely. The idea is that readers have the authority and power to interpret textual meaning. The power of textual construction lies with the reader, not the writer. Russell Hunt (2004) also supports the notion that the most helpful connection for students to make is to learn "how to weave someone else's language into your own voice" (p.8). He is concerned that what educators are now doing is "punishing people for not knowing what it's our job to help them learn" (p.8).

These ideas are also supported by academic writing researchers in the field—Patricia Sullivan and James Porter.[5] They argue that the rise in the role of the reader leads to "instability of the notion of writer as 'author'" (1997, p.29). They claim that an examination of the role of the reader in light of the destabilization of the role of the author is warranted. To examine plagiarism from a reader's perspective is useful where the focus is on the reader as active constructor of textual meaning. In the context of plagiarism, Sullivan and Porter are suggesting that scrutinizing the teacher-reader's construction of the student-writer's text as plagiarized is essential as meaning has been attributed by the reader not the writer. An examination of the teacher's role as reader and interpreter of textual meaning is appropriate and may assist us to reflect upon our positions in the plagiarism debate, as advocated by Foucault.

The Construction of Text in Plagiarism—The Practice

A number of studies have taken place in classrooms around the globe to ascertain how texts are constructed with respect to plagiarism. In short, how is plagiarism characterized both by students and teachers? Why do teachers regard some texts as "plagiarized" and others not? What factors shape the construction of text? The studies since the 1980s used a variety of methods to ascertain the views of teachers and students. Some studies used surveys to ascertain attitudes of students towards plagiarism and academic dishonesty.[6] Other studies focused on teachers' responses and their strategies to help ESL/EFL students avoid plagiarism in academic writing.[7] Yet other studies discussed the technological responses offered to issues of plagiarism, particularly from the Internet.[8] Previous studies can be grouped into three broad categories:

1 *Definitional studies*—which examine students' concepts and under-standings of plagiarism, including knowledge of the policy and penalties;
2 *Culturally constructed studies*—which examine cultural factors that may influence students' abilities to work within plagiarism policies and guidelines;
3 *Textual studies*—which examine textual writing practices, includ-ing the voice of the writer and technical aspects of citation and referencing.

A combination of the findings from the three categories enables us, as teachers, to see how plagiarism has been studied in our classrooms. Many studies exploring students' definitional understandings were conducted in the 1960s and early 1970s. These studies were concerned with students' abilities to define or articulate their understandings of plagiarism before asking students whether they actually engaged in plagiarism or cheating practices. Surveys of students were often used in these studies. The next group of studies that I have called "culturally constructed studies" sought to explore cultural differences as the major reason for students (particularly ESL and EFL students) approaching plagiarism in academic writing in different ways. Many studies observed student approaches to learning, such as memorization and copying chunks of texts from source materials without acknowledgment, and linked these approaches to "culturally different" concepts of plagiarism. A large number of studies relied on constructs such as "deep" and "surface" learning as articulated by Watkins and Biggs (2001). The final group of studies moves beyond attributing diversity of interpretation to "cultural differences" alone and explores textuality itself. Of interest is how students develop a sense of authorial voice in texts— seen as essential to claim the rights of "author" under the Romantic notion of authorship.

Definitional Studies

Many studies asked students to define plagiarism or gave students multiple-choice questions with alternative answers about avoiding plagiarism to elicit students' understandings about plagiarism. An early study was conducted by Doris Dant in 1986. She surveyed 309 first-year under-graduate students at Brigham Young University in the United States, about their knowledge of correct attribution and plagiarism. One questionnaire of five multiple-choice questions was used. She concluded:

> Not surprisingly, less than half of those answering the last question (47.1%) had an accurate understanding when they were high school seniors about how to avoid plagiarism. 31.5% believed that all they need to do is to put ideas in their own words and possibly supply a bibliography (they feel footnoting is not necessary). 15.4% believed that they may copy information as long as either a bibliography or footnotes are provided (they feel that giving credit for another's wording is unnecessary). 5.8% marked that they had never heard of plagiarism. 34% still copied before and/or during their senior year. However, many more (61%) who believed that paraphrasing was the extent of their obligation to scholastic honesty also copied at least some of their reports.
>
> (Dant, 1986, p.83)

As can be seen from the mixed results of the survey, students were confused, unaware or simply not concerned with correct academic attribution. The fact that 31.5 percent of the 309 students responded that merely supplying a list of references or a bibliography in assessment work was "adequate acknowledgment," indicates that students had a limited understanding of their obligations under academic writing conventions to attribute authorship. The study found that the high percentage of students (61 percent) considered that paraphrasing the text—changing some of the words in the original—was sufficient acknowledgment. This finding also hints at another misunderstanding by students, as paraphrasing without the intellectual exercise of reworking text for overall meaning is unacceptable in most university environments. In fact, Dant (1986) found that less than 47 percent of the total number of students surveyed had accurate ideas about what constituted plagiarism. Clearly, if university and college teachers operate under the assumption that students who enter from senior high school have clear understandings about attribution of sources, then immediate problems arise.[9] Moreover, this study's findings indicate that many students are ignorant of the accepted citation conventions rather than intentionally engaging in acts of plagiarism. It bears keeping in mind that where students enter universities and colleges in which zero tolerance plagiarism policies are in force, these students could be expelled for academic misconduct due to outright ignorance of the academic citation practices embraced by that institution.

Another American survey of 140 ESL/EFL students in a first-year undergraduate writing class was conducted by Barry Kroll in 1988. He wanted to explore students' attitudes, feelings and beliefs about plagiarism. He concluded that students did seem to think about "ownership" of material in talking about plagiarism and he equated plagiarism with the criminal act of stealing. He found that:

> Quite a few students (36%) mentioned concepts of ownership in their explanations, identifying "stealing" as the major moral issue involved in plagiarism. Of the students in this study, 25% ranked concepts of ownership as the sole or most important reason that plagiarism is wrong.
>
> (p.220)

Again, although the survey indicates that some students (only 25 percent) believed that plagiarism was wrong because it contravened a sense of authorial ownership, the study concluded that plagiarism was a deliberate action of intentional wrongdoing. Kroll's (1988) study is mentioned here because it was one of the first empirical studies undertaken that discussed the moral issues perceived to underpin plagiarism—such as cheating and stealing. Again these concepts tie in with legal perceptions of central characteristics of plagiarism and embodied in some of the policies discussed in the last chapter. Moral aspects of plagiarism have been highlighted in later studies where the research has tended to center on teasing out the differences between issues of plagiarism and issues of cheating.[10] In fact, the "moral panic" about plagiarism is the subject of recent writing and much debate in current research (see Macdonald and Carroll, 2006; Clegg and Flint, 2006).

Culturally Constructed Studies

One of the predominant themes to emerge from the classroom studies was the connection that teachers and researchers were making between students' ideas about plagiarism and their different cultural backgrounds. That is to say, teachers attributed student plagiarism in essays to a diverse range of cultural responses. Included in the construction of plagiarism were also varying concepts of what was expected of students in academic writing and what was considered to be excellence in its production. A number of studies in classrooms around the world contributed to the mosaic of growing understandings about plagiarism. The early studies tended to view student constructions of plagiarism as "Western" and "Other," or "Asian," and much of the literature uses these terms. More recent studies have questioned this dichotomy and suggest that although cultural understandings play an important part in framing individual concepts of plagiarism, there are many factors to consider. In short, they argue that "cultural difference" is being used as a label where international students are concerned and often as an excuse to stop short of digging deeper into the multiple layers of the phenomenon of plagiarism itself. Sample studies are presented below to illustrate the ways in which teachers and researchers have brought cross-cultural viewpoints to bear on the issue of plagiarism. These perspectives have helped shape a broader lens through which plagiarism in students' academic writing can be viewed.

At Shanzi Daxue University in 1985, Carolyn Matalene interviewed 50 Chinese students in a third-year English composition class. The students were asked questions about their attitudes and reactions to allegations of plagiarism in academic writing. She concluded that different cultures "define and value different relationships" and used a theory of contrastive rhetoric to compare the rhetorical practices of her Chinese students to her own American notions of rhetorical values:

> Our own rhetorical values are profoundly affected by the fact that we are post-Romantic Westerners, teaching and writing in the humanities. As such, we value originality and individuality, what we call the "Authentic Voice." We encourage self-expression and stylistic innovation. In persuasive discourse, we subscribe to

Aristotle's dictum, "State your case and prove it," and we expect to be provided with premises and conclusions connected by inductive or deductive reasoning. We call this a "logical" argument. We strongly favor Pound's dictum "Make it new," and we insist that our students use their own words in their own unique ways. We allow that original writing involved a chaotic discovery process but require that finished texts be cohesive, coherent, and explicitly unified. We expect rhetoric to help us achieve control and to be a force for change. But Western rhetoric is only Western.

(1985, p.790)

By concluding that "Western rhetoric is only Western," she asserts that a broader understanding of traditions of writing practice that are different from Western traditions is not only necessary, but imminent. Matalene's words capture the argument that many teachers embrace, which is that as internationalization of education spreads, the ethnocentrism that has characterized many classroom practices of writing assessment in the past is fast becoming an inappropriate response. Matalene has a point in arguing that "we need to understand and appreciate rhetorical systems that are different from our own" (1985, p.790). This is particularly true where the marketing literature from many universities and colleges makes claims to embrace truly international ideals and be open to what Edward Said (1978) calls the "Other." If this is so, then perhaps we need to consider the appropriateness of insisting on one particular cultural construction of authorship.

One of the early studies that specifically emphasized the role of cultural difference in terms of the concept of exact copying of original text was undertaken by Jane Sherman (1992). Sherman reflected on the writing practices of her first-year undergraduate students in an Italian university. She concluded that Italian university students did not write in the way their English teachers expected them to. Her students memorized words and gave verbatim answers without analysis or sourcing. In short, she concluded that they plagiarized. She noted, however, "What we all saw as plagiarism, they clearly saw as not only legitimate but correct and proper" (p.191). She argued that there were cultural differences explaining this practice. For example, she said that Italians valued mimetic practice in written text while promoting oral debate for spoken text. She also said that oral exchange was used to negotiate and exchange differences of opinion about meanings, whereas writing was used to deliver the product of those exchanges: "I feel that in Italian, less importance is attached to writing as an instrument than in English. The medium of negotiation and exchange is more often oral and writing is the product" (Sherman, 1992, p.193). This study highlights the view that skills in rote learning and recounting memorized tracts of text are seen not only as acceptable, but also as a desired form of writing. Sherman's study foregrounds the idea that literary practices that are considered to be intellectually demanding and "correct" in some cultural contexts by some teachers and educational institutions are not seen to be so universally. Her study articulates the need to be aware of the role that cultural contexts have to play in framing notions of excellence in academic writing.

An important questionnaire study eliciting Hong Kong Chinese students' views of plagiarism was undertaken by Glenn Deckert in 1993. His aim was to investigate Chinese students' concepts of plagiarism and their opinions of students who commit acts of plagiarism in writing. The questionnaire gained responses from 170 first-year students and 41 third-year students in science studies at Hong Kong University. The first-year students answered the questionnaire before any teaching about plagiarism had occurred. The results indicated that these students had little idea of plagiarism and what it entailed as well as poor abilities to recognize plagiarism in the sample texts on the survey. He claimed that these students saw the problem not in terms of cheating the original author, but in egocentric terms of their loss of learning opportunities:

> Most Chinese students overuse source material through an innocent and ingrained habit of giving back information exactly as they find it. They are the proverbial rote memorizers or recyclers ... In other words, egocentric concerns of learning well and feeling right about oneself together far exceed concern for either the college, the original writer, one's own classmates, or one's relationship with the teacher.
>
> (1993a, p.140)

Deckert (1993b) also claimed that these students copied strings of words in writing, as, in Hong Kong, it is acceptable and even thought excellent writing to copy from the masters. He noted, "the student is simply pursuing the writing task in a manner consistent with her educational background and broader cultural experience" (p.95). It is in this sense that the student is engaging in what Deckert (1993b) termed "learned plagiarism" (p.95):

> Many students may enter tertiary-level institutions with virtually no notion of written ideas being someone's property. Neither do they have much awareness of copyright laws about rightful ownership, borrowing and distribution of published materials.
>
> (p.101)

Deckert's conclusions drew criticism from Alastair Pennycook in 1996. Pennycook suggested that Deckert operated from within a "Western" framework of the notion of plagiarism, which does not account for cultural differences in concepts of value in academic writing. He asserts that there is no universally applicable Western notion of plagiarism and he contrasts Anglo-Western ways of learning and valuing individual notions of authorship to that of Asian cultures—where rote learning and huge feats of memorization of texts are regarded as displaying intellectual superiority. Pennycook further argues that Deckert's framing of the notion of plagiarism and ownership of authorial work has been protected by English-derived laws of intellectual property:

> Given the emphasis on the creative individual as producer and owner of his or her thoughts, it seems that the borrowing of words is often discussed in terms of *stealing* [author's emphasis] of committing a crime against the author of a text. This particular connection presumably has its origins in the peculiarly Western conjunction between the growth of the notion of human rights and the stress on individual property, thus making the reuse of language already used by others a crime against the inalienable property rights of the individual.
>
> (Pennycook, 1996, p.214)

He advocates exploring the "cultural and historical specificity of the notions of ownership and authorship" particularly in light of internationalization of education. The view that Anglo-Western notions of plagiarism are merely one way of viewing the issue has received support from teachers working and researching in the cross-cultural studies field. Joel Bloch and Lan Chi (1995) compared 60 articles by Chinese writers and 60 articles by English writers focusing on citation method. They wanted to explore whether different referencing systems were evidenced and review how citation and plagiarism may be linked in ESL/EFL academic writing. They found that plagiarism may be a "compensatory strategy used by novices" and "Chinese rhetoric does not place the same taboo on plagiarism that Western rhetoric does" (p.238). They also concluded that Chinese writers bring "a 2,000 year old tradition of rhetoric to their second language writing process," which illustrates that "each form of rhetoric reflects the cultural traditions in which it developed" (p.271). The importance of this research is that it highlights the connection between the text and the cultural setting in which it is situated and produced. The text is not seen as something created in a vacuum or in a solitary state, as claimed in legal theory and the Romantic notion of authorship. These comments support the ideas of

Bakhtin (1986) that text is alive and fashioned by cultural, social, political and economic settings as well as responding to the environment in which it is born.

In classroom environments, where some textual writings are born, Sharon Myers (1998) reminds us of the frustration for students who do not understand the "rules of the game," which are shaped and molded by writing traditions. She states that this is particularly true for "Western" writing traditions, as they are seen by many institutions as "the only ones feasible or even sensible" (p.12). Her study examined the difficulties facing Chinese scientists gaining international publication of their work as "Western conventions in writing that are difficult to grasp and take years to accomplish" formed a barrier (p.1). She concluded that traditional notions of plagiarism "splinter on close examination" and "a new order" is needed that is inclusive of the writing traditions of "other" non-Western backgrounds (p.14). Myers' view is most helpful to teachers—particularly those operating in classrooms of greatly diverse student populations. She, like Edward Said, recognizes that "Other" backgrounds and cultural perceptions of textual excellence in writing need to be considered. A 2006 study by the project team of the Chinese University Teacher Training in English (CUTE) in Cambridge indicated that "cultural analytical frameworks" can pose problems for students moving into a different higher education system, such as from China to England.

Cavaleri (2006) said:

> Chinese students in particular often struggle to adjust to Western notions of plagiarism as deference to expert opinion is a deeply routed cultural norm in Chinese society. Indeed, referencing sources has been seen as disrespectful to both reader and "expert" as it presupposes that the source is not widely known and that the audience is unable to recognize source material. Students are often extremely committed to practices learnt at school and require significant explanation before they accept the need for referencing.

Cavaleri's (2006) concern with "cultural analytical frameworks" that differ between students from various backgrounds—here specifically Chinese background—is similar to researchers in the analysis of critical thinking (Kutieleh and Egege, 2004; Moore, 2004) and language evaluation (Chanock, 2002). These ESL teachers and researchers have often used the Watkins and Biggs (2001) model to explore factors that relate to learning for Chinese learners. David Watkins and John Biggs identified six "learning-related factors" for the "paradox of the Chinese learner" (p.3). Their research examined beliefs and myths about Confucian heritage cultural styles of learning and they developed a model of six cultural features that they claimed are conducive to academic learning. The Watkins and Biggs' (2001) model is not without adversaries and some of their broad claims for this mainly cultural approach to learning are in stark contrast to research in the field by Pennycook (1996), Noi-Smith (2001), Skutnabb-Kangas (2003) and others. However, their model is still used by a number of teachers and it provides a point of comparison for teachers to gauge their own perceptions of the influence of culture on the learning approaches of their students.

Watkins and Biggs' (2001) Model of Cross-Cultural Learning

The six learning-related factors that Watkins and Biggs identified as important for Chinese learners are described in the following sections.

Memorizing and Understanding

The authors claim that memorizing is a key factor in learning for Chinese students. They distinguish between memorizing without understanding (which they do not favor and term "rote learning") and memorizing as an aid to repetitive learning. The latter occurs where memorizing is used as a "deep learning strategy in order to enhance future recall with understanding" (2001, p.6). Deep learning occurs where meaning is obtained through processes of understanding and reconceptualization of information in another way. Surface learning is where individual knowledge is quickly increased through memorization and reproduction of information. Many tertiary teachers perceive memorization skills as mere surface rote learning techniques. However, memorization skills that are valued by many Chinese learners are akin to deep learning strategies.

Effort Versus Ability

The authors assert that "Chinese students are more likely to attribute academic success primarily to effort, rather than to both effort and ability, as do Western students" (2001, p.6). In their view, Chinese students, their teachers and parents believe that success indicates an individual's ability to work hard to achieve excellence. Encompassed in this belief is the idea that intelligence is not an innate and predetermined characteristic, but can be improved through consistent hard work. The authors distinguish this position from a prevailing notion in many educational institutions that an individual's innate ability (as indicated by various testing mechanisms such as Intelligence Quotient tests, aptitude profile tests and national skill tests) plays a significant role in ultimate academic success. This key factor illustrates different perceptions about the extent to which success is achieved by hard work.

Intrinsic Versus Extrinsic Motivation

The authors note that there appears to be a divergence between Chinese and Western notions of motivational forces to learn. In Western cultures, intrinsic motivation—the deep desire to learn and understand—is the key to learning success. For Chinese students, however, intrinsic and extrinsic motivational forces may intertwine. The authors assert that:

> For Western students, intrinsic motivation is an antecedent of the desired deep learning strategies . . . but for Chinese students the adoption of deep strategies may be activated by a head of mixed motivational steam: personal ambition, family face, peer support, material reward, and, yes, possibly even interest.
>
> (Watkins and Biggs, 2001, p.7)

It is pertinent to consider motivational forces in light of the rhetoric surrounding many institutions that learners are encouraged to be autonomous and self-directed in their approaches to learning. The idea of self-directed and independent learning is currently favored as best practice in many Australian universities and higher education institutions.

General Patterns of Socialization

Watkins and Biggs claim that cultural heritage endows Chinese students with a deep sense of respect for adults and teachers. They assert that "such dispositions to learn are not cultivated so assiduously in the West, because there is more reliance on intrinsic motivation" (2001, p.6). They conclude that "in short, Chinese, Korean and Japanese children are groomed for the demands of schooling before they get there, in a way that Western children usually are not" (2001, p.7). However, this broad claim that students from these South-East Asian nations are prepared to engage in learning with deep respect for the institution of school is difficult to accept. This is because there are many forms of social behavior and norms of engagement in learning around the globe. Exposure to different approaches to learning and studying will influence students' views of the historical truths Watkins and Biggs claim, such as respect for elders and teachers.

Achievement Motivation: Ego Versus Social

According to Watkins and Biggs:

> In Western societies, achievement motivation is highly individualistic and ego-enhancing, characterized by individual competition, where winning is its own reward. But in East Asian societies the

notion of success needs to be reinterpreted in a collectivist framework, which may involve significant others, the family, peers, or
even society as a whole.

(2001, pp.7–8)

The authors note that although individual ambition is present, a far
greater force is at work in terms of family, face and status, as children are
expected to succeed academically, "irrespective of the parents' educational
level" (p.7). The authors also note that failure to succeed is costly in
terms of "family face" (p.8). The importance of "face" and fear of failure
are also discussed by Noi-Smith (2001) for groups of Malaysian-Chinese,
Singaporean and Chinese Hong Kong students studying via distance
education. Although Watkins and Biggs (2001) refer only to Chinese Hong
Kong students, their notion that society's pressure to achieve success is more
influential than personal motivation to succeed, may be a concern relevant
to ESL and EFL students on a broader scale.

Collective Versus Individual Orientation

Watkins and Biggs (2001) explain that the preceding five categories
focus on the dimensions of individualism versus collectivism. They accept
that there is a great deal of controversy in this area but argue that their
research indicates these learning-related factors play a role in relationships between students and teachers in "collectivist East Asia" (p.8). They
explore differences such as Hong Kong students' expectations that their
teachers will take an interest in their personal wellbeing and their personal
lives, whereas teachers in many Western institutions consider that asking
students about their personal lives is invasive and flouts students' rights
to privacy.

In an interesting approach to analyzing the discourses of plagiarism,
Ashworth *et al.* (2003) use phenomenology to delve into the "lifeworld" of
12 students in different faculties at Sheffield Hallam University in England.
They reported on three students' responses and identified a number of
different ways in which students described their educational, social, ethical
and personal reactions to plagiarism. A number of different discourses
emerged. One, a *discourse of morality*, the authors depict as a "sense of
vertigo at the very idea of accusation" (p.268) and describe a student's fear
at the very real possibility of unintentional plagiarism "due to lack of skill
in referencing" (p.268). Another is the *discourse of "the canon,"* in which a
female student acknowledges the historical contingency of scholarly
research and says that the core material provided by teachers is drawn upon
by students as they rely on "leading authors as a way of learning" (p.268).
Ashworth *et al.* conclude that:

The vexed question of plagiarism is often tackled in terms of policing measures or of the institution of moral codes. The variety of understandings of plagiarism—sometimes seeing it as an unskilled lack of referencing or material, sometimes as a necessary stage in the process of learning, and sometimes noting its varying meanings in different disciplines—means that the focus in dealing with the problem must be on *enculturation*. If we view the norm of plagiarism-avoidance as a special feature of academic culture, then it becomes plain that students must be introduced to it as part of their *membership* of that culture.

(p.275, italics in the original)

It is particularly relevant that Ashworth *et al.* note that students need "membership" within an academic culture, as this point is elaborated on by teachers, particularly CheeLing, see Chapter 5 of this book. Students obtain membership of academic culture by demonstrating mastery of certain discourse structures, as explained by Gee (1990) and many researchers argue that re-examination of traditional values of academic excellence in writing is overdue.[11] There is a suggestion that in addition to cultural factors influencing perceptions of excellence in writing traditions, outmoded and inappropriate ways of judging textual proficiency are in place. Indeed, some researchers, such as Phan (2006), argue strongly against some binaries used, such as that of "Asian and Western" constructions of text. Leading researchers claim that there has been cultural monopoly of writing through the dominant position of English as an international language.[12] Some theorists go so far as to suggest that the domination of English as a global language is a form of "cultural genocide" (Skutnabb-Kangas, 2003). Indeed, Edwin Thumboo (2003, p.236) responds that the English language is "the real jewel in the British Crown" because its expansion into every corner of the world ensures that there is widening economic dependence on English as the international language. Naturally, where English is seen as the imperial *lingua franca par excellence,* to use Simon Marginson's (2003) term, perhaps ESL and EFL students subjugate the Eastern "Other" to the Western "Occident" view of authorship, as suggested by Edward Said (1978).[13] Successful ESL writers such as Suresh Canagarajah (1993, 2001) and Ryoko Kubota (2001) indicate that in making the choice to utilize one set of writing conventions over another is a betrayal of their original notions of excellence in writing. If the dominant and powerful vision of academic writing is not adopted by ESL students, entry to the academic discursive community is difficult, if not impossible to attain. Successful ESL writers remind us that "language is power"

(Thumboo, 2003, p.237) and it follows that ESL students must acquire the requisite skills deemed appropriate by Western academic discourse communities. Without the necessary skills, ESL and EFL students are merely linguistic fringe-dwellers on the edge of academic discourse communities.

Following the post-colonial view that English has forced certain academic norms to be followed, Betty Leask (2006) suggests that the metaphor of war is appropriate where the view that plagiarism is a battle to be won by Western scholars is apparent. She suggests that plagiarism be viewed as an "intercultural encounter" and, using Said's (1978) notion of "Other," urges academics to work with the idea that "all students are to some degree strangers to the culture of the academy" (Leask, 2006, p.191). In this way, ESL and EFL students can be seen as "efficient learners in an unfamiliar environment rather than as deficient learners who need to be taught a better way of doing academic work" (2006, p.194). These ideas broaden the scope in which "culture" is seen to play a part in construction of plagiarism by students, and are expanded by teachers considering elements of textual dexterity by ESL and EFL student-writers.

Textual Studies

In 1990, Margaret Kantz wrote about the problems that "Shirley" had in first-year undergraduate writing at universities in the United States. Shirley was a student that Kantz had created as a pastiche from an unspecified number of students at a community college, a public and a private university. She used Shirley to explain why students found it hard to synthesize text and therefore appeared to plagiarize material. She explained that Shirley was not really plagiarizing, but displayed a lack of technique in using textual sources persuasively. Kantz attributed such textual borrowing to be a problem of immature writing technique rather than a moral wrong. In this situation, Kantz argues that plagiarism may have little to do with intention but more to do with lack of specific citation techniques and strategies—the mechanics of citation and referencing are lacking. In other studies, students express similar concerns about the ramifications of plagiarism being found in their work; when they are not confident they possess the requisite referencing skills or argue that they are novices in terms of academic writing (Counsell, 2004; Handa and Power, 2004; Marshall and Garry, 2006; Sutherland-Smith, 2005a,b).

The idea that part of the issue of plagiarism in academic writing, particularly for international ESL and EFL students, is due to inadequate skill in using citation and referencing conventions is supported and extended by Canadian teachers Ishbel Galloway and Marti Sevier in their year-long study of 60 ESL/EFL students. Galloway and Sevier's (2003) work not only supports the idea that there is a lack of skill in academic citation but also points to a theoretical scale of degrees of copying—sometimes intentionally and other times unintentionally but all without attribution. They found that many ESL and EFL students considered it "the mark of an educated person to have huge tracts of text in memory," which they expected to recycle in their work.[14] This study again echoes the sentiments of Pennycook (1996) that "memorization of texts is not a pointless practice . . . because the issue is not one of understanding the world and then mapping language onto it but rather of acquiring language as texts as a precursor to mapping out textual realities" (p.222). The idea that plagiarism can be a situation of insufficient skill is also seen in work in the United States. Cherry Campbell (1990) examined the work of 30 composition students in ten subjects at the University of California, Los Angeles (UCLA). She found that the scale of plagiarism began with straight copying of text for the beginner writer, then moved through to copying with a sense of purpose—such as copying for a set project. As the writer became more experienced with techniques of summarization and paraphrasing, the process of composing began and the final stage of synthesis was reached only after these initial stages had been completed. She concluded that her study lent "conceptual support for a multistage model of skill in using background information" (p.211). Campbell's conclusions that students copy text as part of the learning process in academic writing development, which is refined and honed with time and practice, are supported by many other ESL/EFL teachers and researchers from different classrooms around the globe.[15] It is not just the mechanics of referencing and citation that are of concern—it is also the question of students' identity and voice in their work (see Ivanič, 1998; Ryan, 2000; Scollon, 1995[16]).

Many teachers require that students come up with "original" ideas or ask students to give their own opinions and justifications for viewpoints they express in their written work. Leaving aside the question of whether any work can be truly considered to be "original" (as detailed in Chapter 2), part of the problem for some students is actually knowing how to present their own opinions alongside the literature. Attaining the delicate balance between reliance on the literature and their own voices weaving the thread of argument through the text can be daunting for students—particularly for students trying to manipulate words in a foreign language. This is a key point that tertiary and college teachers need to take into account—both when setting and marking work. Navigating the mystifying labyrinth of academic writing takes time, constant practice and knowledge of writing skills. Inherent in this learning process is the students' awareness of themselves in the word maze. Researchers such as Ramanthan and Atkinson (1999) claim that voice is linked to identity and a sense of the individual. They say students convey their "essentially private and inner selves" through their choice of words and phrases and this is the individual sense of "voice" (1999, p.47). Diane Belcher and George Braine (Belcher, 1995) agree, and argue that the danger for ESL and EFL students is the problem of losing their own voices once they are initiated into the discourse of academic writing. Sylvia Cher's (2007) study of ESL postgraduates' use of sources in academic writing also highlighted the importance of voice in academic writing. Her research study found that the ability to be able to write in a meaningful way is essential if students are to feel any sense of empowerment in their writing. She says that "not being able to express one's voice gives a sense of powerlessness and a feeling of invisibility" (2007, p.12).[17] Phan (2006) also supports this idea and says her voice was silent until she was able to develop her "hybrid discourse" (p.132) for academic writing purposes—which communicated her Vietnamese self, mediated through the English language. These ideas are also espoused by most teachers in this study, who said that students' academic writing was often "stilted" and that a sense of the writer "being at one" with the text was missing. One teacher, Georgiou, captured the essence of concern in his comment:

> The problem is that when a student reads multiple texts, as a novice writer he or she is confused by which text is the major one or leader of the pack. When the teacher comes to read the stuff, there are a multitude of voices leaping off the page and the voice of the student, who should tie it together, is silenced, overshadowed or lost completely.
>
> (Georgiou, teacher at South-Coast University)

Learning to differentiate between the varying nuances of argument and opinion in texts is a developmental skill and takes time. Students also need to develop considerable proficiency in deciding how to give textual weight to varying perspectives in writing. Many teachers as well as researchers allude to the fact that students need time and practice as they are mere "novices" learning the craft of academic writing. James Wertsch (1991) refers to this as the act of "ventriloquism" and says, "the process whereby one voice speaks through another voice or voice type in a social language is one of the fundamental processes of development" (p.127). Finding a sense of academic voice is an important part of the language learning and sub-suming process. The conscious process of internalizing academic language into an individual educational perspective is one that many teachers and researchers acknowledge is difficult for students to achieve.

Summary

In contrast to the legal notions of plagiarism presented in Chapter 2, this chapter focused on cross-cultural views of plagiarism drawn from literary theory and cross-cultural studies. The notion of "authorship," as adhered to in law, is contested through the work of Mikhail Bakhtin (1986) and Roland Barthes (1977). The very concept of "authorship" is questioned and the views presented in this chapter offer alternatives to a narrow construction of plagiarism. The roles of both the reader and writer in textual relationships were also explored with the specific aim of highlighting the critical role of the reader, rather than the writer, in textual construction. Key ideas from previous studies about plagiarism in students' academic writing were detailed under three broad headings: definitional studies, culturally constructed studies and textual practices. The aim of this chapter is to draw teachers' attention to the complexity of plagiarism "in its appearing"[18] as a textual phenomenon and to suggest a re-examination of ways in which we see reading and writing relationships. The next chapter probes textual relationships even further when Internet plagiarism is discussed.

CHAPTER 5

Plagiarism and the Internet

A battle is shaping over the future of the Internet. On the one side are those who see its potential as a threat to traditional notions of individual proprietorship in information, and who perceive the vigorous extension of traditional copyright principles as the solution. On the other side are those who argue that the network environment may become a new cultural "commons" which excessive or premature legal control may stifle.

(Peter Jaszi, 1994, p.56)

The Internet is a new space for the creation of writing (Barlow, 1994; Bolter, 1991). Traditional legal notions can protect stable print texts, but in the hypertext environment, where texts can change and move, it is difficult to apply traditional notions of authorship to the Internet (Kress, 1997, 2003). Internet "works" can be created as text, images or graphics in an intangible medium. Additional problems arise where the Internet provides for rapid and easy copying of sections or whole works (Gurak, 2001; Lankshear and Snyder, 2000; Larson, 2001; Lincoln, 2002; Litman, 2001). As the Romantic view of authorship has previously relied upon the idea that a work has specific boundaries, it becomes problematic to apply these views to an environment where, as Fitzgerald (2000, p.4) states, "the fences are too easily removed." Digitized information can also be considered intangible property, which strains traditional notions where "ownership" has always applied to tangible works.

Whether the Internet is seen as a battleground, as suggested by Jaszi (1994), or as a contested intertextual space (Howard, 2007), there is little doubt that the Internet has been linked to plagiarism. Research reports that plagiarism, as well as cheating, is increasing in universities (James and McInnes, 2001; Maslen, 2003; O'Connor, 2002; Zobel and Hamilton, 2002). Often, media headlines such as "Foreign students in plagiarism scandal" and "Dirty marks" hint that plagiarism is flourishing at tertiary institutions and point the finger both at international students and the Internet.[1] Indeed, Russell Hunt (2002) declares that when plagiarism or cheating is found at a university, "the headlines leap across the tabloids like stories on child molestation by alien invaders" (p.1). The media frenzy over the issues of plagiarism at Curtin University in Western Australia (Malatesta, 2001), Monash University (Madden, 2002a, 2002b), RMIT (Hunt, 2003) in Victoria and the University of Newcastle in New South Wales (Davis, 2003a) have pressured universities to publicly react—often in a punitive manner. Teachers have been sacked, external investigations instigated and independent commissions of inquiry held in order to allay fears that academic integrity has diminished to a point of non-existence. Many universities overhaul curricula and assessment practices, amend plagiarism or academic misconduct policies and overtly introduce technology in order to reduce plagiarism. Chapter 5 focuses on the perceptions of Internet plagiarism by teachers and students in my study[2] and links their ideas to previous teachers' comments and also research in the field. The aim of this chapter is to outline the challenges that the Internet poses for traditional concepts of plagiarism and highlight some of the issues for teachers, students and policy-makers that hypertext environments pose in our classrooms.

The Internet is often touted as the source and reason for perceived increases in plagiarism. Some research studies indicate that plagiarism has not actually increased exponentially (McCabe and Drinin, 1999; Park, 2003) and it is not clear that the advent of the Internet can be attributed as the "cause" of plagiaristic activities by students (McCabe, 2003). Other researchers claim the Internet is a primary force pushing an increase in student plagiarism (Atkins and Nelson, 2001; Kitalong, 1998; McLafferty and Foust, 2004; Szabo and Underwood, 2004). James and McInnes (2001, p.28) argue that "the incidence of plagiarism has risen dramatically" adding that "electronic technologies lend themselves to the grosser forms of cut and paste cheating." There continues to be debate about the connections between the Internet and plagiarism. Well-known American researcher,

Don McCabe (2003), claims that the incidence of plagiarism has risen with the increasing use of new technologies. However, he considers that the Internet itself has not led to a significant rise in new cases of plagiarism, but the Internet has provided a space for those students already plagiarizing to increase their plagiaristic activities. McCabe's (2003) large study in the United States and Canada indicated that the percentage of students reporting plagiarism by using "cut and paste Internet sources" jumped from 13 percent in the 1999–2000 academic year to 41 percent in the 2001–2002 academic year. His survey of 35,000 students on 34 campuses found that students reported a 28 percent increase in plagiarism because "the Internet is simply too vast, too convenient, and in some sense, too anonymous to ignore" (p.6). Although McCabe does not consider the Internet has led to a dramatic surge in the total number of students who plagiarize, he is concerned that the "ambivalent feelings" many students display towards the concept that plagiarism is academic dishonesty is alarming (p.6). He foreshadows that with younger students using the Internet as a "primary reference tool," Internet plagiarism will become "the dominant form of cut and paste plagiarism" in the future (McCabe, 2003, pp.6–7).

Similarly, a report published in 2002 of 698 students surveyed between 1999 and 2000 across nine institutions in the United States found that 25 percent of students indicated that they plagiarized online. Students responded that they plagiarized "sometimes" to "very frequently." Researchers Patrick Scanlon and David Neumann (2002) concluded that this "should be cause for concern" but that the numbers did not indicate "an epidemic of Internet-facilitated plagiarism" (p.376). Students were "more apt to plagiarize" if they perceived that "a majority of their peers are going online to plagiarize" (p.384). Scanlon and Neumann argued that it was not yet clear how technologies such as the Internet would shape new generations' conceptions of fair use and appropriate attribution, but they saw this as "the critical issue" (p.384). Although they found that there was not the "epidemic" proportion of plagiarism associated with Internet information that the media suggested, researchers such as Attila Szabo and Jean Underwood (2004), Susan Stoney and Mark McMahon (2004) and Mark Warschauer (2004) tend to disagree. Stoney and McMahon suggest that "cybercheating has become so prevalent in Australian universities" that institutions are treating plagiarism as "a battleground, where a war is waged between students and institutions and played out using all the means afforded by contemporary digital technologies" (pp.81–82). Szabo and Underwood (2004) argue that their study in the United Kingdom shows that "the threat of use of the Internet for academic dishonesty by a substantial number of students is very real" (p.195). They claim that the alarming figures of Internet plagiarism demanded "a call for preventative action to curtail students' academically dishonest activities through the Internet" (p.180). Mark Warschauer (2004) writes:

> There is little doubt that the rapid diffusion and growth of the Internet facilitates students' plagiarism by making available millions of texts around the world for easy cutting and pasting, many of them commercially-provided and tailored to high school and college students' needs. Online plagiarism takes a variety of forms from the blatant and intentional (e.g., purchasing an essay online) to the accidental and ill-informed (e.g., quoting small amounts of online material without proper citation).

Warschauer's (2004) comments support much of the prior theoretical debate covered in Chapter 4; that plagiarism can be both intentional and "accidental" or "ill-informed" in print-text and also in Web-text, as denoted on the plagiarism continuum.

Although some researchers indicate that the Internet is a juggernaut for academic dishonesty, other researchers disagree and urge us to consider broader notions of textual space (see Carroll, 2002; Howard, 1995, 2000; Hunt, 2002, 2004; Leask, 2006; Macdonald and Carroll, 2006). Most recently, Rebecca Moore Howard (2007) states that "the near-universal belief that the Internet is causing an increase in plagiarism" is simplistic and uncritical (p.4). She says that although "the Internet makes texts readily available for plagiarizing" (p.4) our fear arises "from a belief in widespread plagiarism—plagiarism that, because of boundless access to text, cannot be controlled" (p.7). She argues that the standard response to our fear that students will access limitless textual forms available on the Internet is one of increasing scrutiny and control, whether that be through policy, technology or external intervention. She persuasively contends that these assumptions ignore the role that the teacher plays as co-constructor of textual meaning. Howard maintains that the Internet must be understood in terms of textual relationships, not just a source of textual appropriation and it forms part of our "culture of authorship" (2007, p.4). She says:

> The biggest threat posed by Internet plagiarism is the widespread hysteria that it precipitates. With an uncritical, oversimplified understanding of intertextuality, teachers subscribe to plagiarism-detection services instead of connecting with their students through authentic pedagogy.
>
> (Howard, 2007, p.12)

She further contends:

> What is being called "Internet plagiarism" is presently understood almost exclusively in terms of access to text with expanded access itself believed to be the primary cause of the phenomenon. . . . If, however, we consider not just access to text but also textual relationships, we can gain a more tempered, critical understanding of Internet plagiarism.
>
> (Howard, 2007, p.4)

Howard's stance is supported by Russell Hunt (2002) who wrote a paper titled "Four reasons to be happy about Internet plagiarism" in which he outlines the necessity to critically examine pedagogical practices in order to change teaching for the better. Howard's (2007) assertion that any new form of communication that revolutionizes access to text is met with "a new round of anxiety and resistance" (p.6) is supported by a teacher in this study. Georgiou asserts that the Internet is merely a new source of information, and, like any technology, will take time to work with its potential as a resource. He says:

> It is a difficult issue because it's a new technology and normally a philosophy takes a long period of time to develop, and we're talking the Oxfordian method which has taken 600–800 years for tradition to evolve. The Internet is a new phenomenon, basically, since 1995 really, it's grown logarithmically, so the philosophy that would normally take several hundred years to develop is still forming, it's embryonic, and so things are not set in concrete. So, yes, the issue of ownership suddenly grays but we will work through that. The potential of the Internet far outweighs any hiccups we are experiencing now.

Carrie Leverenz (1998) also pre-empted that the Internet as a new textual space would challenge ideas of authorship and meet some degree of opposition. She says:

> The fact that writing on the Web allows authors to constantly revisit and revise their ideas means that knowledge can grow at an exciting pace that none of us can hope to keep up. The fact that any text can be connected to any other text through hypertext linking opens up the possibility for boundless collaboration but also increases anxiety about intellectual property right and fair use.
>
> (p.197)

She concludes by asking a very pertinent question in relation to source acknowledgment, which is bound to the issue of plagiarism. She ponders whether our traditional ways of citing print-text sources can be relevant to online sources, or "whether we need to rethink the whole notion of what it means to consult and cite sources, to make knowledge by drawing on the knowledge of others" (p.196). Certainly, as teachers, we know that our students can and do mine the vast quarry of rapidly changing information on the Internet. We also know that Internet sources require acknowledgment, following standard academic writing conventions. But the question remains, do our students also know and understand this? What are our perceptions of Internet sources compared to those of our students?

Internet Plagiarism: Views of Teachers

Teachers have opinions about a number of different aspects of plagiarism and the Internet. Teachers overwhelmingly believe that the Internet is used as a source of information by students—many teachers arguing that it is over-used by students in their academic writing. Although it may seem banal to make the comment that students actively use the Internet, it is often assumed that students use the Internet more for social rather than university or "serious" study purposes. The student comments in this study show that this assumption is a misconception. Students not only use the Internet for study, information gathering and downloading images and diagrams, but also access sites such as Wikipedia, and use information contained there as "facts." In addition, students use video-clips on Youtube and Myspace to "get direct quotes for assignments" (Ari). Student comments also support teachers' perceptions that they consistently use Internet information for academic work. Ninety-one percent of the students surveyed (n=170) indicated that they use the Internet as a major source of material for assessment tasks. Students were reluctant to say how much Internet information they used but one student did say he probably used the Internet for 80 percent of every assignment he submitted. Although other studies have also shown that students use quantities of Internet source material in academic assignments (Marshall & Garry, 2006; Sutherland-Smith, 2005b; Szabo and Underwood, 2004), the extent to which students rely on the Internet as a sort of "one stop shop" for information is worthy of further research. Of particular interest is to ascertain how students use, check and verify sources of Internet information for academic work.

All teachers interviewed in this study consider that the Internet gives students the opportunity to plagiarize, whether students do so or not. Teachers often express feelings of helplessness with the inability to keep track of Internet information and a sense of frustration that despite every effort to read widely and keep up to date, that "just keeping abreast of the explosion of information is increasingly difficult" (Georgiou). Similar sentiments have been expressed by other teachers in classrooms around the globe (see Gardiner, 2001; Johnston, 1991; Whiteman and Gordon, 2001). Many teachers feel that it is part of their professional responsibility to keep up to date as much as possible, so that they can share current views with their students. Teachers are very concerned that some students are using Internet sources without reference, but say that the pool of material on the Internet is so immense that students can find sources that teachers are not aware of. As Kate noted:

> The difficulty is that it's so much easier to plagiarize online because you can cut and paste just about anything. And of course, the other difficulty is that online is so vast I can't keep abreast of everything there—so I guess an enterprising student could cheat and plagiarize more easily without detection.

CheeLing raises a number of issues about material from the Internet. She is concerned by the prospect that "hidden" and "remote" sources are used by students, and also is suspicious about the dubious nature of some of the information on the Internet. She says:

> I think it's difficult to reference material from the Internet unless you know the whole site and in which case—it looks a little bit unprofessional. But the students don't know the proper referencing in the first place. I found overseas students where they got information that would be so remote and so hidden, therefore they will just put the information down without giving references. I don't know—I always have a doubt about people's work from the Internet—even with the right address. If students download, I don't know whether they've read it or not, but I do with the textbook. It becomes easier to copy each other's work I think. My view is it's difficult to police plagiarism, but we can just emphasize we are not going to tolerate it, but to what degree we are policing this policy? I think it depends on each case—if it's a couple of minor paragraphs or it is the whole thing downloaded—which is ridiculous and give them a zero.

Here, CheeLing proposes that the degree to which students plagiarize should affect the penalty—if only a little. Presumably the penalty would be less for "a couple of minor paragraphs" than when an entire work is downloaded and submitted for assessment, as is the case with Birmingham

University's plagiarism policy (see Chapter 3). Inger agrees and is also concerned that, as the Internet is increasingly providing for languages other than English to be used, students may take articles in their own language and translate them into English for assignments. She continues:

> I mean one of the things I worry most about is that some of my students seem to have amazing "facts and figures" at the ready. The information all seems to be really genuine and it's not in any text I've ever read, so I'm wondering where they might have got it from. You know, there are so many bits and pieces up there that are in other languages, I'm a bit concerned that they might be just taking something in their own tongue and giving me a translation of it for the assignment. Again—how would I ever know? What can you do about that sort of thing?

Inger expresses her fears that she cannot personally check the sources of information because of the vast amount of material available. She is concerned, as a young teacher, that she may be seen by her immediate supervising staff as not fulfilling her role properly. This could affect her ability to gain tenure. She says:

> I mean anybody out there could be just pinching somebody's essay from cyberspace, I mean they could be going to any of these commercial sites and finding an article that I'm not going to know about and half the people in the world aren't going to know about, but could be plagiarized . . . yet they can just take it on board and write it up, send it and it's not theirs. How can I ever really know?

Staff concerns about students who gained information by downloading from the Internet in a form of cut and paste plagiarism are also supported by previous studies. Justin Zobel and Margaret Hamilton (2002) conducted a study at RMIT in Melbourne into instances of plagiarism over ten subjects ranging from first- to third-year level. They found a high instance of plagiarism across all subjects and year levels, particularly in one subject where 17 percent of all students engaged in cutting and pasting Internet information without acknowledgment. Helen Marsden conducted research into dishonest academic behaviors at the prestigious Australian National University in 2001. She found that very high levels of self-reported plagiarism existed, which supports the earlier findings of research conducted in Canada and the United States by Don McCabe and Linda Trevino (1996). She also documented the expected high correlation between low levels of academic self-efficacy and high levels of plagiarism. One surprising finding in her study related to the measures of dishonesty having no significant relationship to students' being informed about plagiarism. Marsden (2001, p.42) reports:

> None of the three measures of dishonesty were significantly related to a student having been informed about the rules and penalties for cheating or plagiarism. In an American study, Kerkvliet and Sigmund (1999) found that students given verbal reminders about cheating were significantly less likely to cheat than those who only received the standard written warnings in handouts. Huge resources are expended in Australian universities every year in an effort to inform students about their responsibility to behave honestly and ethically, and yet the message is falling on deaf or selectively deaf ears.

Marsden's words "yet the message is falling on deaf or selectively deaf ears" mirrors findings in a number of studies arguing that providing students with detailed information about plagiarism does not appear to impact upon its prevalence. In other words, merely telling students not to plagiarize and directing them to information about plagiarism is not an effective strategy to reduce plagiarism (Howard, 2002, 2004; Hunt, 2004; Macdonald and Carroll, 2006; Sutherland-Smith, 2005a).

Detection of Plagiarism

Most teachers believe that "cut and paste" plagiarism is easy to perform and probably difficult to detect. Some also say that they will check or trace sources used by students, but locating Internet source material is often too hard and too time-consuming to pursue, so they prefer to "let it go" (Renuka). Teachers use various strategies to detect plagiarism. Some employ technology, such as Google or Dogpile search engines, and they type in "suspect" phrases or references. Kyle says this is the fastest and most effective way he knows of locating "the one or two students who play the system." Other teachers, such as Naomi, try to locate the "authentic voice" of the student writer and employ that as a yardstick by which to measure plagiarism. Naomi says that it is particularly easy to locate plagiarized sections of text where the text changes from fluent, eloquent prose to text with slightly colloquial expressions, evidence of grammar errors and the occasional lack of sophistication in phrasing. Naomi finds that the movement between passages of considerable dexterity in the use of vocabulary, high levels of manipulation of grammar and error-ridden sections of poorly written text always alert her. According to Naomi, this is "a dead give-away." However, she is concerned that this useful method may be negated in time, as she believes that an increasing amount of work by students is published on the Internet. With this happening, Internet sites and sources may, she feels, incorporate the language and vocabulary used by students—including inappropriate or misleading information. She is troubled because "anyone is able to write on the Net" and this fact may make it more difficult for many students, particularly ESL and EFL students to distinguish between credible and less credible Internet sources.

Rane supports Naomi's view, claiming, "I think that it's getting worse and the expectations are downgraded because of the Net. More online published work that is written by students will become available for other students to download. Plagiarism will become much harder to detect." The youngest and newest member of the South-Coast University teaching team, Fiona, expresses her concern about detecting plagiarism. She indicates that she is worried her colleagues will think that if a higher degree of plagiarism is detected by her than by her peers, it will somehow reflect negatively upon her. She is anxious that her colleagues may deem her inexperienced, overzealous or just incompetent as a teacher if she detects significantly more or significantly less plagiarism than they do. Fiona says, "In terms of cutting and paste plagiarism, I just hope that I can know the students' style and work it out and try and spot it. But in terms of trying to prove it, that's where it becomes problematic and I feel knots in my stomach just thinking about it." Further issues for the detection and reporting of plagiarism are canvassed in Chapter 8.

Quality of Internet Sources

Not only did teachers express concern about "the cut and paste plagiarism generation", as Kate called them, they were also uneasy about the quality of Internet information used.[3] Teachers were anxious to know whether students had read, understood and critiqued the information, or just downloaded vast quantities of text from the Internet, without undertaking active processes of understanding that information. Larry Cuban (2001) describes this tendency as "a long stretch from thoughtfully considering the information and turning it into knowledge, or in time, forging that knowledge into wisdom" (p.189). For example, Tim said that students "just search it, download it and print it" and Lars said "I've watched them in the computer labs. They just find one site, get a hit that's near enough and copy it into their Word document." Students often admit to just cutting and pasting information without really trying to verify its authenticity or validity. Many students, when asked about how they verify the quality of Internet information, appear surprised and admit they have never thought about it. Others say they only check Internet information against other websites or use Wikipedia. One of the common anxieties for teachers is student use of Wikipedia and teachers' ongoing uneasiness about students' understandings of the need to use quality information. Most students in this study said that Wikipedia was like an online encyclopedia and they gave it the same status and authority as reference works such as the *Encyclopedia Britannica*. Overall, students did not seem to know that authors of Wiki entries might be experts, but equally, could be anybody with Internet access.[4] The fact that so many first-year undergraduates had no idea that people who wrote for Wikipedia were not necessarily scholars or academics is alarming for teachers and educational institutions. The level of awareness of the necessity for critical evaluation of websites, and the means by which students can assess the authenticity of Web information, is clearly an area in which a great deal of work has to be done, both in schools and in the tertiary sector.

Reporting Plagiarism

Reporting allegations of plagiarism is fraught with difficulty. This is because of the variety of ways in which plagiarism policies detail (or fail to detail) how plagiarism should be handled once it is detected. As can be seen from the myriad of approaches outlined in Chapter 3, allegations of plagiarism are handled differently across universities and tertiary institutions. Within universities, plagiarism might be treated differently by individual teachers. Sometimes this is the result of unclear or non-specific policy provisions and, at other times, it is because individual teachers do not support the institutional policy or their own pedagogical stance is incongruent with formal processing requirements. For example, although the policy at South-Coast University states that cases of plagiarism must be immediately reported to the Head of Department, who will send out a letter warning a student that an allegation of plagiarism has been lodged by a staff member, some teachers consider it is better to "get to the bottom of the matter themselves." For example, Sarah relates an incident and says:

> I had an example only a couple of weeks ago. I called them [students] both to my office, one at a time, and one admitted straight away he'd plagiarized from his friend. He said, "I didn't have time to do it and so I just copied." So I pointed out that copying in whatever situation is wrong and it is plagiarism and plagiarism isn't accepted and as a consequence you are getting zero because you let him copy from your work and you are just as responsible as he is. And they both accepted it and I think they

both knew that what they'd done was wrong. They seemed to be
a bit repentant before I even gave the consequences.

Although Sarah knows that the policy states she should direct the matter
to the Head of Department, she justifies her action as follows:

> Yeah, I know I'm supposed to tell Dick but the way I figure it is
> that it's easier and more effective to show the students I can deal
> with this myself. After all, I'm their teacher and if I appear weak
> by just passing the buck to someone else, what will they think of
> me? Another thing, I just don't want the hassle of filling out the
> report for Dick and then having to go and explain it all to him (if
> he even asks me!) when I can sort it out very quickly this way. I
> also think the students need the opportunity to own up or say
> whatever it is they have to say. This is not necessarily guaranteed
> once you send it up the line in a formal sense. I had an experience
> last year when I referred it to Dick, where the students weren't even
> heard at the Department level—it just went straight to the Faculty
> Disciplinary Committee before they even got a chance to speak and
> I think that's really poor.

Other teachers speak similarly about the dilemma of finding plagiarism
in a student's work but then being torn as to what to do about it. Some,
like Sarah, want to "sort it out" quickly with the students themselves and
other teachers are not confident that if the cases of plagiarism are reported,
the university processes and mechanisms will be effective. Teachers are
particularly apprehensive that where they have detected plagiarism, often
taking onerous hours of time to search websites and find the original
sources of the plagiarized material, that reporting plagiarism through the
bureaucratic channels might not be the best way to handle the situation.
The vexed question of handling plagiarism, as well as other ongoing issues
for teachers, are explored more in Chapter 8. One of the arguments behind
the drive to purchase commercially available anti-plagiarism software is
that it will take the mundane and time consuming task of identifying
plagiarism away from teachers and make detection and reporting of
plagiarism more effective and consistent.

Anti-Plagiarism Software—Turnitin

Anti-plagiarism software has been successfully marketed to universities as
a means through which to detect and deter plagiarism. Although there are
many packages in the marketplace, as well as the free online services, such

as Google and Dogpile, one commercially available product, Turnitin, has been embraced and implemented in many educational settings around the globe. Turnitin is an anti-plagiarism software program, developed by Dr John Barrie of iParadigms (2007), which checks Internet sites and also trawls four billion websites searching for matching text. The Mission Statement of iParadigms states:

> Recognized worldwide as the standard in online plagiarism prevention, Turnitin helps educators and students take full advantage of the internet's educational potential.
>
> (www.iparadigms.com)

Turnitin is aggressively marketed around the globe and is used by six million students at universities and schools in 51 countries around the globe to detect and deter plagiarism (www.turnitin.com). Although Turnitin has been heralded as an effective measure to combat plagiarism, some empirical research has been undertaken to examine user perceptions of its effectiveness. In 2002, an Australia-wide study examining the extent of student copying of texts was undertaken by Steve O'Connor. O'Connor used Turnitin and reported detecting large-scale copying of texts from Internet sources in 70 percent of participant universities. His research showed 1,125 or 58 percent of the total essay pool had more than 5 percent of the submitted essays copied, with 9 percent of those having information copied from the Internet (from 131 different websites). Furthermore, he concluded that student copying covered activities ranging from downloading a free research paper from the Internet to inadvertently leaving out quotation marks for embedded references. He concluded that Turnitin was able to detect plagiarism in a large number of cases. Against the backdrop of universities seeking effective, cost-effective and timely detection of plagiarism, Turnitin has been adopted, even lauded, as a solution to forms of academic misdemeanor by many educational institutions.

In the wake of other Australian universities adopting the software, South-Coast University decided to trial the software during 2004 with 2,000 students across its four campuses as a pilot research project, which I led. All teachers involved in undergraduate programs from five different faculties—Business, Education, Health and Physical Sciences, Law, and Science and Technology—were involved. The aim of the study was to explore teachers' perceptions of the usefulness and applicability of Turnitin in tertiary classrooms. In addition, staff were asked to comment as to how Turnitin might be used as an educative tool with respect to plagiarism. The purpose of the research was to inform the University Academic Board whether staff considered Turnitin would be a worthwhile investment of university funding, and, if a license was purchased, whether staff would find it user-friendly and therefore actually use the software.

Teachers were interviewed at three stages. Initial interviews ascertained their expectations of the software, and most teachers supported its acquisition and use. They expected the software would highlight passages of text and identify those passages as plagiarized with very little effort on their part. The majority also believed that the software would probably detect plagiarism more efficiently and consistently than they could. They also assumed that the online detection tool would be quicker and would search more widely than an individual teacher. Their comments are captured in the response of Glen, a psychology teacher from the Faculty of Health Sciences, who said:

> This is going to be great. It should save me hours because it will trawl through thousands of pages of material on the databases and find spots where text has been lifted. I hope it will be a quick and relatively thorough means of finding out where students plagiarize and highlight those spots for me. It takes me so long at the moment and even though I can spend a couple of hours checking suspect papers, I'm never really convinced that I've got everyone. This could be the answer.

Only one teacher, from the Faculty of Education, expressed reservations about using Turnitin. He was concerned about the way in which such a tool could be used to punish rather than help students overcome issues with plagiarism. Burt said:

> You know, I'm worried about the application of this software. I hope we as a university don't invest in it. I think it makes it all too easy to rely on technology as empirical evidence of plagiarism and this will allow staff not to check out with students what's going on with their writing. It offers an easy solution to academics to point the finger at students and in a way there's an abrogation of our responsibility to teach the students not to plagiarize in the first place. I think it will be used as a stick rather than a carrot.

Generally, at initial interview, teachers were positive that Turnitin would be more efficient, quicker and more thorough than they could be, as well as time saving. Interviews and observations took place when all teachers had been trained in the use of Turnitin's anti-plagiarism software. The majority were disappointed that the software did not discount text that was correctly referenced. Comments are aptly summarized by Deb, from the Faculty of Business, who said:

> I had thought that the text-match would pick up text that was not correctly referenced. It hadn't occurred to me that ALL text that matched would be identified. Really, in terms of effort, I have to now go through and see whether the text that has been identified as "match" has been correctly cited or referenced by the student or not. If it has, then there's no question of plagiarism. I didn't expect this, as I said, so it will take a bit more time than I thought initially.

The overall expectation of these teachers was that the software should have done more of the hard work for them. They commented that the software certainly matched the student's text against those it trawled from the Internet, and matches were easily understood by the color scheme used in the reports generated by the package. However, teachers still needed to scroll through the identified text-matches and ascertain whether plagiarism occurred or not. This was a time-consuming task that teachers had expected the software would do. Although this expectation may be naïve, teachers were not convinced that the marketing pitch that the software saved time was accurate. They were all convinced that the software found source matches as well, or better, than they could, but that this was only the starting point of the investigation. Decisions as to plagiarism still needed to be made. Final interviews and observations took place when teachers used Turnitin on student work.[5]

Overall, teachers said that Turnitin was useful to detect text-matches. Observations of teachers using the software also confirmed that they had little difficulty using it, although some became frustrated with the time delay in receiving the originality reports from the United States, as there is a time-zone difference for the southern hemisphere. Teachers considered that the color-coding system used to identify text-matches was excellent. Reports generated by the software assisted them in deciding whether to check the assignment further for plagiarism. Most staff, after checking through some papers with the full range of colors, decided that checking only yellow, orange and red cases was worthwhile. They found that in most cases, where red coding indicated 100 percent text match (i.e. the entire assignment matched another text) that it was because of human error, for example, the assignment had been sent to the Turnitin twice. However, in the case of one teacher, Craig, a red text match was because an assignment contained an OECD economic report that had simply been "cut and pasted" into the student's work. The student had only added a brief introduction.

Overall, the majority of teachers said Turnitin was a useful tool but they also strongly urged that it should not be the only means of plagiarism detection. Very few teachers thought that Turnitin alone would deter students from engaging in plagiarism and some were nervous that it may only encourage students to resort to more subversive activities, if they had decided to cheat.

A number of teachers also voiced their apprehensions that a number of their colleagues could, and would, view the software as a "stick not a carrot," to use Burt's words, and use it as a purely punitive tool. By this they meant that some would use the software to detect mere text-matches and then, as Thom said, "wash their hands of the issue and pass the buck upstairs" to formal disciplinary proceedings. Thom and others feared that the students would not have the opportunity to explain themselves until the stage of formal hearings, which was, in his opinion, unfair. Other teachers felt that the tool was primarily useful as a deterrent and should be used as such. By this they meant that the university should let students know that Turnitin was available for staff to check for plagiarism, should they so desire, and that this alone was sufficient for the university to discharge its responsibilities. These teachers felt that if students were caught through the Turnitin process, and penalties applied, that was the primary educative value of the software, as students would be unlikely to re-offend. Teachers were also adamant that no staff member should be forced to use Turnitin; it should be available if people wanted to use it.

Most teachers also said that Turnitin should be available for students to use to check their work before submission. Teachers favoring this option said that students could take more responsibility to ensure their work was not deemed to be plagiarized. Some teachers considered that Turnitin would thereby be used in a more "positive educative manner." Chris said:

> Students need to link the concept of intellectual honesty through checking their work. They need to do more than just run their assignments through the Turnitin site to see whether they'll be picked up or not. It's much deeper than that. They need to accept responsibility for understanding why they need to cite the sections that Turnitin has picked up, or go away and try to reword these parts in their own words, with appropriate citations for the ideas, of course.

These teachers considered that Turnitin could form part of the raft of existent support services for students. They were keen that Turnitin be positioned in such a way that it was not just a tool to "catch cybercheats"

(Ryan, 1998) but marketed by the university as a device through which students could learn how to engage with textual attribution conventions. However, a few teachers said that permitting students to use Turnitin would only encourage them to seek ways to "beat the system" and "students would, most likely, just change a few words here and there until the color-coding does not turn up as yellow, orange or red" (Lili). A couple of teachers, Ann and Marg, also thought that it was a deliberate challenge to students to see "who can beat the new techno-system" and they did not favor purchasing licenses for student use of Turnitin at all.

Although teachers thought that, overall, Turnitin was a useful tool, they did not consider that it really saved them all that much time. By the time they downloaded the "originality reports" generated by the system and scrolled through those that matched yellow, orange and red, they said it was just as time-consuming as the previous manual methods they employed. As Jo said, he felt overwhelmed by the workload and felt it was a question of "choosing whether it's the devil or the deep blue sea" in terms of effective plagiarism detection. Teachers' perceptions that the software would identify plagiarism and take that responsibility away from them was, of course, unrealistic. The software carries out text-matching functions but cannot determine whether plagiarism has occurred or not. That decision remains with the teacher. Teachers are also worried about the increasing availability of commercial sites from which students can purchase either generic or custom-written assignments and submit them for assessment.

Cyber-Pseudepigraphy (Buying Commercially Available Papers Online)

James Page (2004) uses a term "cyber-pseudepigraphy" to refer to the phenomenon of students using the Internet for others to write an academic paper for them, without this being acknowledged.[6] In other words, he is referring to websites providing academic papers for sale. Page (2004) argues that most websites market themselves as "research or editing services— thereby keeping ethical respectability and safeguarding against litigation" (p.430). These sites offer either generic papers for sale, or custom-made essays and assignments, where individuals can provide background information on the task, including lists of the references that are expected to be included, formatting requirements and key words to be included to ensure a personally tailored essay is produced for purchase.

Indeed, one site I visited recently[7] offered not only undergraduate papers for sale in a 14-day turnaround time, ranging in price from US$14.95 per page, but also Masters papers at US$22.95 per page and Doctoral dissertations at US$25.49 per page—prices increased if you wanted a "rush job." The website also has a special section titled "How to cheat Turnitin" with video-clips on beating anti-plagiarism software and teachers. The service assures customers that the essay is guaranteed plagiarism-free and is written by experts in the field. Investigating the "testimonials" section proved interesting: it is claimed there are over 300 satisfied student customers from around the globe—many of whom stated that they had used the service in all their subjects and intended to do so for the remainder of their degrees. Naturally, it is difficult to verify whether the information on such sites is genuine or not but some of the sites are certainly professionally presented. Although such essay-writing services exist, there are other websites that alert students to fraudulent practices of term-paper mill sites and contain "horror" stories of students who have paid money and not received their essays at all.[8] As always, the choice to act rests with the student, and some of the "market culture" influences on students' notions of cheating and plagiarism—such as plagiarism as consumptive practice—are discussed further in Chapter 8 (see particularly Saltmarsh, 2004; Vojak, 2006).

Student Attitudes to Internet Plagiarism

Students were asked whether they used the Internet as a source of information for their assignments and whether they could define or explain what plagiarism means. A Chi-square test was conducted to examine whether the response rates were different with respect to students' use of the Internet for source material and their abilities to explain what plagiarism meant.[9] The overwhelming majority of students, in fact 91 percent (n=170) of students, used Internet materials in their studies and only 9 percent (n=16) said that they did not use Internet information in their academic work. A further 48 percent of students (n=81) said they understood what plagiarism meant, which meant that more than half the student cohort studying this first-year writing unit (52 percent, n=89) responded that they did not understand what plagiarism meant. The findings showed that students who used the Internet were more likely to be able to explain what plagiarism meant than the students who did not use the Internet. A graph at Figure 5.1 illustrates the nature of the relationship between the variables.

Although this finding is not of statistical significance, it is of educational interest. The fact that 91 percent of the cohort use Internet information in their academic writing, supports comments made by teachers that they believe students are increasingly using the Internet as an information source. Furthermore, the findings show that the 52 percent of students

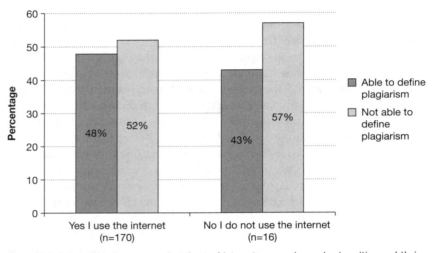

Figure 5.1 Relationship between students' use of Internet sources in academic writing and their ability to define or explain what plagiarism meant.

who use the Internet as a source of information are not confident that they can define or explain what plagiarism means. The question then remains that if students use Internet information without understanding the concept of plagiarism, do they know that they should reference this information? If so, how do they do it? How do students perceive cutting and pasting information from the Internet?

Students' Perceptions of Cutting and Pasting from the Internet

Thirty-two percent of students in my study indicated that they cut and paste directly from the Internet into their essays, although teachers consider that the proportion of cut and paste information is much higher than students ever admit. In an effort to elicit how much Internet information students believe they actually reference in their academic writing, a Likert scale was used in the student survey. If students believed they cited "all" the information they took from Internet sources, they circled "90%" on the scale. If students believed they cited "nearly all" Internet sources, then "85%" was selected; where students estimated they cited "most" of their Internet source information, "75%" could be chosen. Students who thought they cited "some" of their Internet sources could elect "65%"; for half "50%"; less than half "40%"; and for one third of Internet information cited, students could choose "30%."[10] The results showed that students who used the

Internet for sources in their academic writing were more likely to cite them than students who did not use the Internet, or said they did not use it.

In addition, students were asked about how they used Internet information—specifically about their cut and paste practices. Although the majority of students, 68 percent (n=126) indicated that they did not cut and paste information directly from the Internet, 32 percent (n= 60) of students did cut and paste Internet sources straight into their academic work. This represented almost one third of the total student cohort of 186 students undertaking the first-year writing unit. What is interesting is that almost half the students who admitted to using Internet information, although they said that they did not cut and paste directly into their work, also said that they did not understand what plagiarism was, nor could they explain it or how to avoid it.[11] The findings indicate that where students are able to understand and explain plagiarism, they are less likely to cut and paste Internet information directly into their academic work than students who do not understand plagiarism. This means that with better understandings of plagiarism, students will be able to utilize Internet information more effectively and appropriately in their academic work and the amount of cut and paste plagiarism should be reduced. Figure 5.2 is the graphical illustration of this relationship.

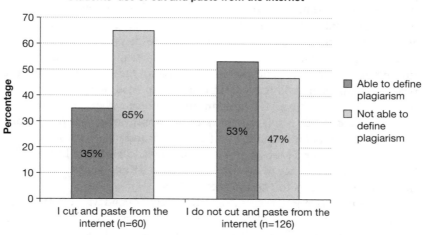

Figure 5.2 Students' ability to define or explain plagiarism and their concepts of cutting and pasting information from the Internet.

Although it may not be surprising to find that teachers' and students' views differ as to how much cut and paste from Internet sources is occurring, what is of concern is that 52 percent of the students (n=89) engaging in cut and paste activities with Internet information admit they do not know what plagiarism is, nor do they understand citation conventions. A further 15 percent of these students (n=25) indicate that they do not consider it necessary to cite information taken from the Internet at all. Clearly, many students are not making a connection between Internet information and the requirement to cite sources. In short, they do not understand that Web material still requires citation in their academic work. Students did not indicate that they relied on the Internet as a major source of material, but teachers are anxious that the Internet may become, for some students, the sole point of reference for academic assessment tasks.

These student responses echo the concerns expressed by most teachers that Internet source material is not being cited correctly, if at all. Teachers expressed the fear that students are cutting and pasting Internet information without understanding the need to cite it, and they are deeply concerned that students do not realize that plagiarism applies to Internet texts as well as to print text materials. Students' comments at interview provided some insight into reasons why students may not consider there is a need to cite Internet sources in their academic writing. Zhao, a student from China, said that there was no need to cite Internet information and, indeed, cutting and pasting information from the Internet is, in his opinion, quite permissible. He said, "If it not meant to be taken, it would be 'read-only' protected. This mean I cannot download it or print it out at home." Zhao believes that unless Internet source material is securely protected against actions of cutting and pasting, then it is able to be appropriated without acknowledgment. Similarly, Yan, a student from Singapore, said that the Internet is "a free zone" and there is no need to cite information in "the public domain." She said that any information posted on general websites is "there for the taking." These comments indicate that some students consider the concept of plagiarism does not apply equally to the "public domain" of Internet information as it does to information in print sources, such as textbooks and journal articles. Comments such as the Internet is a "free zone" give credence to the "grave concerns" (Kate) held by staff about the failure of students to cite Internet sources.

These findings support recent research in New Zealand where "plagiarism from web sources is considered generally less serious by students than plagiarism from books" (Marshall and Garry, 2006, p.31), as well as others such as Park (2003) and Scanlon and Neumann (2002) that students do not see taking information from the Internet as a particularly serious problem. Indeed in Deborah Straw's 2002 study, the general attitude of students in "generation why-not" is that teachers are particularly naïve or "clueless" in students' eyes when it comes to copying information from the Internet. It is "fair game" in their opinion. The problem remains, as Aly Colon noted in 2001, that students consider Internet information is "free for the taking" and the difficulty is how to convince them otherwise. This is a major challenge for teachers and institutions in the age of "academic cyber-sloth" (Carnie, 2001) also called the "mouse click" age of plagiarism (Auer and Krupar, 2001). Some suggestions and approaches that have been taken by different universities, as well as individual teachers, are described in Chapter 8.

Internet Plagiarism: Teachers' and Students' Responses

When comparing students' notions of how to define and explain plagiarism, to that of their teachers, it is not surprising that teachers have a far clearer notion of what constitutes plagiarism than their students. This is expected. What is unsettling is that teachers assume that having discussed the notion of plagiarism in class and given the students' exercises to complete, most of their pupils will now understand the term "plagiarism." From students' questionnaire responses, the data indicates that these assumptions are largely incorrect. A staggering 61 percent (n=81) of the 133 students did not demonstrate clear understandings of plagiarism. Some members of staff admit that students are "experts in training" (Belcher, 1995, p.137) as they learn to navigate through the labyrinth of textual complexities and styles in academic writing. Other teachers point out that understanding writing conventions and processes takes time, as does attaining the requisite skill level to manipulate language in sophisticated ways. A number of staff applaud Howard's notion (1995, 1999, 2000) that students when grappling with unfamiliar discourse structures use imitation and copying— "patchwriting"—as part of the learning pathway. However, for 61 percent of the 186 first-year students in this study, the explicit instruction was insufficient to enable them to grasp any real understanding of plagiarism and be able to apply it. Prominent among the findings in this study is that some students do not agree that Internet sources require referencing in their written work to the same extent as print-based texts. A number of students believe that Internet material does not need to be cited at all. In stark contrast, the participant teachers said that Internet sources *must* be cited and do not distinguish between Web-based and print-based texts in terms of referencing. It is these points of divergence in perception about plagiarism that must be addressed in open discussion, otherwise progress towards greater understandings of how to negotiate issues of plagiarism in the Internet Age will remain unresolved.

Summary

Chapter 5 detailed some of the competing viewpoints about plagiarism and the Internet. It began by highlighting perceptions that Internet plagiarism abounds in epidemic proportions in our higher education institutions and that there is little academic integrity left. The chapter then detailed the viewpoints of teachers in this study, interspersed with findings from previous research as well as current points of debate. All teachers in this study acknowledge that "cut and paste" plagiarism is a phenomenon and they witness it in classroom practices. They also voice their concerns about the use of Internet sources and the demands placed upon them to detect and deter plagiarism. However, their approaches in dealing with student plagiarism differ enormously. Some teachers adopt the stance that their professional responsibility is to detect and deter plagiarism and penalties cannot be strong enough where students are caught. Some teachers agree that plagiarism is part of their responsibility but disagree with punitive models of handling it, saying that it does not deter plagiarism. Yet other teachers argue that approaching plagiarism from the current viewpoint of authorship is futile and more thought needs to be given in policy and practice to implementation of pedagogical practices that deter plagiarism. They argue that through critically engaging with and examining ways in which academic integrity can be promoted in partnership with students is more likely to overcome issues of plagiarism in the long term. One of the main purposes of this chapter was to highlight the divergence of perspective about the roles of the teacher and student in the textual relationship—which was explored in Chapter 4. Here, in the world of hypertext, the differences in perspective are played out. The Internet has re-articulated the role and meaning of authorship in a number of complex ways. In that process, traditional notions of textuality are confronted in the hypertext environment of the World Wide Web.[12] Students' perceptions of plagiarism are not the same as teachers, despite explicit teaching about plagiarism in this first-year undergraduate course. Students not only use Internet information in academic assignment work, but many cut and paste directly from the Internet without citation. The students who adhere to the idea that the Internet is a free public space and therefore Internet information does not warrant citation pose the greatest challenge to notions of authorship held by staff.

Teachers who adhere to Romantic notions of authorship often support the view that plagiarism by students is intentional, and their role is one of detection with resultant punishment to follow. Other teachers consider globally linked hypertext and hypermedia not only provide new ways to explore textuality, they also shape new paradigms of teaching and learning. Consequently, they support the view that plagiarism is a joint responsibility between all parties in the educational arena. Their focus is more on education than punishment. These views will be explored more in the next chapter in which teachers' perspectives of plagiarism in academic writing are presented.

CHAPTER 6

Teachers' Perceptions of Plagiarism

> Plagiarism by students is a moral maze, because it raises important
> ethical and moral questions about good/bad or right/wrong behav-
> iour and about acceptable/unacceptable practices. Who decides it is
> wrong, on what basis and for what reasons? Who is responsible for
> deciding on behavioural norms in the context of plagiarism?
>
> (Chris Park, 2003, p.474)

In Chapter 1, the snapshots of six staff discussing their responses and
perceptions of plagiarism in the Board Room of South-Coast University,
Melbourne, Australia were presented. These mini-portraits were drawn
from detailed responses of 48 teachers involved in my research study from
2004–2005 at South-Coast University. These teachers were asked to
define and explain their understandings of plagiarism and also discuss how
they applied these understandings in their approaches to teaching and
learning. In other words, their conceptual frameworks and their pedagogical
approaches to the issue of plagiarism in their classrooms were sought.
These views were then mapped onto the plagiarism continuum model that
was drawn from the literature and previous studies (see Chapters 2–4).
The teachers who give voice to their ideas in this chapter are selected from
those 48 teachers in the study. They teach university undergraduate courses

in the faculties of Arts, Business and Economics, Health and Behavioral Sciences, Law, Science and Technology as well as the undergraduate English Language Bridging Program, operating through the language support arm of the university. Some of them also use anti-plagiarism software (specifically Turnitin) as one of their plagiarism detection strategies. The teachers, male and female, range in age from 27 years to 55 years and include those who are both very experienced teachers as well as those relatively new to the tertiary sphere of teaching.

As mentioned, some of the teachers are involved in teaching in the English Language Bridging Program at the university. This program is a pre-entry bridging course that provides a pathway from the university's Language Center to mainstream university study. The Language Center is charged with provision of language support to both undergraduate and postgraduate students wishing to enter university, but who do not meet the set English Language Proficiency requirements,[1] as set by individual faculties. These students undertake intensive English language instruction for a period of 10 to 15 weeks, depending on their initial entry score, and they are assessed in their English language preparation courses both on a video-taped oral presentation about a specific research interest in their proposed field of study, and a written literature review task of 3,000 words. The final assessment grading certifies that a student possesses sufficient English language proficiency skills to cope with mainstream academic study within the faculty, or not. The readiness of the bridging program students to enter mainstream study is assessed by teachers, like those in this chapter, in the specific faculties to which the students seek entry.

Teachers in this research study share a great deal of common frustration, anxiety and concern about plagiarism, not only in relation to their students' writing, but also with respect to institutional policy and processes. Their responses are framed, not surprisingly, within their understandings of plagiarism. Naturally, these understandings vary between individual members of teaching staff and also across discipline areas—as do their reactions and their action in pursuing instances of plagiarism. In discussing their understandings, reactions and processes with respect to students' acts of plagiarism in academic writing, a rich multi-textured picture emerges that provides a platform from which the plagiarism continuum can be more easily understood. It is interesting to compare the teachers' responses both to the official university stance on plagiarism as well as their perceptions of plagiarism compared to Pecorari's (2002) model, described in Chapter 3. The reason for this comparison is to identify shared ground in conceptualizing plagiarism among teachers and policy, as well as points of divergence in perception. Such a comparison helps both teachers and policy-makers understand the tension between the rhetoric and the reality of managing plagiarism in educational settings. Table 6.1 provides a summary of the 48 teachers' understandings of plagiarism in comparison to the six-element definitional model outlined in Chapter 3.

As can be seen from Table 6.1, although teachers use different words to describe plagiarism, most differences are minor. The labeled elements in the model tend to be broader than teachers' responses. For example, the first element of plagiarism is generically described as "object." Most of the teachers are more specific in their descriptions of the "object" of plagiarism and use the following: "words," "work," "ideas" and "assignments." Another minor difference appears to be around element three, the "source" of the plagiarism. Again, the language of the model is broad and the term "source" is used by Barry, Jon, Kris, Jac, Pipi, Kristian, Hesha, Ben, Lili and Naomi. These teachers conceptualize the "source" of plagiarism to be quite wide-ranging and include both places and people. For example, they list "sources" as the Internet, textbooks, lecturers' notes, other students and microfiche theses. Other teachers, Athena, Eli, Wai-Mei, Siobhan, George, Graham, Sarah and Bernhard, believe that the source of plagiarism is a *human agent*—"someone else" and "another person." This is similar to concepts that are often embodied in university plagiarism policy—which often refers to the source of plagiarism as "another person." The other 30 members of the teachers' group did not refer to element three—the source of plagiarism—at all. Any differences in teachers' concepts of the "source" of plagiarism and "any other person" appear to be minor, as people can often be considered to be the "source" of information as well as print or electronic sources. In the six-element definitional model, the person instigating plagiarism is described by element 4—the agent. Although the term "agency" was not used by any of the teachers, there was overwhelming support for the definitional model's notion that the agent of plagiarism would be a student or a number of students. Teachers used words such as "they," "them" and "students" to indicate who they thought would be perpetrating acts of plagiarism.

Although there are slight differences between teachers in defining the term "plagiarism," overall, their notions of plagiarism appeared to fit within the parameters of Pecorari's (2002) six element model. The major difference in understanding between teachers and many university policies is centered around element six—whether plagiarism is intentional or unintentional. It appears to be of great importance to teachers to ascertain whether plagiarism has been an intentional action by the student, or not.

Intentional Plagiarism

Many teachers regard "intention" as a necessary element for a student to have committed an act of plagiarism. This means that the student has

Table 6.1 Comparison of teachers' responses to Pecorari's (2002) six-element definitional model. Teachers are asked to define or explain their notions of the term "plagiarism" and their responses are mapped onto Pecorari's model

Plagiarism as defined by the six element model and teachers

Element number	1	2	3	4	5	6
The six element model	object	taken	from a source	by an agent	without adequate acknowledgment	with/without intention
Athena/Eli/Wai-Mei/Siobhan	words	using; copied	someone else	they	without acknowledging	naïve; unintentional; sometimes intentional
Barry/Jon/Kris/Jac/Pipi/Kristian	words; ideas	mis-appropriated	from sources	you	without acceptable acknowledgment	intention is irrelevant
CheeLing/Martina	words; work; ideas	borrow; copy; take	x	students	without references	unintentional
Colleen/Miki/Jake/Will/Nikolas	ideas; words	copied; stolen	x	they	unacknowledged	intentional
Fiona/Kyle/Juanita/Andi/Laini	words; ideas	taken; claim; pass off	x	students	don't acknowledge your source	intentional
Georgiou/Graham/Sarah/Bernhard	text;	cheating;	another person	they	omission to credit source	intentional
Hesha/Ben/Lili/Naomi/Ann/Marg	the same material	using	another source	students	x	always intentional
Inger/Kat/Antonio/Jack/Jesse	x	x	x	they	x	usually intentional; can be unintentional
Jane/Elin/Emilio	words; texts	taken	x	students	don't cite	intentional
Kate/Vlad/Renuka/Rane/Thom	ideas	using	x	they	without proper acknowledgment	intentional and unintentional
Thivanka/Lars/Tim	what you write	to pass off; deceive	x	students	x	intentional

to have intended to deceive the teacher. This is also true of some policies, where intentional actions delineate whether plagiarism has occurred or not. These teachers support the idea that plagiarism must be an intentional act of appropriation of text and anything other than an intentional taking of the words or ideas of another is some lesser form of academic misdemeanor. Some teachers in this study variously describe "intentional" plagiarism as "deliberate," "willful," "calculated" and "premeditated" action, which is using the language of criminal law. They indicate that, in their opinions, the students know exactly what they are doing when plagiarizing the work of others and these actions are tantamount to a form of cheating. This group of teachers believe that plagiarism is a deliberate and calculated action, so it is always intentional.

These teachers also agree that where plagiarism is established as a deliberate action that is intended to fool the teacher or deceive an examiner, then it is more than plagiarism—it is cheating. These members of staff say that if cheating is able to be proven against students, then the severest penalties available to the institution should be applied, as the students clearly demonstrate there is no intention on their part to engage in any thinking themselves. Kat and Siobhan, for example, who are teaching in the same first-year unit in the Business faculty, set one assessment task of a 3,000-word research essay. Both teachers are involved in marking the work from across the three campuses at the university that offer this unit of study. They detected three essays that were exactly the same. Investigation revealed that three students emailed the same essay response to each other (on different campuses and in different time zones) and, as Kat said, "Foolishly, they expected that they'd get away with it." The students involved did not expect the same person to be marking their work, but because all the marking had been centrally allocated, the same teacher did happen to mark all three pieces of work. Both Kat and Siobhan argue that in these circumstances, there is clearly an intention by these three students to deceive the assessor into believing that the essays are the result of each student's individual research efforts. Siobhan had no doubt that this was plagiarism "in its worst colors" and she and Kat recommended to the Disciplinary Committee that severe penalties apply for this action— suspension from the university for 12 months. These two teachers categorized this act as more serious than plagiarism—it was cheating.

Some other teachers in this group had similar instances to relate, although not quite so clear. For example, Jack is a lecturer in environmental science in the Faculty of Science and Jesse is the tutor for that subject. Jesse also, however, tutors in the Faculty of Education in a science education unit. When Jack was on sick leave and Jesse marked his students' work, Jesse noticed that one student had submitted an essay that bore a remarkable resemblance to one of the essays he had just marked in the Faculty of Education's science education unit on environmental science. Jesse found that the student was enrolled in a double degree and had submitted nearly the same piece of assessment in both faculties—where the topics were similar, but not the same. Jesse recommended that the student fail both pieces of assessment with a grade of zero, as there was no attempt to answer the question on one piece and the other piece was plagiarized. Jack supported this recommendation and the penalty was applied.

Hesha, Ben, Lili, Naomi, Ann and Marg claim that plagiarism is always intentional. In the opinion of these teachers, students are "faking it" if they claim otherwise. This is based on their viewpoints that students are provided with ample information about plagiarism and the expectations of student writing to either know what to do or seek assistance if unsure. They do not accept the view that plagiarism can be unintentional. They argue that students should have been taught correct citation conventions in secondary schools or college preparation courses. If any student is unsure about referencing practices, then, these teachers argue, there is sufficient informa- tion in student handbooks, online tutorial self-help packages, library support systems and information given by lecturers and tutors in individual subject areas to assist. All orientation handouts, information sessions and enrolment materials also point to additional sources of help if students want more information or advice about plagiarism. The point these teachers are making is that there is sufficient information, advice and support for students in the current system and that students must access these support mechanisms if they are uncertain of referencing conventions. These teachers assert that it is too late for students to allege ignorance of conventions once the assessment has been submitted and graded.

These same teachers declare that this situation holds true for inter- national students studying abroad—that either they have already been introduced to citation conventions in their home countries or if they have not, they may take specific study support programs within the university. Support programs include citation and referencing workshops, on-campus and guided online tutorials in referencing conventions and regulations and processes on dealing with plagiarism and academic misconduct. All students can access these programs, should they so desire. Some support programs exist specifically for first-year undergraduate courses and specialist ESL staff are available for additional advice and support in the general international student support network. Therefore, these teachers consider that as additional support exists for students who are unsure of referencing or citation conventions, any deviation from correct citation procedures must be an intentional action by students. Hesha, a male academic from Sri Lanka, says he thinks plagiarism is a form of "intellectual laziness" where students are not adding their own perspectives to information they have learned. He explains that he expects a student to engage "actively" with the material or "other sources" so that the student's writing is not a copy of the original. Hesha says he wants student work to evidence the student's ability to comprehend or analyze the original text. Other teachers support Hesha's view, saying that plagiarism is intentional because students who copy the work of someone else are not attempting to "have a go" at an intellectual task or assessment piece themself, so they are plagiarizing deliberately.

CheeLing and Martina—two teachers who consider that plagiarism is often unintentional—also delineate strongly between plagiarism and cheating. They consider that cheating is limited to activities such as taking unauthorized materials into exam situations or concealing formulae in electronic calculators, where there is a clear intention to gain some sort of unfair advantage over other students in examination settings. Were these two people teaching at Monash University, their views would be supported by the Monash University policy, where cheating is distinguished from plagiarism in the examination situation (see Chapter 3). Indeed, a number of academic researchers such as Russell Hunt (2004) in Canada, Rebecca Moore Howard (2007) in the United States and Peter Levin (2006) in England agree that there is considerable confusion by conflating actions of cheating and plagiarism. Hunt (2004) argues that "our thoughtless equation of plagiarism with cheating and dishonesty puts all of us in a position that's not very useful" (p.5). He advocates setting up learning situations that are rich in opportunities for students to develop their own voices in texts and in which plagiarism has no room or motive to exist. Rebecca Moore Howard (2007) is even more adamant, saying that the tendency to "lump" together activities from "bungling citations and downloading term papers" under the one label of "plagiarism" thwarts pedagogical excellence. She says that if, as teachers, we regard plagiarism as "the reader's awareness of unacknowledged but significant intertexts" (p.9) we can engage in pedagogies "from which students derive a heightened sense of academic values and a heightened sense of their own possibilities as writers" (p.13).

Unintentional Plagiarism

Teachers interviewed who fell into this group consider that plagiarism can be either intentional or unintentional, but it is up to the individual teacher or teaching team to decide the intention of the student. Once intention has been decided, the teaching approach is determined, but for that process to occur, the student must be involved in the discussion. This stance is different from many of the teachers who consider that plagiarism is always an intentional action. This is because for those who consider plagiarism is always an intentional act, the appearance of plagiarism in a student's work is sufficient to prove intention.

Athena, Inger and Kate believe that plagiarism can be an unintentional action. Athena describes plagiarism as being both a "naïve" approach to writing by ESL students as well as a convenience, if not checked. She explains:

> I think there are some naïve students who don't know what they're doing and some who are so desperate that they do whatever they can to try and survive, like a sort of drowning approach to their academic work. Other students, and I've only started to believe this recently, try and do as little work as possible, and if they don't really have to do these difficult things [referencing and acknowledging authorship] then they will quite happily not do them at all.

Athena believes that students who are unaware of correct citation conventions, or who are "desperate" and do not attribute authorship in their academic work, are not committing acts of plagiarism. Her sentiments are shared by Inger and Kate. Inger explains her point of view with reference to her years of teaching senior high-school students in Borneo, Indonesia. She described the incredulity of her students to her explanation that the ideas of others require acknowledgment in academic writing. She said, "I was flabbergasted that they simply had no idea that acknowledgement was not only necessary but essential. They seemed to think citation was a novel idea and certainly an optional one." Kate, too, thinks that students can plagiarize material without intending to do so. She points out:

> Some students read a lot and carelessly over time and put an assignment together because they haven't been attentive to the need to acknowledge, they have used the words from an article or paragraph, perhaps not deliberately in a way that is cheating but rewritten and ended up at the end with sections more or less drawn from other people's work without acknowledgement. If the student has worked hard and inadvertently not included citation then that's more acceptable than outright cheating. I also teach postgrads and later degree students and they don't seem to know how to acknowledge sources properly and which sources need to be acknowledged or even understand which are primary and which are secondary sources. They plagiarize without knowing what they're doing and their note-taking skills are so poor, as I said, that they have no idea where the material came from.

Two teachers who assess work for the English Language Bridging Program believe that students make mistakes as to referencing and citation and should not be penalized for those errors. They also claim that many students have not been taught to reference in high school and that as first-year university students or students in English Language Bridging Programs, they should not be penalized for lack of explicit instruction on appropriate academic conventions. CheeLing and Martina claim that it is the teachers' role to ensure that academic expectations of referencing and citation are explicitly made clear to students—in whatever educational setting. They both relate this to their own experiences as second language speakers of English, who completed Masters courses in their home countries (China and Poland respectively) and completed doctoral studies in Australian and New Zealand universities. They state that academic expectations vary enormously between academic institutions and that where there are specific academic conventions to be followed, these should not only be spelled out in policy and unit guide information, but that there should be explicit teaching of these in class. CheeLing explains that in her own circumstances, although she graduated with a Masters degree in Law from a university in Beijing, when she embarked upon a Doctor of Philosophy in Melbourne, she could not understand why she was required to cite material in-text. She says:

> At the time, I didn't see why my supervisor wanted me to ruin the flow of the sentence and the overall argument by putting in a whole heap of references. To me, it looked clumsy and ugly, as if I, as the writer, had no finesse to be able to weave the arguments of others into my work. To me, that was the skill—to be able to show my supervisor how much reading I had done by seamlessly weaving the words into my own sequencing of writing.

CheeLing advocates that not only did it take a great deal of time for her to realize that she was required to write using in-text citations and acknowledge the authors she used each time she quoted them, but that there was unnecessary frustration both for herself and her supervisor in the process. She says that she remembers coming away from some of her supervisory meetings very upset because she thought her female supervisor was angry with her for "not getting referencing right," but did not really understand why she needed to repeat the same bibliographical information in the body of the text. She remembers feeling embarrassed and felt she could not ask for further explanation from her supervisor because she thought she would appear stupid. CheeLing says her supervisor knew she had completed volumes of reading and could articulate key points and divergences of perspective between authors, so she was confused as to what more she needed to "reference." She says she did not really grasp the importance of referencing conventions in the Australian system and found it very difficult to adapt to the form of academic writing required in Australia. She adds that even when she did feel she managed to develop ways of maneuvering within formal academic writing constraints, she did not feel much at home writing either in English or in Mandarin. She laughs and describes her writing as a "hybrid-text" a sort of "in-between both kinds of writing" practices. Her frustration is similar to Suresh Canagarajah's (2001) experiences of "shuttling between discourse communities" in moving between writing in Tamil and English and his clear description of the "painful personal experience" (p.37) this can accord for individuals.

CheeLing says that for students learning a specific writing genre, plagiarism is acceptable and even expected in China. She says that students copy words and ideas without attribution as part of the learning process, but the important distinction between plagiarism and using the words of others as part of learning is whether the student tries to claim public credit for the content or not. A section of the interview transcript illustrates this. CheeLing says:

> I have to think if I translate that [plagiarism] into Chinese, that means you copy someone's work and put your name down. For instance, if I found someone was writing an article and I just more or less copy everything and change a few minor things and try to publish then that's plagiarism—try to claim other people's work in my name . . . if you just use for education purpose, for myself, I probably would not worry too much. I was learning and I would try to learn those words or ideas or knowledge—I wasn't trying to do anything to make myself more famous. So why? There's no action there. But what was my intention? Just try to learn things. I wouldn't worry if I use someone's writing in my own writing. I probably wouldn't worry because my point is that I read this and I wouldn't worry about someone saying that you haven't quoted that. So proper referencing wasn't a concern if I didn't claim it publicly.

CheeLing distinguishes acts of direct copying attributed to plagiarism from learning a new writing style by imitation. She highlights the importance of intention in an act of plagiarism by asking the rhetorical question, "But what was my intention?." She immediately answers her own question with the words, "I just try to learn things," as the rationale for direct copying of text. For CheeLing, there must be deliberate intention by the individual to claim another's work in some public arena before plagiarism can be alleged.

Martina describes feelings of being an outsider to the closely guarded secrets of academic writing success. She says her experiences of her postgraduate course in Poland, where the oral defense was considered a key feature of demonstrating academic competence led to serious confusion when studying for a doctorate in New Zealand. She says the passion and subjugation of various authors' works into a coherent argument was what she expected in her doctoral candidature—with heavy emphasis on the oral defense. Instead, she found that she was expected to demonstrate an ability to directly state prior research and justify how her research added to the broader understandings of the field. Martina says that anxiety to observe referencing conventions meant "I wrote my spirit out of my work and there exists only a ghost of myself on the pages of my dissertation." She feels that her doctoral dissertation is not really a true acclamation of herself and has a lingering sense of disappointment in her written thesis.

Both CheeLing and Martina assert it is the individual class teacher's responsibility to go over referencing and citation expectations explicitly with students—either in an introductory lecture or in tutorials at the start of each teaching semester. Both claim this is necessary, as merely directing students to written materials or online packages is not immediate or explicit enough and does not provide the necessary impetus for some students to take plagiarism seriously. These comments echo similar sentiments from the research (see Ashworth *et al.*, 2003; Counsell, 2004; Handa and Power, 2004; Noi-Smith, 2001). CheeLing and Martina state that copying and appropriating text is part of the usual learning process for many second-language students, and should not be seen as plagiarism. They claim it is a process of imitation that is not underpinned with intention to deceive— rather it is an intention to sound more like first language speakers. Unintentional plagiarism, as described by these teachers, mirrors the ideas in much of the research literature and also some university plagiarism policies. For example, at Monash University the university-wide policy denotes intentional plagiarism as cheating (under the University Disciplinary policy—Statute 4.1, Part III), which is handled by Faculty Academic Misconduct Panels whereas unintentional plagiarism is handled within faculties by the Associate Dean of Teaching under the plagiarism policy. The mechanisms across the university set up at the policy level are required to treat one end of the plagiarism continuum (cheating) as an offense that is immediately punishable, and the other end of the continuum (unintentional plagiarism) as a "lesser form of academic misconduct" where the faculty is required to determine how and why the student plagiarized and whether there will be a penalty other than a recorded warning. Some of the literature also reflects this dichotomy where plagiarism is considered to be "less an intentional violation of a cultural code, than a survival measure in the face of perceived difficulties or deficiencies" (Hafernik *et al.*, 2003, p.45). For many ESL and EFL classroom teachers, plagiarism is seen as a desperate action by students to submit work without penalty. For some, although not all students, there is also recognition that there are particular academic barriers facing ESL and EFL students that run much deeper than a failure to cite references. It is useful to examine how these teachers approach issues of plagiarism and learning in their classrooms.

Classroom Teaching Approaches

This section examines the approaches adopted by teachers to instances of plagiarism in the classroom. This means that often the ways in which teachers handle instances of plagiarism can give us a great deal of information. This chapter links comments made by teachers in this study with views expressed in the literature and perspectives of teachers in prior studies. Here we examine how teachers deal with plagiarism in light of their theoretical perspectives and map their teaching approaches onto the plagiarism continuum. This is where a more complete understanding of the plagiarism continuum is garnered—from the teachers' points of view. When discussing teaching approaches to plagiarism, it is also possible to compare the reactions by universities to issues of plagiarism. These institutional responses can be grouped into three broad categories: technological responses; procedural responses; and holistic responses, and these institutional responses will be discussed in Chapter 8.

Transmissive Approaches to Teaching

Some teachers indicated at interview that they firmly believe plagiarism is intentional and is a deliberate action. When describing their approaches to teaching, these teachers display an instructional orientation to learning that has knowledge "acquisition" as its foundation. In observing their lectures, I noted that lectures are often highly content-driven, with numerous PowerPoint slides or overhead transparencies that are full of information. In engaging in an information-delivery style of teaching, these academics seem to expect that students will copy down their lecture notes and use the set readings or textbooks to acquire further information. Some teachers permit questions from students at certain points during the lecture— usually only once or twice—and others talked for the entire period, where no questions were taken from the floor at all. I observed most students busily copying down the information on the PowerPoint slides and many struggling to keep up with the pace of delivery. There were few students who sat and listened to the lecture and only jotted down notes occasionally. The majority of the student body worked at a frantic pace to copy down every possible word.

These teachers also indicated that the lecture was the place in which the basic content was "covered" and that the real space for student interaction was in tutorials. There were often 25 to 30 students in each tutorial and these were frequently "problem-based" sessions, where students used their collected notes in order to apply the principles or formula to other cases. Again, teachers described the tutorial sessions as a means of fine-tuning information gathered in lectures and from reading textbooks in order to reproduce principles at a later date. Observations of tutorials indicated that in only a few cases was there discussion by students. Most tutorials (usually one hour blocks of time) were teacher-driven and the main forms of interaction were question–answer responses. A typical tutorial consisted of very specific questions that the tutor posed to students which often required merely fact recall or location of certain information from lecture notes or in the textbook in order for students to respond. Rarely was an extended response required and, if so, the response from the student was usually one of describing a particular principle or application rather than analyzing or questioning why a principle would or should apply at all. In some cases, questions were initiated by the students, but not often. ESL students seldom initiated questions or volunteered answers in tutorials—most of the time they remained as silent as they had done in the lecture. This is not to suggest that dynamic and active questioning is not taking place by students sitting silently—they may well be engaged in self-dialogue, or reflection at a later time and place—however, they did not take part in public discussion. Most teachers favoring transmissive forms of teaching indicate that they require students to demonstrate their learning in competency-based assessment practices, such as examinations or lengthy problem-based assignment questions.

When asked about detecting plagiarism in their students' writing, a common response of these teachers is that students should know better. One teacher, Lili, said, "The policy and process is plastered everywhere around them, so they can't say they don't know about it." Almost all teachers adopting a transmissive form of teaching had undertaken some kind of plagiarism awareness activity either within lectures or in tutorials. These activities include: highlighting the links to the university plagiarism policy in subject materials, explaining in writing or verbally that plagiarism was unacceptable and that correct referencing strategies needed to be adopted. A couple of lecturers also covered samples of plagiarized and non-plagiarized responses to questions in their introductory lecture. However, once this initial information session about plagiarism had taken place, the issue was not explicitly canvassed again by teachers in formal classroom situations. Most of these teachers regard the responsibility for understanding the nature of plagiarism and adopting strategies to avoid it lie with the student. One of the key issues for these teachers in detecting plagiarism is the fact that students memorize and regurgitate slabs of text without references or citation. Particularly distressing for these teachers is where students reproduce the teacher's lecture notes or class notes verbatim in assignments or on exam papers. Kate said, "I can't believe they have the cheek to copy down my lecture notes and then cut and paste them into assignments to hand back to me! Where's their intellectual input?" Teachers clearly linked memorization and rote-learning of information as a pathway to plagiarism.

Memorization is perceived to be a degree of resistance to intellectual engagement with ideas and an overall reluctance to question or analyze content deeply. The teachers who refer to memorized text in this way allude to the "rote learning" model of memorization, which they claim requires little thinking on the student's part, but highly skilled techniques of memory retention and recall. Some teachers do not distinguish between memorization for *deeper learning* purposes—where meaning is obtained through the processes of understanding and re-conceptualization of information in another way—and *surface learning*, where individual knowledge is quickly increased through memorization and reproduction of information (Watkins and Biggs, 2001). Teachers made comments such as:

> Students appear to think that as long as they memorize everything they can, they can reproduce it in an exam. What they fail to realize is that often the exact materials don't answer the question they're being asked . . . so their answer is largely irrelevant. It just doesn't pay to memorize because it's not really learning anything. It might help in some science areas, but in management and law subjects, it's not good enough. You need to apply the knowledge, not just to memorize it.
>
> (Kate)

One teacher, Jane, commented: "Some students predominately have been taught to rote-learn and take whatever the authority had said and repeat it as if that would be alright, as if it's enough." She explained that "so much more is required of students in our system." By "our system" she means a "Western" university system founded on principles of direct questioning and interrogation of information. She later clarified this and said:

> Our system prides itself on being intellectually rigorous and we want our students to question and argue and generally debate ideas. There

is no room just to sit back and absorb information like a sponge. Students have to actively interrogate sources and in the process, their own ideas will be developed and emerge. Mere memorization has no place in this kind of intellectual environment.

Most teachers agreed with Jane that memorization is not "appropriate" for the level of analysis needed in tertiary subjects. In addition, teachers said rote-learning is an "unthinking" skill or a "second class form of learning" (Angelil-Carter 2000, p.44), therefore to be discouraged as an academic learning strategy. However, these teachers did want students to "acquire the facts" (Vlad) and be able to apply those facts to various scenarios presented on exams and in assignment problems.

It is pertinent here to draw a parallel between teaching approaches and teacher expectations of student learning. If in most sessions, teachers talk and students write—there appears to be little opportunity for students to engage in dynamic questioning and interrogation of ideas. This teaching approach encourages students not only to copy down teacher-formulated ideas and words but often rewards the memorization and regurgitation of such principles in tutorial and assessment work. Transmissive teaching approaches often belie the ideals that teachers have in terms of students' intellectual engagement with ideas. Although teachers want active oral participation by students in their classes, as discussion and understandings of principles are crucial for future application, transmissive approaches to teaching do not create the space for such learning to occur. In other words, oral interaction as part of teaching and learning pedagogy was not evident in practice. The very pedagogical approach adopted hampered the kinds of learning outcomes teachers professed they wanted their students to achieve. This point is made in order to increase the awareness of teachers that their pedagogical practices may not encourage the key skills they deem valuable and require their students to demonstrate as part of their learning. In fact, if teachers model an information-focused pedagogy, where vast tracts of text, factual data or formulae are demonstrated to be the epitome of learning, then it is impossible to see how students would engage critically with such matter. If teachers really want students to engage with ideas, then pedagogical models centered around shared experiences, dialogue and critique are essential.

CheeLing offers a contrasting perspective to a transmissive construction of memorization, copying and rote-learning as a route to plagiarism. She views memorization as an essential skill in order to have sufficient breadth of content to be able to interact with those already situated in the discourse community—often teachers. According to CheeLing, memorization of content enables a student, particularly a second-language speaker to "have enough to say about some topic" when participating in class or trying to gain access to the discourse community. CheeLing claims memorization and rote learning are part of her educational heritage and have been useful strategies to assist in her learning process and pathways to date. She explains how memorization, copying and rote learning are used as part of the learning process, in an anecdote about her early secondary years of schooling in Beijing, China:

> I remember memorizing quotes from Mao, and I think they give people an indication that you know that and other people's sayings are insignificant so you don't bother to say where they come from. They have sayings that are minor and unless someone is so important, you don't quote them, so why you want to individualize that this is say by Professor Wong or Professor Lee? So why you want to emphasize the individual's ideas? Certainly in China, from early days—from learning how to write—there is a little handbook of style of writing Chinese characters—and if you want to write well, then you need to copy from this. So as soon as you see this writing you know which style. You learn to copy other people's writing and when someone comments on your writing, great writing, they say, "Whose style?" and people in their young age, they still write calligraphy and you never really come out and write your own, you copy other people's style. How possible to have your "own" style, how can you do that? It's the same theory for other writing and you really need to start from learning to copy other people's work and then wean to your own, but without copying other people's work you don't have the foundation.

For CheeLing, rote learning, memorization and copying are all necessary learning strategies and are essential in order to participate in academic life. She sees these skills as a "foundation" or cornerstone of learning from which spring individual ideas or, as she says, "your own style." Her views are consistent with many ESL researchers, such as those of Xu Fang and Mark Warschauer (2004) who outline a progressive means by which individuals operating outside their mother tongue come to make their own meanings. They describe a five-year research study on project-based instruction using technology at Jinhuang University in eastern China. They comment that "in China deep-rooted cultural norms and beliefs mandate the teacher's control of the classroom and deserve utmost student respect" (pp.315–316). They state:

> Language learning involves a quantitative increase (*liangbian*) in knowledge. Traditional wisdom suggests that memorizing the target

language's vocabulary and studying its grammar will automatically foster fluency, flexibility, and appropriate use of language, the final qualitative change (*zhibian*). This view holds that creativity will flow naturally, in time, from discipline and proficiency in rote memorization, so the teacher does not need to encourage it.

(p.303, italics in the original)

Fang and Warschauer (2004) explain that although rapid changes in China's curriculum reform with respect to English language teaching for international communication purposes are taking place, they conclude that project-based courses "ran counter to professional, cultural and institutional values and reward systems in the university and in China" (p.317). The authors, using Larry Cuban's (1993) model of "situationally constrained choice," write:

Deeply-held cultural beliefs about the nature of knowledge, how teaching should occur, and how students should learn—all reinforced by educational systems that reward traditional forms of instruction—tend to mitigate against radical reform in teaching and learning.

(Fang and Warschauer, 2004, p.315)

Fang and Warschauer suggest that the "clashes" between culturally valued approaches to teaching and "more traditional norms" of learning provide one explanation for the lack of enthusiasm at faculty level to implement the changes trialed during the study (2004, p.1).

It is important to recognize that where approaches to teaching have been in place in faculties and departments for considerable time, perhaps with little change, there are bound to be the sorts of "clashes" that Fang and Warschauer (2004) spoke about. It is equally important that teachers and faculties engage in reflective discussion about the kinds of teaching approaches teachers are using and whether such approaches are commensurate with expectations of learning. Different approaches to teaching and learning should be openly discussed, as they are of consequence. It is crucial that particular teaching approaches, as well as individual philosophical justifications for using such approaches, are debated. Open acknowledgment of differences in teaching approaches can stimulate greater understanding of the consequences for learning. Suzie Scollon (1999) argues that discussing differences such as the Socratic method of learning, which "emphasize the art of rhetoric as a search for knowledge," (p.15) in comparison to the "Confucian educational philosophy, [where] rhetorical reasoning is secondary and the primary goal is to gain wisdom and act in accordance with the moral code that the teacher communicates to the student," (p.10) promote understanding that different approaches to learning have different aims:

> The main difference between Socrates and Confucius is that the former was interested in truth and universal definitions, his method centering on following out the consequences of a hypothesis, whereas the latter was more concerned about action. One learns in order to gain wisdom so that one may act appropriately. Instead of emphasizing truth, Confucius emphasized the consequences of using the right names in the doctrine of rectification or *zheng ming*.
>
> (p.17, italics in the original)

Scollon (1999) therefore suggests that whereas the Socratic approach to learning, which is highly favored by many teachers in this study, values students' search for truth in knowledge through inquiry, Confucian approaches to learning value knowledge in order to gain wisdom to act in a virtuous manner. As she notes, "the emphasis on reasoning was not a high priority of Confucius" (1999, p.17). Her comments echo literary theorist Kenneth Gergen's (1991) views that the Romantic or Enlightenment notions of the early eighteenth century are based on the divine right of the individual to use reason and observation to determine truth and, as such, paved the way for "the grand narrative of Enlightenment" and cultural imperialism of the West (1991, p.30). The reason for highlighting two such distinct approaches to teaching is that they clearly demonstrate different visions of learning as outcomes. It often seems that teachers remain blithely unaware that the very way in which they approach teaching and assessment in the classroom will have a direct and palpable effect on the way in which students choose to tackle their learning. Transmissive teaching approaches with a strong reliance on content-driven courses in which factual information recall and application is rewarded in assessment tasks can shape reproductive or instrumental learning rather than analytical approaches to learning by students. As a result, students may choose to use techniques to produce content-rich but thinking-poor work, including plagiarizing the words of others to boost the credibility and amount of information in assessment pieces.

Most teachers in this study were confident that they knew the reasons why students adopted reproduction or rote-learning strategies in learning. They said that many students approach learning with an expectation that they can, and indeed should, merely reproduce information for assignments and exams. Teachers referred to the practice of student reproduction of information as "copying" text. They commented that students "copied wholesale" (Jac) or "copied slabs of text" (Ann) from textbooks, course materials, lecture notes given by lecturers, PowerPoint slides used in lectures and prominent journal articles. Teachers were convinced that students are familiar with this approach, as it has served them well in the past. The teachers, however, argue that direct copying of text indicates a lack of intellectual engagement with texts or with learning processes. Many are disappointed and some are annoyed that students can consider copying text directly from sources without acknowledgment to be a legitimate form of learning. Renuka said:

> My concept of why students plagiarize is based on a difference in culture. These cultures are not intellectually dynamic in the sense that they value copying and respect of teachers. And that Western ideas of learning from respected sources and then questioning and querying and challenging what those sources say is not something that is done or valued. So what is valued is emulating the learned people of your culture and it's in fact rude or disrespectful to question or challenge the teacher and so what you do is reproduce what you are given as faithfully as possible. Which is very much not what we're on about. We want students to bring a critical questioning to class.
>
> (emphasis in the original transcript)

Renuka's distinction between "not intellectually dynamic" and "Western ideas", which she says embody intellectual rigor, supports Edward Said's (1978) claim that many academics view the "Other" as culturally inferior approaches to teaching and learning. The assumption here is that approaches to learning where criticizing, analyzing and questioning—as promoted in Ballard and Clanchy's "analytical learning styles" (1988, p.26)—are prized in our institutions but not valued by students using other approaches to learning. Colleen, a curriculum materials writer, echoes Renuka's sentiments. Colleen has over 30 years of teaching experience in many different countries and says that using the work of learned "sages" is prominent in ESL undergraduates' writing:

> Within many Asian traditions, let's say Chinese, there is a notion of the sage. Along with that, there is a respect for the wisdom of the sage, but an inherent kind of conservatism which leads to a conservatism in writing. An effect of an oppressive, totalitarian tradition in imperial literature at the ordinary individual level is

that people think ideas of difference are dangerous and also that individuals do not have the expectation of being unique.

Colleen believes that one reason for students engaging in copying or exact reproduction of texts is the influence of factors such as prior schooling and cultural expectations of what is valued as excellence in writing. Teachers such as Colleen, Jac, Ann, Jane and Renuka speculate that copying texts is steeped in a tradition of writing that ensures accurate reproduction from previous scholars. Additionally, they claim that students do not expect to challenge authority or articulate a sense of individuality or a difference of opinion. Colleen describes the reproduction of text as a valued form of "conservatism" and believes that "individual difference" is frowned upon, or regarded as "dangerous," in particular educational contexts. The view that students adhere to textual reproduction out of a sense of respect for the accumulated knowledge or wisdom of their forebears has, rightly or wrongly, been described as a "Confucian" heritage approach to learning (Noi-Smith, 2001; Scollon and Scollon, 1991; Watkins and Biggs, 2001). There is much debate about this learning approach. CheeLing, who was educated to Masters level in Beijing, describes her experience of the approach to learning in China in the 1980s:

> In China it was very, very different. I remember when I was doing paper and presentations I gave for my lectures to classmates . . . I certainly was not afraid of . . . you know . . . just borrow the idea and put it in my writing because the other writings I look at they would not have references. And lots of the reference I look at unless they quote from very famous person like Mao's writing from a particular volume, they won't have reference—in whole article I won't find more than say about five footnotes or endnotes. So it wasn't really seen as you need to give reference . . . I remember quotes from Mao and I think they give people an indication that you go there and other people's sayings are insignificant so you don't bother to say where they come from. They have sayings that are minor and unless someone is so important, you don't quote them, so why you want to individualize that this is say by Professor Wong or Professor Lee? So why you want to emphasize the individual's ideas? . . . International students find themselves a bit more difficult to adjust because their own cultural backgrounds and their training from high school is to copy everyone's work.

CheeLing's personal insight into the way in which writing and, indeed, learning is valued and approached supports the comments made earlier by Colleen and the other teachers in this study. CheeLing also explains that she thinks that approaches are changing in China, but it will take time for wholesale acceptance of "other ways to do things," as Fang and Warschauer's (2004) work demonstrated. She describes the cultural expectation that "famous people," such as Mao, will be quoted in academic work and that there is an assumption that the reader will know the source of famous quotations, so that there is no need to reference such quotations.

There is an expectation that such an overt form of acknowledgment draws attention to the individual writer and that is not necessarily considered to be desirable. Her question, "So why you want to emphasize the individual's ideas?," supports the views that some teachers in this study share—that there is a reluctance to identify individuals as sources of information. The teachers note that in this particular approach to learning, there is a tendency for some ESL and EFL students to present information from the collective whole and assume that the reader is familiar with the source. CheeLing notes that inventive or analytical work may be interpreted as irreverent or cheeky, rather than innovative, particularly if the writer is of a "young age." When CheeLing says, "How is it possible to have your own style?," she indicates that there is a perception that older people who have learned certain "styles" or approaches to learning of previous generations are capable of creating new approaches.[2] Her expectation that wisdom is the result of age is implicit in this statement. Although agreeing with the sentiments of other teachers, that many students reiterate the writings of former masters out of a system of respect for traditional knowledge, Inger objects to the practice being attributed to a particular approach to learning. She says:

> Well what I see is that label that people often use is "Confucian" though and I think that's a bit clichéd for me. What I do see is what many students do, is revere or have been taught to revere what they read and they think it's quite OK to reiterate what somebody has written. It shows that you have engaged yourself in that person's thought and you have actually assimilated to it and you have replicated it because it is such important knowledge, according to some people. I don't think it's necessarily linked to one particular learning or teaching approach—I remember doing the same in high school chemistry years ago!

Some of the teachers in this study are concerned that certain teaching approaches may be encouraging students to reproduce and copy work as a learning approach. This, from their viewpoint, is a sure road to plagiarism.

Although some of the teachers prefer to see the tendency to reproduce or copy work as a particular cultural norm, others see it as inherent in poor practice. One teacher (Ann) said that she refused to put her lecture notes on the university intra-net site because:

> I don't want my own words coming bouncing back to me in student work. I expect they will listen in lectures and go away and do their own reading to make their own meanings. I don't expect to see the meanings I have made from my own experiences and understandings come back to me in their work—that's just not on!

Ann said that students needed to engage with materials and make their own meanings in order to foster understanding. She was adamant that she would not engage in any teaching strategy that encouraged or enabled what she termed "non-thinking engagement" with words. Another teacher (Marg) agreed and said she would only place dot points of material covered in class for the same reason. She said, "I get so distressed that students quote my words back to me. I have to find a way to stop that practice—it's not good learning for them, if learning at all and it stems from the way in which I do my teaching." These teachers clearly view copying text as a reproductive approach to learning and are taking steps to try to enable students to get the gist of lecture notes, without providing slabs of texts that are able to be copied.

The comments of these teachers as well as observations of their practices allow some of the following characteristics of a transmissive approach of teaching to be drawn out. This list is not intended to be exhaustive but to indicate that these are the major characteristics to emerge from this study. There are clear links between content-driven approaches to teaching and types of assessment tasks set that reflect expectations of information-based responses by students. The connections as interpreted by students are that content, rather than understanding, is what is required. They then use learning approaches that have supported information-laden responses successfully in the past.

Characteristics of a Transmissive Approach to Teaching and Plagiarism

- assumes all students have similar understandings of plagiarism—particularly when given the policy or told where to locate it;
- assumes the responsibility to understand the university plagiarism policy rests with students;

- assumes teacher responsibilities are complete once plagiarism has been referred to as an issue of academic misconduct and formal references to the policy given in lectures or unit guides;
- assumes plagiarism is intentional—penalties automatically follow.

Transformative Approaches to Teaching

A number of teachers in this study and in the previous studies discussed earlier consider that multiple lenses of inquiry can be bought to bear on the issue of plagiarism. Teachers adopting transformative approaches to teaching build their pedagogical practice on the notion that students' construction of meaning is when learning takes place. That is to say, the teachers provide classroom experiences that allow students to engage with information, events, laboratory experiments or other stimuli in order to make their own understandings of these experiences and transform mere information into knowledge. Many of these teachers do not tend to run formal lectures, as such, but rather, they run large-scale seminars. These seminars can be conducted with anywhere between a handful of students and up to 300 students in a lecture hall. The teachers engage in a dialogue with students and often the seminar provides some space for students to engage in reflections or share experiences with their peers, as well as the whole group. These reflections are often in response to a particular question posed by the teacher. Students engaging in this kind of forum do not respond in the same ways as they would in the content-driven traditional lecture. In this forum, students were not scrabbling for pens to copy down the words on the PowerPoint slides or to take copious notes, trying desperately to write down every word the lecturer uttered. Here, students noted down some key points—and certainly the questions that were posed for reflection—but a great deal of time was spent in listening, not only to the lecturer but also to each other and various shared views on the topic. Most of the lecturers referred to multiple readings as well as the set texts and the list of additional readings was available for students to go and read in their own time.

When I asked about this technique, Kat, who teaches economics, said that she believes it is better for students to read the articles themselves and draw their own meanings from them, related to their own experiences and reflections. She maintains that her understandings of the article will necessarily be different from her students and she does not want to give them the idea that there is only one approach or only one way to reach their solutions. She encourages them to discuss their varied interpretations of articles in tutorial classes and to highlight similarities and differences between their interpretations and explore them. She says that this makes for a much richer engagement with various perspectives offered in the literature. Kat argues that it is important for students to understand that perspectives in the literature will also differ and that they need to come to grips with the fact that there are multiple ways of looking at the same issue or problem. She stresses that her expectations of students in their assessable work is to explore a multitude of voices in the literature and justify their particular stance. A similar approach was taken in tutorials—where student numbers ranged between 20 and 47 in different faculties. Tutorials, or symposia as some teachers prefer to call them, are arranged so that students are responsible for leading certain reading discussions and the teacher is one of the participants. Pairs of students work together to flesh out and respond to issues in the readings and tie various different readings into an overall topic framework, set up by the teacher at the start of semester.

It was interesting to observe that in the English Language Bridging Program teachers often gave students "practice" at taking certain roles in a "mini symposium" role play. Students were given small cards with their role printed on them, such as "Chair," "asking a question of clarification," "summarizing a discussion section," "interrupting" or "presenting a different opinion." Students would then focus on a particular academic text—usually a journal article and assume their roles for the discussion. Roles were then swapped and students were asked to take a turn at each role. When I asked participating teachers about this activity, they replied that it was their experience that second language students in English-speaking tutorials felt silenced. They were unsure how to act and uncomfortable with the notion of interrupting or putting across a different point of view. The teachers believe that students certainly did not feel comfortable in the position of Chair, as this had not been their prior learning experience and they were unsure what the role entailed. The "mini symposium" was designed to allow students to experience different ways of interacting in a tutorial and also to gain some experience, in a supportive environment, in undertaking roles that were difficult for them. Students seemed to respond well, although my observations showed that many of them were reluctant to interrupt or disagree with a point of view, even after many opportunities to practice in the program. However, it is pertinent to note that the Bridging Program was taking positive steps to give students experiences so that they would be able to more fully participate in student-led kinds of tutorials or symposia.

As part of their transformative pedagogical approach, teachers assume a joint responsibility with students and the institution for enabling students to understand plagiarism. This is borne out in their classroom approaches, where they do not assume that plagiarism is necessarily intentional and insist that the student be involved in the determination of the outcome of alleged instances of plagiarism. Often teachers talk about expectations of most tertiary academics when it comes to written work, and they engage in guided practice with samples from the field. A key component of their approach is to show, often during the seminars, that a myriad of perspectives exist in the literature and that problems and issues can be approached in a number of different ways. Each method of approach may result in a different conclusion, but the important point for students to grasp is that their conclusions are valid, provided that those conclusions are balanced and consider the different points of view of "experts" in the field. Many of these teachers adopt Bahktin's (1986) stance and contest the role of the author as the giver of meaning. They believe that the teacher constructs notions of plagiarism when reading a student's text as well as intention, so the idea of students always intending to plagiarize is fraught with difficulty for them. They tend to assume that meaning is made by the reader rather than the writer of text. Before making any decision about plagiarism in a piece of written work, these teachers discuss the work with the student—whether that is provided for in the policy procedures or not.

Some of these teachers (although not all) consider that copying the words of others is a means for students to learn how to use new words appropriately in a specific discipline. In this study, for example, Eli, Wai-Mei, Siobhan and Antonio agree that students appropriate or take the words of others to try them out within a discourse framework within a specific field. In this way, it is an "apprenticeship" model of academic writing, where copying is not seen as plagiarism but as a means to learning specific writing genres. For example, Eli said, "Of course they copy words in law! How else are they going to learn where to put the phrase 'doctrine of precedent' in relation to judicial decision-making processes? It's not the sort of phrase that you'd use in the supermarket!" Siobhan says she adopts a teaching approach that promotes a culturally diverse view of writing, by suggesting that through reiterating past writers' views, students are not merely reproducing text but rather developing understandings of the text and including ideas with which the writer agrees. She says:

> Often students use words from previous writers. They do so, in my opinion, not so much to just copy out words, but to try and demonstrate what the "authorities" have to say on the matter. It's clumsy and often rudimentary at the analysis level, but I think they do this to show that they agree (as a writer) with what the experts in the field say. In assignments where students tend to have a coherent set of such "experts" copied into their work—I think it demonstrates that they actually understand what's going on and they are choosing the experts that best fit in with their understandings. Where students have a complete mish-mash of all

different opinions and nothing holds together—then they have demonstrated to me that they have not yet reached an understanding of the topic or material.

Siobhan's comments echo the ideas of Suresh Canagarajah (2001) where he says that he learnt about "appropriating the dominant conventions or developing multivocal texts, not from postmodernist academic scholarship, but from the painful personal experiences of shuttling between discourse communities" (p.37). Ryoko Kubota (2001) also supports this view when she says that "reading articles on the topic of my research helped me discover patterns of arranging materials at the sentence as well as the larger discourse levels" and that this writing development is important when "using an appropriate form of discourse for the language one is writing in" (pp.104, 105). Similar arguments are to be found in Rebecca Moore Howard's (1995, 1999, 2000, 2002) work over many years and other teachers working with ESL and EFL students—such as Vijay Bhatia (2001) and Paul Matsuda (2003). These teachers and researchers suggest that a time of acculturation into a language and familiarity with ways in which discourse is used is essential before a student can even exist as a fringe-dweller in a specific discourse community. They claim that "patchwriting" (described in Chapter 4) is a process in the learning cycle of some students and, in itself, is not an act of plagiarism. These teachers justify their approach by arguing that students seek entry to specific discourse communities, such as law, as legitimate members. They must acquire and be able to use specific language of that particular discourse community to be seen as authentic members of that community. Such views resonate with the notions of James Gee (1990) in his use of the term Discourse (with a capital D) to mean "ways of being in the world." If we view CheeLing's situation in this light, although she is now an academic, she clearly remembers what it is like as an ESL student at postgraduate level to study in a foreign country. From her comments, we are able to appreciate her struggle to appropriate the language of the law in order to gain entry to what she perceived as an elite social grouping of legal academics. In CheeLing's case, copying and imitating appropriate Discourse is one of the ways in which all students (not just ESL and EFL learners) gain entry and seek to fit into a specific academic community. Many of the teachers adopting a transformative approach to teaching incorporate an awareness that some students need time to ingest information, reflect upon it using their own experiences and then construct their own understandings of information. These teachers believe there is a period of "transition" in academic writing, where students need to come to terms with the expectations of academic writing both at South-Coast University and generally. One of the teachers, Wai-Mei, also points out that some students enter universities and colleges with different expectations about the actual purpose of writing. Her previous experience at undergraduate level in China was to describe the subject matter of the assessment piece rather than engage with any other genre of writing:

> The expectations of writing are different in first year of courses in China to here. If we talk about writing, here, you're not supposed to just describe other people's writings even for educational purposes. But in China, it's OK to do that. So we look at it differently, to start with. You're not allowed to just borrow other people's ideas or writing because it's not yours. I think we need to tell the students our expectations or our way of the doing things, is quite different from their expectations. They need to believe they haven't done anything wrong when they copy or plagiarize and they don't try to cause any harm to you, for instance. It's just that they don't know exactly what you want from them in writing.

Wai-Mei's comments are important on two levels. First, because her insight indicates that there is a need to be aware that different writing traditions exist among their students and these different traditions are accompanied by different expectations about what academic writing entails. The second point is that she advocates that teachers must be explicit about their expectations for synthesis, analysis or critique within the assessment tasks set. Wai-Mei says that often students demonstrate a kind of "transitory" writing process during their first or early years of tertiary study, particularly ESL and EFL students, because they are not accustomed to producing sustained critical or analytical pieces of writing. By sustained, Wai-Mei was talking about the length of the assignments, as many students had not written more than 1,000 words in their secondary school assignment tasks. Excerpts from interviews with one female and one male academic exemplified the kind of comments teachers made about perceptions of academic writing purposes. Elin, an experienced female academic at Central campus, said:

> Well some of that comes down to the concept of argument. I look for students incorporating other people's ideas in a synthesizing kind of way and applying them in a unique kind of way rather than simply to regurgitate ideas or information, which the primary writers are producing. So from my point of view, a more appropriate way is to take it a step further rather than just simply reproducing material. Students need to understand that we

expect them to work with multiple opinions in texts and critique and synthesize these opinions—that is the whole idea of written assessment.

Antonio, an experienced male academic at Riverside campus, noted:

Students are now dealing with a mode of communication that's not intuitive to them. Consequently they're having to go to Western texts written in English and English texts are written in a particular way, whereas Chinese and other ones are in a culturally specific style which may reflect their academic or intellectual tradition. As a consequence, the students are compelled to draw on their summary skills or whatever, so they're either going to be either less likely to plagiarize or extremely likely to plagiarize, depending on their level of desperation to succeed. Students see the final product as the goal, so they're missing the point of what our expectations are in marking their assignments and essays.

These comments suggest that students are not clear about the purpose of written assessment. They are, as Elin says, "simply reproducing material" rather than expressing "some form of argument" on the subject matter, which is clearly what she (like many of us) expects her students to do. Elin sees a disparity between her expectations of students' role as interrogators of texts using skills of synthesis and analysis and her views that students see their role as merely reproducing a variety of material from the course reading lists. Antonio's comments indicate that there is an understanding that there are different perceptions of writing, but he believes that for these students, the level of desperation to succeed is the key factor in plagiarism. Antonio perceives plagiarism as a last resort for students—a situation in which students unfortunately find themselves, but due to their understandings of the assessment requirements in some subjects, one in which they must succeed. Most teachers using a transformative approach to teaching have discussed situations of plagiarism explicitly with students, and many indicate that assessment is one of the key ways in which plagiarism can be deterred (see Chapter 8).

These comments and observations of teaching practices allow some of the characteristics of a transformative approach of teaching to be drawn out. Once again, this list is not intended to be exhaustive but to indicate that these are the major characteristics to emerge from this study. For teachers using a transformative approach to teaching, the key is that students make their own meanings from texts. Teacher expectations of student interaction in class and engagement with materials and ideas are high. The aim is that students will transform mere information from a conglomeration of sources into a coherent whole—and demonstrate their understandings of the field.

CHARACTERISTICS OF A TRANSFORMATIVE APPROACH TO
TEACHING AND PLAGIARISM

- assumes diversity in student understandings of plagiarism;
- assumes joint responsibility for understanding plagiarism (institution, teacher and student);
- assumes if plagiarism is found it is not necessarily intentional—the student must be involved to determine intention;
- assumes students lack technical skills (such as paraphrasing, summarizing, referencing) to avoid plagiarism;
- assumes plagiarism is largely due to lack of practice or developed skill in weaving "self" into academic writing;
- assumes students are apprentices in academic writing and teachers are facilitators to aid growth in academic writing.

The very approaches teachers use in their daily teaching and assessment practices influence the approaches students take to learning in various fields of study.

Summary

Chapter 6 examined different approaches and perspectives of plagiarism held by teachers in this study. Although most teachers perceived plagiarism to have similar characteristics, there was dissent on the issue of determining students' intention. Some teachers regard plagiarism as an intentional act and believe that students have enough information to enable them to follow academic referencing conventions and avoid the issue. Many of these teachers adopt a transmissive approach to their teaching and often assessment is set up in such a way as to enable content-driven approaches to learning. A number of teachers thought that students could be involved in both intentional and unintentional plagiarism. Where the act was intentional, many of these teachers considered it to be cheating but where plagiarism was unintentional, teachers believed the issue was more to do with lack of understandings of course readings or problems of engagement with ideas. However, most teachers also thought that students needed to be part of the discussion to determine intention and that it should not be an automatic penalty. Teachers adopting a transformative approach to teaching aim to set up their classrooms to promote student responsibility for intellectual engagement with readings. A primary focus is to enable students to reflect upon and listen to various perspectives. Assessment is designed to require students to reflect on the literature and draw clear parallels to their understandings in light of their experiences. These teachers argue that this approach helps students to avoid producing information-laden essays where course materials are regurgitated. All teachers are concerned that plagiarism appears to be rising and that there is increasing demand on teachers to monitor and report cases of plagiarism. Importantly, differences in interpretation of plagiarism as well as its detection and reporting, exist among individual members of teaching staff, and the implications of this are discussed in Chapter 8. The next chapter discusses students' points of view on plagiarism.

CHAPTER 7

Students' Perceptions of Plagiarism

> In general, plagiarism is a far less meaningful concept for students
> than it is for academic staff, and it ranks relatively low in the student
> system of values.
>
> (Peter Ashworth *et al.*, 1997, p.201)

Many students have quite clear views on a range of unacceptable
academic practices, including cheating, collusion and plagiarism. Although
many students are fairly clear on what they consider to be cheating, often
it is not the clear-cut line that university policy assumes it to be. In addition, the term "collusion" can appear daunting to many first-year tertiary
students. Collusion is difficult to distinguish from collaboration at times
as, for many students, collusion is just a stronger degree of collaboration
and does not amount to cheating or misconduct. Students appear to have
shades or gradings of behavior in terms of use and acquisition of the work
of others—as with the University of Birmingham's plagiarism policy, where
the university considered plagiarism could be categorized from "serious"
to "slight" (see Chapter 3). A number of students find the concept
of plagiarism quite confusing, based on prior learning experiences of what
was expected of them and what was valued and rewarded in terms of
high grades in their secondary schooling years. Plagiarism presents the most

difficulty for students because for many it is a new concept, whereas for others, although the notion of acknowledgment of sources is not new, the actual point of such acknowledgment continues to elude them. In other words, some students understand that they should not take words or ideas without attribution to the source, but they do not understand why not—other than to avoid university penalties. Plagiarism often presents great difficulties for students in operational terms, for example, how do students know what needs to be referenced and what does not and what constitutes "common knowledge" that does not require citation and what is not "common knowledge" and therefore does require citation? It is important for teachers to understand that students can and often do view plagiarism through different lenses from staff. Although students may read the same plagiarism policy, attend the same sessions on academic referencing and be provided with the same set of instructions about plagiarism, cheating or collusion—they perceive plagiarism differently from their teachers and from each other. This is not a new phenomenon. Peter Ashworth, Philip Bannister and Pauline Thorne concluded in their UK study in 1997 that student perceptions of plagiarism do not start from the same premises as academics, and one problem with many of the studies is an assumption of shared understandings of plagiarism between students and staff. According to Ashworth *et al.*, students tend to value factors such as protecting friendship groups, interpersonal trust and also "us" and "them" attitudes towards institutional power in their decisions on whether to plagiarize or not. My own research builds on the previous studies which suggest that many students, particularly those for whom English is a second or foreign language, are fearful that they may be unwittingly plagiarizing and can tend to over-cite sources in a bid not to be labeled a "plagiarist" or a "cheat." By understanding varying students' perceptions of plagiarism, particularly in relation to Internet sources, teachers may benefit in understanding plagiarism in light of issues of academic integrity.

This chapter will introduce you to the views of 186 international students about plagiarism in general—their concerns and practical dilemmas as well as their views on Internet plagiarism. These students participated in a research project from 2004–2005 at South-Coast University, which is a medium-sized university in Melbourne, Australia. South-Coast University has one rural, two regional centers and three city campuses in Australia, as well as partner campuses in Malaysia, Singapore and Hong Kong. It offers studies in arts; business; computing; education; health and behavioral sciences; law; and science and technology. The student population is around 32,000 students and this includes students who study both on-campus (59 percent) and in off-campus (41 percent) modes. The student population is drawn from across Australia as well as internationally.

Table 7.1 Participant students' countries of origin

Country of origin	Number of students	Percentage of total cohort
China	78	46
Malaysia	26	13.2
Indonesia	15	8
Cambodia	12	6.4
Singapore	12	6.4
Thailand	10	5.1
India	9	4.8
Zimbabwe	8	3.9
Korea	7	3.6
Sri Lanka	5	2.1
France	1	0.5
Romania	1	0.5
Sweden	1	0.5
Total	186	100

Students completed questionnaires and then 30 of the 186 students volunteered for interviews that were taped and transcribed, so the words appearing in this book are the students' own words. These students are all English as a Second or Foreign Language (ESL/EFL) students from the 18 countries listed in Table 7.1, who came to Australia to undertake studies in business and law at South-Coast University. They are all first-year undergraduate students who have not studied overseas at an English-speaking university before.

Method of Collecting Student Information

Two hundred and fifty-five students were asked by means of a questionnaire about their perceptions of plagiarism, and 186 responded. The breakdown indicated that 53 percent (n=99) of participants were male and 47 percent (n=87) were female. Of these students, 30 also wished to speak about their experiences in interviews with me and these interviews were taped and transcribed with students' permission so that the words appearing in this book are the words of the students. Seventy-four percent of students (n=138) were between the ages of 18–19 years (n=83 were male and n=76 were female) and 26 percent (n=48) were between the ages of 20–21 years (n=16 were male and n=11 were female). This means that students were either straight out of high school or they had worked for a couple of years before beginning a tertiary course of study in Australia. All students were in their first year of study in an undergraduate academic writing unit in the Faculty of Business and Law.

The Questionnaire

There were 32 questions on the questionnaire. Three questions asked students for information about their language backgrounds and country of origin. The responses to questions about students' first language corresponded to their countries of origin, with the exception of students who indicated that their first language was Hokkien (n=2), a language variation of Malay. These two students indicated their country of origin was Malaysia so were included in the Malaysian language grouping (n=26).

Students were also asked 10 general questions about their English language learning experiences in their home countries. Of the 186 students, 97 percent (n=180) responded that they had continued with English in their final year of schooling and 3 percent (n=6) of students responded that they did not study English in their final year of schooling in their home countries. These six students (n=4 were male and n=2 were female) came from different countries. One male came from Romania, another male from Sweden and the remaining two male students came from Cambodia. The two females came from Zimbabwe. Students were also asked whether English was the language used for their final written exams in their home countries. The purpose of this question was to check whether students had experienced writing responses in English under exam conditions. Four percent of the 186 students (n=5 male and n=3 female) responded that their final exams had been in the English language. Seven of these students came from Malaysia and the other student came from Sri Lanka. The other 98 percent of students (n=180) responded that their final examinations were in the national language of their country. In response to questions about formal testing in the English language in their home countries, 86 percent (n=159) of students indicated that they had completed short tests in written English during their specific subject "English" classes. However, only 14 percent (n=27) of students responded that they had undertaken written exams in the English language. The remainder of the questionnaire asked students about their understandings of plagiarism, as well as their use and sourcing of Internet information.

In illustrating the results of this study, I have chosen to use bar graphs (see Figure 7.1). These graphs represent a visual picture of the data collected, which was analyzed according to a Chi-square formulation.[1] The graph shows the number of students as a percentage of the total pool of 186 students on the vertical axis and the columns on the horizontal axis indicate the variables compared. Percentages of the total pool are given within each column in the bar graph and the numerical count is given on the horizontal axis. An explanation of the relationship of the variables follows the graph.

Plagiarism and Students' Prior Learning

One of the most frequent criticisms in the higher education sector is that students enter university ill-equipped to study at tertiary levels. Many teachers as well as institutions consider that students do not possess the necessary writing and oral skills to embark upon a serious course of intellectual inquiry. One of the criticisms is that students plagiarize at secondary school and then continue the practice at university. Interview responses from international students indicated that in their secondary schooling years in their home countries, students were mostly instructed not to commit acts of plagiarism. However, students reported that they had been taught few skills and given scant practice.

Students who indicated on their questionnaires that they had been taught about plagiarism in their home countries said at interview that the instruction had largely been in the form of a directive "not to copy" (Tai, Hong Kong). They said that in their home countries teachers generally did not elaborate on this instruction. Some of their teachers preferred to tell them to "use your own words" in their writing tasks (Khoti, Zimbabwe) but did not give examples of how or when to do so. Typical student responses included: "They [teachers] say no copying and use own words to write, just like that" (Jason, Hong Kong), while Johan from Indonesia said:

> We didn't have anything like plagiarism at school. First of all, we don't really do things like compare opinions so you didn't need to do the citation. We just write our personal story or letters but not have to think about other opinions. Our teachers just used to say "Don't copy" but, yeah . . . they never tell us how not to copy. We still just copy and not losing marks for it, so, yeah, I think it's maybe OK for here.

Although these students indicated on the questionnaire that they did have prior knowledge about plagiarism, upon probing at interview, "knowledge" appeared to be largely a list of prohibitions about plagiarism: for example, "Don't copy" (Daniel, Hong Kong) and "Copying is illegal" (Marjorie, Malaysia). Students at interview could not explain why universities, such as South-Coast University, considered plagiarism to be unacceptable—in other words, they really did not understand why the university wanted sources acknowledged. Furthermore, students' prior knowledge of plagiarism did not include strategies or techniques that are commonly expected to be used by tertiary students to avoid it, such as summarizing, using quotation marks and paraphrasing. Most students had been taught how to summarize, to greater and lesser extents, in their home countries. The problem was that these students did not realize, nor had they been explicitly taught, that summaries of factual content still required acknowledgment using academic citation norms at university. An extended response about prior learning experience of plagiarism within the specific learning context of Korea was provided by Lee-Kim:

> I think that you must understand the schooling in Korea to understand how this works. In school, we have very large classes, not like in here. In my school we had around 60 or maybe 70 children in classroom. This is a lot of kids for the teacher to handle, so we have to sit quietly so that everyone can hear teacher. It is not the case of just sitting and doing nothing but we have to give everyone the chance to learn, so we need to remember what the teacher says. Every Friday we would have tests. They would be on what the teacher had told us for the week. We had to study every day at home and for me, I lived a long way from the school and had to walk and take bus. I would get home very late and then have to study late before going to school at 7.30 in the morning. So the best way to study, to give the teachers the right answer was to memorize. It was not because I liked it, but it was most convenient way for me to learn. The main thing to get through the exams in Korea to get into university was passing exams. The work during the year didn't matter really—just exams. So we studied hard. In the exams, you had to give the right answer. The right answer was what the teachers said to you in class and also what was in the book. Our teachers followed the book very well and so we had to match our answers to the book. They were the best answers. So when I come here and teachers say not to give the answer straight from the book, but to use my own words, because to use the answer from the book is stealing words I am shocked! This is only what I know how to do. So I worry that I don't know how to study well here. Teachers ask me to use my own words when writing down work but I know my English is not good and I don't have the words to use. I sound stupid! Like baby! It is much better writing to use the words from the book because the writer he knows what sounds very well in English. How to improve on his words? I can't! It's very confusing to me and I don't know how teachers here can ask that because they know we are international

students and our English is not so good. How they expect that we can pass exams using our words when native speakers have advantage in that. It's very hard for me to do that. I think that in Korea, I know exactly what I need to do to pass exams. The teachers were good because they taught us what we needed to pass the Korea State exams and successful in that. Maybe it's not learning like here but I remember many things and have knowledge. Here, I don't think I can pass exams because I have to use my own words and my words are not good enough. I don't really understand what teachers want me to learn here to pass exams and I don't have much knowledge after studying hard for one years here, I think.

Lee-Kim's powerful narrative illustrates her experience of inherent differences in academic expectations of writing between the Korean and Australian education systems. She highlights the fact that her previous experience in extensive use of memorized learning techniques gave her a sense of absorbing a great deal of knowledge. South-Coast University staff require that she use her own words to express her ideas, and she claims that this does not provide her with the same sense of "knowledge" achievement. She has no tangible outcome (amount of text memorized) by which to measure her learning success and she equates this with a lack of learning "knowledge." She also mentions that the teaching aims in Korea and Australia are different, in that the teaching staff in her home town of Chŏnju teach for the purpose of passing the all-important national exams and gear their assessment tasks to that end. At South-Coast University, examination success is not necessarily driving teaching methods, and assessment tasks reflect a range of learning outcomes, not just exam success. In Lee-Kim's eyes, an assessment task that is not directly related to exam preparation is not seen to be "good teaching." Her comments relating to plagiarism are particularly salutary. She said, "Teachers say not to give the answer straight from the book, but to use my own words, because to use the answer from the book is stealing words. I am shocked! This is only what I know how to do." Her comment points to both a misunderstanding of plagiarism and a fear of the outcome of plagiarism allegations. Lee-Kim understands plagiarism to be an expectation that every single word she uses must be her own, and she cannot utilize any words from textbooks or other sources. Clearly, the concept of citation is not clear to her at all. Her assumption is that teachers expect her wording to be better than that of the original authors, rather than as a means of indicating her understanding of their ideas. These assumptions fill her with fear: the fear of linguistic inadequacy, the fear of failing exams and the fear and uncertainty synonymous with not understanding what is expected of her. Her responses indicate that Lee-Kim does not know how to prepare for her exams, as the learning system at South-Coast University does not bear a similar relationship to her previous learning experiences in Korea.

Similar sentiments were expressed by Ratan (India) who said that he preferred to copy the direct words in the text because:

> The words are strange and not easily part of my way of talking. So how can I put in my own words? What words are the correct legal ones and which ones should I find other words for in the dictionary? I do not know that, right at this minute.

Ratan is concerned because as a first-year law student he is unsure which particular words are legal words and should be copied from texts verbatim and which words he could look up in a thesaurus to find synonyms. Many words are unfamiliar, but he is anxious that he does not appear less knowledgeable than his classmates. Correspondingly, Budi said that his English teachers at home in Ipoh, Malaysia, expected, "Good grammar, sentence structure and then the content of the essay. I think they didn't value the knowledge very much, just more the structure." Budi said that he had not heard about plagiarism until he started his studies at South-Coast University and was not sure how to action the principles of citation he had learned. Budi continued:

> I mean, do teachers here really want my words in place of the textbook? How can I say it better than the writers of a book? If that is not what the teachers want, then I don't know what they want me to write.

In terms of writing practices in their studies, some students were inclined to place citations at the end of each sentence and over-use referencing conventions. When asked why they adopted these practices, they said they were so afraid that the reader would think that the ideas were not theirs, that they wanted to be sure they acknowledged everything so plagiarism could not be alleged. Their responses reinforced the findings in Ashworth et al.'s work (1997) that they had little understanding of the mechanics of referencing or the meaning of plagiarism.

These students' responses indicate that a lack of practical skill in citation conventions is a learning hurdle for them. The other point is that teachers and the university are assuming that students come armed with such skills, which is clearly not the case. There is an immediate tension evident in different expectations and realities here. University citation conventions are strongly linked to the legal framing requiring acknowledgment of authorship in plagiarism policies. The data findings from student responses at both questionnaire and interview indicate that where students are unfamiliar with citation as a style of acknowledgment, they may be disadvantaged because they do not utilize the discourse markers of academic writing. Problems that students encounter when learning in a different environment, such as a university abroad, may bring about confusion where there is dissonance between what is valued as "good learning" in their home countries and what is valued as "good learning" in their new university. However, if we compare these perceptions with the views expressed by the teachers in this study, there is quite a difference. Teachers attribute ESL and EFL students' inability to demonstrate citation and referencing skills almost exclusively to cultural differences in learning (see Chapter 4). Student responses, however, indicate that the issue is much more complex, because a central conflict is the tension between different perceptions of what is valued as learning and the difficulties for many students in demonstrating their learning in writing.

By contrast, some students (n=3) who also noticed a difference in learning expectations, as highlighted by Lee-Kim, were not afraid to tackle it. As Zhen, a female student from China, said, "Australian teachers like most to learn English activity but in China teachers always say remember the words and do homework but not to learn." Zhen elaborated on this: "This way learning is better because here you must always use it. There in China it [English] is just subject." Zhen clearly distinguishes between learning for information and learning for skill, which Lee-Kim does not. Lee-Kim equates "knowledge" with the degree of content she is able to memorize. She takes comfort in her ability to study successfully when she has accumulated content in her mind. Zhen, on the other hand, finds the "subject" English to be just "words" or "homework," but she does not equate it to learning. Zhen believes learning to be more than demonstrated lexical competence. She claims that learning gives you a degree of skill that can be applied in other contexts, when she says, "You must *always* use it." Zhen is also confident that she understands plagiarism and its role in attribution of authorship:

> Plagiarism is only you copy the another author's ideas and the meaning so I think it's illegal because so the information is another's not mine. So if I use the another's ideas I must paraphrase or use the quotation mark.

When probed further about conventions of paraphrasing or use of quotation marks, Zhen is a little more vague. She understands paraphrasing as "changing words" but she considers that using her thesaurus to substitute a few words as synonyms is sufficient to paraphrase the original section of text. Here is an example of a practice that Zhen feels is acceptable in academic writing, but many teachers and university policies do not. Teachers in the last chapter were annoyed that students indulged in the practice of word substitution and called it a paraphrase or summary and said they would penalize students who engaged in such approaches. University policies also often give specific detail about "correct" paraphrasing, which suggests that there is an "incorrect" method as well. Zhen also had clear ideas about the use of quotation marks, although she was not sure "how many" quotes she could use in a piece of academic work, and sought an answer in percentage terms for the whole text. Zhen queried, "I know I can use those marks [quotation marks] but I do not know how many times I can use. Is there a rule about this? Can it be more than five times or 20 times in my essay? I just don't know that." Zhen's comments indicate that she, like some other students interviewed, is aware of the role that understanding different academic expectations plays in student perceptions of learning. She also claims that merely being aware of the different understandings and perceptions of learning is not enough. Students need the space and opportunity to practice acquiring the skills demanded in their new learning environment without fear of failure. Supporting Zhen's comments are those of a male student from Thailand, Naraporn:

> I understand plagiarism is when you use of others' ideas or words without acknowledgement so you need to change them and put in a reference. What I don't understand is how to do this. If I do just copy, then it's plagiarism, but how *many* words do I need to change and how *many* quotes do I use in my Economics assignment for it to be good? I don't want to fail after doing all these changes.

Naraporn, like Zhen, has an idea of what plagiarism entails that would mesh with university policy definitions and also the explanations of most of the teachers as seen in the previous chapter. Both students, however, lack practice and application of these skills. Neither student is comfortable or familiar with strategies to develop an individual sense of voice in academic writing, in order to display understanding or analysis of the set material. Similarly, Mei from China said:

> Teachers give us some information and they asked us to just do the comprehension and then after that maybe lots of material, maybe three or four articles about the same topic and then do the writing. Most of them is quite concerned about the structure

of the writing, you know, the grammar structure and complex sentences. They tell us to use our own words but they did not really to show us how to do that.

Like Mei, Endi is concerned that although he was told about plagiarism in his home country of Indonesia and instructed not to plagiarize, he did not come to Australia with sufficient skills to avoid plagiarism. Endi said:

Basically we were told that we should just use our own ideas and not copy other people's things. The trouble is that we don't have enough good words to use, so we copy because the assignments are due and we have to put in something.

Yet another student, Peng, a female from Cambodia, wrote, "The whole theory of plagiarism is base on cultural concept of tolerance or not." Peng did not choose to elaborate on her statement at interview other than to say, "Here is not understanding that we do differently in home and it's OK. I think Australia is not very tolerant of international students." Peng said that she had not learned about plagiarism in her previous schooling at home in Cambodia. She found that although she had been introduced to the concepts of plagiarism and authorship attribution in the academic writing unit at South-Coast University, the teachers in her other subjects made no allowance for the fact that these academic notions were new to her. This may help to explain why she considers there is a lack of "cultural tolerance" at South-Coast University.

Peng's point is worth some further discussion as she raises a central concern that academics, such as Peter Levin, have written about—the moral and ethical responsibilities of a tertiary institution to provide assistance for students. Levin (2006) claims that where there is a disparity between the university's expectations of a student's skills and their actual skills, the university has deemed the student is able to undertake tertiary level studies and has accepted students who meet a certain "entry" level. If the student does not have the necessary skills in writing to succeed at university, then it is the university's responsibility to provide explicit instruction and practical assistance to help the student at least be able to stand a chance of succeeding in tertiary level studies. Levin says:

It is not plagiarism that is the key issue, but the fact that students—at all levels in the education system—are being tested on their use of skills that they have not been taught. The key issue is: How can teaching and learning in our education system be improved? We can then go on to assess whether, if they were improved, there would be a need for the plagiarism police as presently constituted.

(2006, p.20)

Although Levin is open to criticism in suggesting that plagiarism is not a "key issue" he does raise the issue of how plagiarism is handled in our educational institutions, which is explored more in the next chapter. Not surprisingly, the 106 students who said they were taught about plagiarism during their secondary school years in their home countries felt more confident that they understood plagiarism than the students who claimed no prior knowledge of plagiarism in academic writing. However, 42 percent (n=45) of the 106 students said that they still did not have strategies to overcome plagiarism in their writing. Of the remaining 80 students who said that they had not been taught about plagiarism in their home countries, 34 percent (n=27) of students said they knew what plagiarism meant but 66 percent (n=53) of students indicated that they could not understand the concept.

The problem for teachers is that most staff expect that students have some idea about plagiarism when entering university study. The excerpts from teachers indicate that teachers construct and mark assessment tasks based on this assumption, which is clearly not the case in reality. Such divergence between expectations of students and the reality of student understandings will inevitably lead to misunderstandings and punitive action. It is also evident that teachers expect that students will understand plagiarism to be the same thing—a shared understanding between teachers and students. This is not the case, as was seen in the marked difference in perceptions of plagiarism between staff and students.

The fact that 57 percent (n=106) of students' responses indicated that plagiarism was canvassed to some degree in their home countries was in direct contrast to the perceptions of the staff interviewed at South-Coast University. Teachers believed that many students from the participants' countries of origin had little instruction about plagiarism before commencing courses at South-Coast University. Teachers viewed students as either "naïve" or "ignorant" about plagiarism and textual attribution before arrival in Australia. Mistakenly, they suggested that for many students, their first exposure to the concept of plagiarism was in the first-year academic writing unit offered by the Faculty of Business and Law at South-Coast University.

What is Plagiarism?—Students' Responses

As was seen with teachers, students also have a variety of understandings of plagiarism. Students were asked to give their own definition or explanation of plagiarism in both the questionnaire and also to expand on that definition at interview. The aim of this was not to seek a reproduction of any particular definition as written in dictionaries or the university policy, but rather try to elicit whether students had grasped the concept of plagiarism. Of the 133 students who wrote definitions or explained the concept of plagiarism, 39 percent (n=52) did so in similar ways to the university policy definition, which corresponded to the explanations of plagiarism given by teachers. Responses in this category included: "Plagiarism is to copy exactly others' word but without any quotation" (female from Cambodia) and "Plagiarism is using other peoples' work without their knowledge" (male from Malaysia). A further 29 percent (n=39) had definitions that were "partially similar" such as "Plagiarism is cheating or copying" (male from India) or "Plagiarism is use other people idea and haven't notice" (female from China). Thirty-one percent (n=42) of students responding defined plagiarism in a way that was not at all similar to the university definition. Sample responses falling within this category were, "Plagiarism is a bad attitude in all over the world" (female from Zimbabwe) and "I don't know, doesn't matter, I am not going to plagiarize anyway" (male from Sri Lanka). Table 7.2 summarizes the students' responses and shows there are differences between students' concepts of plagiarism.

These responses are of particular interest because all of these students had been studying the first-year academic writing unit that had specifically covered the issue of plagiarism in previous weeks. The unit of study included not only discussion of the university policy and the issue of

Table 7.2 Summary table of students' responses to question 24: "How do you define or explain the term *plagiarism*? Please use your own words to indicate what you understand the term to mean."

Students' definition of plagiarism compared to definition in study materials	Students' responses by first language background													
	Cambodian	Chinese	French	Indian	Indonesian	Korean	Malaysian	Romanian	Singaporean	Sri Lankan	Swedish	Thai	Zimbabwean	Total
Similar	1	23	1	3	3	1	11		7	2				52
Partially similar	4	19		2	2	2	7				1	1	1	39
Not similar	3	21		1	2		6	1	3	1		2	2	42
Total	8	63	1	6	7	3	24	1	10	3	1	3	3	133

academic integrity, but also a series of diagnostic class exercises on a case study, where sample texts contained both plagiarized and non-plagiarized examples. Although 68 percent of the 133 students had understandings that were mostly (n=52) or partially (n=39) similar to the university definition, 32 percent (n=42) or one third of these students had understandings that were not similar to either the subject materials or the university policy. This is similar to the findings in other research studies (Ashworth *et al.*, 1997; Carroll, 2002; Howard, 1999; Marsden *et al.*, 2005; McCabe, 2004; Pecorari, 2002) that indicate students do not understand the term plagiarism in either similar ways to their teachers, or in similar ways to each other. It is surprising, given the prevalence of research that suggests that students understand plagiarism in a myriad of ways that often are not congruent with either policy or staff understandings, that universities do not accept this as a base point. If it were an acknowledged situation that plagiarism was not a sort of universally understood truth for all parties, then students do, however, tend to have two distinct categories: students who intentionally plagiarize and those who do so unintentionally or unknowingly. This dichotomy aligns with the plagiarism continuum model, described in Chapter 1, because students perceive there is a range of intention upon which the decision of plagiarism is based. However, where teachers viewed all intentional acts of plagiarism to be a form of cheating, students said only some forms of intentional plagiarism could be cheating and other forms were not cheating. This is quite a marked difference from the teachers' responses, as almost all teachers said intentional plagiarism was equivalent to cheating.

Intentional Plagiarism = Cheating

Students are clear that where there is a deliberate or calculated attempt to gain some sort of unfair advantage over other students by taking words or work of another person, then that is a serious action and it is cheating. This means, for example, that where a student orders a custom-designed essay from an online provider and pays for the service of having their assessment task written for them, or takes a fellow student's memory stick with an assignment on it and submits it as their own, then that action amounts to cheating. Students consider this the worst form of plagiarism because it is unashamedly deceptive. The students use the language of criminal law to describe it, such as cheating, stealing, criminal, penalties, intentionally deceptive, taking property and deliberately dishonest. Students in this study generally support the notion that such action should receive the full weight of sanctions available under university regulations. Li, a student from Taiwan, said:

If they're cheating—I mean real deliberate stuff so that they will get better marks than the rest of us who are just struggling to do it ourselves—then that's not fair and it's not learning. They should be expelled from the course and the university because they're not trying anything themselves. It's the easy way out!

Students in this study did not distinguish between cheating in assignments, essays, group work or examinations. For them, where there is an intention to gain unfair advantage and no attempt to actually take part in the learning experience provided, then all offenders deserve the same penalty. A number of students supported Sandeep's eloquent statement that:

To be a student is to be taking part in the intellectual activity of the course. For people who intentionally and knowing what they are doing, choose to steal work from others, then they are not using their minds and not even engaging themselves intellectually with the task. They are guilty of cheating and misusing the status of being a student. They should have the whole penalty thrown at them by the university.

Sandeep's statement is similar to Ashworth *et al.*'s (1997) findings on ethical learning, where the authors say, "Part of this condemnation stems from a moral view of cheating as entailing the willful squandering of educational privilege" (p.198). It is the concept that there is an educational opportunity being wasted that these students say really irks them, as, for many, it is a very costly choice to come to university in the first place. The students are quite clear about "cheating" and, of course, describe it as an intentional act, but they also perceive there can be situations where students can intentionally take the work of others where it does not amount to cheating. This "other" form of appropriation the students claim is not misconduct.

Intentional Plagiarism = Not Cheating

Students were able to distinguish between intentional plagiarism that was deceptive and therefore cheating and a lesser form of intentional plagiarism that was acceptable practice. Commonly, students said that taking and using the written work of others in a group study situation or with their consent was intentional plagiarism but it did not equal cheating. For students, these practices were part of the learning process in which they had engaged for years in their secondary schooling and they did not harbor any doubt that these practices were legitimate learning strategies. For many students, group sharing of individual assignment tasks is common and also standard practice in their home countries. They do not liken it to cheating or academic misconduct in any form. Marish said:

> It is usual for me to get together with my friends back home and we sit and do our study together. We all talk about the work and make notes and even write things down for each other and then we sort out what we think. We have always done it this way and our teachers say to us that this is good thing. We co-operate together so we learn things better and that can't be cheating or anything bad, because we have no bad thoughts or intentions to cheat—only to help each other with work and get a good mark.

Yvette confirmed this by saying:

> I have always worked in study groups. It is common practice in Trioletian schools to do these things together—orally and in writing. It does not mean that we are cheating at all, it is the best way to learn from each other and to talk things through—isn't that what you want us to do here in the group work? They even have assignments that say "peer review" for things, so the university wants us to work together and share ideas and work. It is the same, I think.

Further questioning about what was involved in co-operative learning, such as this kind of group work, revealed a list of common practices that these students considered promoted learning. These group-study practices include:

- reading and using each other's work for the same assignment;
- taking and sharing notes on work;
- reading and using past students' work (older sisters, brothers and friends) who have completed the subject in previous years;
- helping each other with vocabulary and construction of sentences, so many sentences will appear to be the same;
- taking their work to the university Language and Learning Support Staff for checking and assistance (as they are encouraged to do by many staff) and sharing the feedback with the group;
- sharing their teachers' feedback and comments and discussing what else they could have done to improve the assessment piece;

- if a student is asked to resubmit work, often the group will help that student complete the task which involves discussion, helping with grammar and vocabulary and making detailed suggestions as to how and where the assessment piece can be improved; proofreading is also done by the group before resubmission.
- collaborating and working together in practical situations, such as laboratories or other practical components of the course—sharing tasks and notes.

Generally most students regard these actions as shared practices of learning. Furthermore, many regard sharing their ideas, notes, past assignments and feedback as their social obligation or even as a duty to be performed. In some cases, students have a great deal of difficulty understanding the difference between collaboration (which is often encouraged in various university settings) and collusion (which is academic misconduct in most institutions). Brinna said:

> Actually, I don't get it. The university and teachers say to work together on an assignment and ours was a practical IT component but then they say if you share your work and ideas and words, then it's illegal collusion! On the one hand they want us to share and discuss work and on the other hand, they penalize us if we write it up together. I don't get it—what are we supposed to do?

Brinna's concerns have been voiced by students in other studies.[2] It is apparent that the fine distinctions universities make between co-operative learning and collusion are clouded for these students. There is another aspect of group learning that can be more difficult for teachers to come to grips with because it is not necessarily transparent. These are cases where there is a strong social and moral obligation to provide any assistance requested by an older student holding a position of social dominance. In the case of Lim from Korea, the issue of collusion and plagiarism was of ongoing concern. He said:

> Well of course I must help him if he asks me and I must help him as much as he want because he is older than me and must be respect. He is most senior Korean man here and we all do as he ask. It is my duty and Korean way.

Lim went on to explain that as all young men had an obligation to serve in the Korean army, there is a strong sense of social and moral obligation from junior to senior males (as determined by age) and this does not stop once you leave the army. He further explained that there is an expectation that it is your duty to help and support your senior colleagues and it is dishonorable to shirk this duty and brings shame not only upon yourself, but also upon your whole family network. In this case, Lim felt obliged to take notes for the older Korean student and write parts of his assignment for him, as he was asked to do so. Although he felt uncomfortable being placed in this role, he considered it probable that the older Korean student would tell others if Lim failed to assist him, which would bring great discredit upon Lim and his family, should word get back to Korea. This insight sheds light on a possible tension between a specific social expectation for some students—that all assistance requested is rendered—compared to teacher expectations—that each student has completed the task individually. Punishing students for collusion or plagiarism, where these students are observing their social and cultural norms, is problematic, particularly where many tertiary institutions claim to embrace global views of education and internationalization of the curriculum. However, the dilemma remains for many teachers and students about how to proceed in situations such as this.

Similarly, students did not regard copying the work of another student with their consent to do so as plagiarism. For many, they regarded this as fair practice and as a kind of peer teaching. Juan said:

> Of course if he says I can use his work then I will. Why wouldn't I? Anyway, if the teachers are too lazy to change the task, then they deserve to get the same things in writing back again.

Other students say that it is common practice in their home countries for teachers to pass out sample and model answers and students are encouraged to replicate them as a process of learning the style and means of constructing excellent work. Many of them flounder when they are not given a sample to follow, as they say they need that sort of framework to understand what is required. Kiki said:

> I need to have a model answer. I used all the time in China because then I know exactly what teacher wants. I feel teacher in China understand us and are good teacher because they give us what we need, but in here, teacher don't and just say "Write your own opinion." But how to know what to write when I don't know what teacher want me to say and I have no example to follow?

Kiki's comments were echoed by many of the other students, who regard "good teaching" and "helpful teachers" as those who provide model answers.

For most teachers, this practice is regarded as a method that encourages plagiarism and a reliance on the teacher that they do not wish to create. As Kate said: "No way would I give out a model answer. It's bad enough getting my lecture notes quoted back to me but to give out a model answer would only give license to unbounded acts of copying and plagiarism." On this point, there is a considerable degree of difference between teachers' and students' concepts of "good teaching."

Other students were confused that some teachers seemed to regard writing techniques such as paraphrasing to be equivalent to a form of plagiarism (see Hesha's comments for example), and yet other teachers encouraged their students to use such writing strategies. Teachers, such as Hesha, said that what they found as common practice was students substituting one word for another in a sentence (usually through means of an online thesaurus) and claiming it was a paraphrase. Hesha was particularly critical of this and called it an "intellectual short-cut" that students were taking instead of really trying to explain things in their own way. However, teachers such as Mina actively encouraged students to paraphrase. She said it was an accepted writing practice to help students to learn how to use academic writing conventions. Indeed, as Mina claimed, it was also permitted and encouraged as a legitimate practice under the university policy. Such differences in interpretation by teachers of what is acceptable and what is not acceptable in academic writing is clearly confusing and often intimidating to students—particularly those in their first year of undergraduate study.

Reasons Why Students Choose to Intentionally Plagiarize

Students elicited many reasons as to why students intentionally plagiarize or cheat in their academic studies. Common reasons are:

- Universities do not seem to take cheating all that seriously because some people are "let off."
- Universities do not take responsibility for teaching students what is acceptable practice, so taking short cuts by cheating is acceptable.
- University regulations are sometimes unclear—what is the difference between collaboration and collusion (one is deemed to be acceptable and the other an offense?) so cheating occurs.
- Poor time management—students who get overwhelmed by their workload and are desperate to finish set tasks by a given date cheat or intentionally plagiarize.
- It is worth taking the risk of not being caught—ineffectively policed.

- Lack of interest/difficulty in a particular subject—this is often true where there are compulsory or core units in a course to be taken. Students who are not interested in these particular units or find them exceptionally demanding will risk being caught and take other work and pass it off as their own. Usually this is in response to their poor performance in the subject.
- Students feel the original text is so well written, they could not possibly say it better themselves and see no need to interpret the original text.
- Students feel "Everybody else is doing it, so why don't I?"—the perception exists, among students in this study, that cheating is prevalent among undergraduate students. They say they need to balance the risk of being caught with the fact that those who are cheating (and getting away with it) are getting better marks than students who do their own work. This causes a situation where students are worried that if they do not cheat, then they are not putting themselves in the best position to succeed.
- Fear of failure and disappointment to family—one of the most common given by students, particularly international students, for cheating. They fear that failure will bring great shame upon them in the eyes of their families, many of whom are working very hard to support their overseas studies financially. The fear of disappointing family and friends is too great and students report that they know of friends who cheated just to avoid failure. Often such actions result in greater fear of being caught, or deep-seated depression that they cannot cope with the demands of study.
- The tasks are so meaningless that cheating seems the best way to avoid boredom. A small group of students feel that where assessment tasks are not related to their experiences or appear to be "rehashed" over many years, then these tasks deserve to be treated with derision. Cheating was one way of demonstrating such contempt.

What is illustrated here is that students perceive there is a spectrum of intentional plagiarism—with cheating being an unacceptable practice—but other forms of intentional plagiarism being more acceptable and at times, appropriate. Students also indicate that intentional plagiarism can be used where students feel universities are shirking their responsibilities in the learning and teaching relationship—particularly in respect to provision of explicit teaching about academic conventions. Some students are aggrieved that the university is happy to take their fees, but does not appear to provide the necessary support for them, as ESL and EFL students, to succeed in their studies. One student, Ari, said:

They say that they're "international" in the way they look at education, but they're not. It's just their way of doing and writing things, but they never tell us exactly how they want it done and they never ask us if we would like to do it another way—like the way we did it in our country. It's costing me a lot of money to be here, so I think I need to find ways to help me pass, if the university won't.

If we compare the reasons students give for intentional acts of plagiarism, to the ways in which staff view intentional plagiarism, there is a marked difference. Whereas students have levels of plagiarism from unacceptable conduct, which they term "cheating," to acceptable plagiaristic conduct, most teachers say that students plagiarize because they are too lazy to do the work themselves, they are pushed for time and plagiarize to finish the assessment task, or they are simply unethical. Teachers' reasons clearly demonstrate their notions that students either do not bother to put in time and effort to complete assessment tasks, or that they manage their time poorly in terms of assessment submission. Although this is true of one section of the student population, for those who admit that they cheat,[3] many of them claim they have a reason for doing so—often claiming the assessment task is a rehashed and boring task that should be treated with disdain. This is similar to the findings in previous research (Ashworth *et al.*, 1997; Whitley and Keith-Spiegel, 2002).

Although most teachers would not accept this reasoning as justification for such conduct, and I am certainly not condoning such action, the point must be made that students may use what Sue Saltmarsh (2004) calls "graduating tactics" as they are consumers of educational product. Saltmarsh effectively uses Michel de Certeau's (1984) theory of consumptive practice to argue that students are consumers of educational products and use tactics, including plagiarism, to increase their agency in consumptive relationships. She argues that we need to understand that students, as consumers, may use "legitimate" tactics in order to complete course require-ments, but also reconceptualize the power relations between themselves and the university through activities such as plagiarism. She says:

> The tactic of plagiarism can thus be understood beyond its current constructions as "cheating" or "academic misconduct" and instead considered as a productive practice which disrupts and subverts the consumption of education as a "product" from which consumers are expected to derive benefits as prescribed by the institutions while simultaneously submitting to its strategic demands.
>
> (Saltmarsh, 2004, p.454)

This means that students will take whatever action is required to meet deadlines, cope with balancing study and work, and strive to meet their own or family pressure to succeed. Colleen Vojak (2006) agrees and claims that there is a market-culture influence on the willingness of students to cheat. She says that "cheating has become both more prevalent and more socially acceptable" (p.177) and market values of competition, private good and self-interest encourage students to engage in practices that promote "getting ahead" of others. She claims that our education system is "attributable to a growing materialism that has fuelled a preoccupation with the economic value of education—one that focuses on the end product rather than the process—thereby eclipsing other important educational goals" (p.184). What Vojak is saying is that the public good and intellectual ideas of education for the sake of intellectual growth are not key values in the market perspective of education. This is because, as she says:

> The market reduces a wide range of values to their monetary worth and as a culture increasingly comes to view economic success as an intrinsic good, many other goods such as critical thinking, civic engagement, interpersonal relationships, service to others and personal integrity can easily take a back seat to future earning power.
> (Vojak, 2006, p.187)

In this competitive higher education marketplace, students now— more than ever before—not only expect but demand a quality educational experience in return for their money. Where assessment practices are seen to be unworthy of student effort, for example in recycling assignment or exam questions, then students may feel justified in taking such steps as intentional plagiarism to counter what they see as the delivery of an inferior educational experience. As Peter Knight says "Plagiarism often shows students responding intelligently to teachers' slack assessment practices" (2001, p.20). Certainly, the students in this study who spoke about engaging in such actions did not do so with any degree of remorse. What this shows us is that students and teachers view plagiarism and assessment in very different terms. For teachers, there are not the shades of acceptability in cases of intentional plagiarism that students hold to exist. Plagiarism is also clearly linked to the quality of the assessment task, in the opinion of many students, which is something that teachers have not alluded to, or perhaps taken seriously. On this point, meaningful dialogue must take place between teachers and students in order to develop higher quality teaching and learning environments for all parties. If transformative teaching approaches are matched with open discussion of ethical values and the "pedagogical power of ethical role-modeling" (Vojak, 2006, p.192) we, as teachers, may be able to reduce dishonest academic practices and help students reshape beliefs in academic integrity. In addition to broadening the scope through which intentional plagiarism and cheating are viewed, students were also quite expansive in their discussion of unintentional plagiarism.

Unintentional Plagiarism

Many students regard unintentional plagiarism as falling outside the ambit of academic misconduct. For some students it is almost an impossible task to decide what needs to be cited and what does not—based on inexperience in referencing and lack of knowledge of what is "common" knowledge in the specialist field in which they are studying. For other students unintentional plagiarism falls into the "So what?" category—where students perceive teachers as being "overly hung-up" (Jess) on academic niceties such as referencing and conventions of attribution. They do not view plagiarism as having anything to do with serious academic endeavor, but more as a form of academic etiquette or polite way of writing in the tertiary context. In this light, students regard plagiarism as a slip of the pen and not a terribly serious matter, which is in direct contrast to the ideas of many teachers that plagiarism is "the academic death penalty" (Howard, 1995, p.788).

In this study, students were asked by questionnaire whether they had been taught about plagiarism since studying in Australia.[4] Of the 186 students who responded, 87 percent (n=162 students) indicated that they had been taught about plagiarism while in Australia. Of these, 50 percent of students (n=81) said they could define or explain plagiarism but 50 percent (n=81) said they could not, despite attending the specific academic writing classes in which plagiarism and the intricacies of the plagiarism policy were covered. Of the 24 students who responded that they were not taught about plagiarism in Australia, 29 percent (n=7) of students indicated that they could define and explain plagiarism. However, the majority, 71 percent (n=17) of the students responding, indicated they could neither define or explain plagiarism nor were taught about it in Australia. Although this means that students who had been taught about plagiarism in Australia were more likely to be able to define or explain it than students who had not, the issue is that of those students who had been taught about plagiarism in Australia, 50 percent were still not confident that they could explain it. The graph in Figure 7.1 illustrates this.

This finding merits discussion. Staff teaching this first-year academic writing unit assumed that students understood the meaning of plagiarism, as they had completed exercises on plagiarism and attribution in week two of the 13-week course. Of the total group of 186 students, 53 percent (n=67)

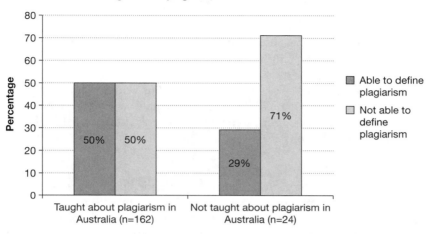

Figure 7.1 Relationship between students' ability to define and explain plagiarism and students' perception of being taught about plagiarism in Australia.

remained unable to define or explain plagiarism at the completion of the course. This is disconcerting for teachers as they had expected a high number of students would respond that they not only understood what plagiarism meant, but could give clear explanations and possibly even examples of plagiarism, after having completed this specialist academic writing unit. This was not the case. Similarly, teachers expected that their students were confident in their capacity to identify plagiarism and demonstrate competent referencing and citation skills. So what was the problem? Students were able to explain these comments more during interviews with me. Ridma, a male student from Indonesia, said:

> Before I came here I didn't know [about plagiarism] because I never told before. But when I studied here it is, well, plagiarism is like copying from someone and ideas and without footnotes. You must do the footnotes, that is very important. It is like that we already quote from that one and it mean that we steal something from someone. Only, I just don't know what should I exactly footnote and I feel very worried about that.

Ridma's explanation shows us that despite learning about plagiarism in the academic writing course, he confuses techniques such as quoting and footnoting with copying and stealing. Although he understands plagiarism is unacceptable, he does not appear to understand that techniques such as quoting and footnoting are acceptable, but actions of unauthorized "copying" and "stealing" are not. He further said, "Plagiarism is mean that we copy and should not copy, it is like steal work that's not our own so it is wrong to do," but he added that he was not confident he had overcome tendencies to copy directly. As he said:

> The teacher, she say plagiarism is wrong but I do not know why is so because in my high school in Kalimantan we do copy all the time and it works to learn some things so now I don't think I really know whether copy is too bad or OK to do. It's confuse for me now.

Ridma was like other students who had attended the 13-week specialist writing course as a preliminary part of their studies but did not come away from the course with clear understandings of how to avoid plagiarism in practice. Two students from India made comments to the effect that plagiarism was a strange idea and they did not really understand it, despite the classes they had taken. Shirani said:

> This plagiarism is being strange to me because how can we learn if not to write things out of the book. I don't really understand when we should write the cites next to the words we reference. I mean, should we be doing this all the time for every sentence or just some of the times. If just some of the times, then when is right and when is wrong? How should we just *know* these things?
>
> (emphasis in the original)

Her friend Nalia said:

> I know that I listened carefully in the class but I just don't get it. Why do we put all these footnotes around and have to say where we get every single word from? It looks like I haven't done any work at all and have just been copying everyone else's thoughts and words. I did do work by myself and I read many things to make the essay but when I have to write where all bits come from, it looks like there is no effort by me at all. I feel small to do this.

For these students, it is clear that the reasons for adopting academic citation and referencing conventions are unclear. The information they have absorbed has led to more questions—particularly about "how much" information should be referenced. In particular, the student's fear that by referencing all sources the student appears to have done nothing because the assignment is full of signposts to the work of others. This means students feel "small," as Nalia says. Students articulate feelings of inadequacy, that despite all their hard work, the end product is not something with which they have any sense of connection. This loss of connection is often referred to as the student's "voice" in the text. Many students in our classrooms are unsure about how to structure academic writing and to highlight their own sense of "voice" in the work. Although "voice" was discussed by teachers in the previous chapter, it seems that many teachers do not give credence to the feelings of inadequacy experienced by many students who struggle to reach a balance between the literature and the self. A number of teachers have advocated that the challenge of creating a coherent whole from linking different ideas, quotations and words of others is a hurdle for many students, particularly when operating in English as a second, third or fourth language. Strategies that students use to help them reach the fluidity necessary for excellent work include what Rebecca Moore Howard calls "patchwriting" (1995), Peter Ashworth *et al.* (1997) call "mosaic technique" and Karla Kitalong (1998) calls "patchcoding" when dealing with Internet texts. However, as discussed in Chapter 4, some of these techniques are deemed to be inappropriate by institutional policies and in tertiary practice they are still perceived to be plagiarism. Students' comments indicated that they found plagiarism both complex to understand and difficult to avoid without time to practice techniques that melded their own voices with the literature.

Students' Responses and the Plagiarism Continuum

Students' responses about how they perceive actions of plagiarism as well as why students plagiarize and cheat connect with the plagiarism continuum. Students wrote comments such as, "Plagiarism is illegal and is punished because it is stealing." Such responses characterize plagiarism as cheating and the action of "taking" falls within legal notions of ownership of text (see Chapter 2). Students also moved towards the right on the continuum by categorizing some forms of intentional plagiarism as plagiarism per se, but not as an inappropriate action and not as action deserving penalty from the university. Much of what students had to say in this area aligned with prior research that students are far less concerned about plagiarism than their teachers or institutions and simply do not see it as a major issue for them to think about in the overall scheme of what is important in their studies. Students' comments also support the idea that "transmissive" modes of teaching and assessment are structured to elevate levels of plagiarism. The very approaches that students see teachers using endorse student practices of copying down information in lectures, tutorials and from readings in order to regurgitate the content in predictable or unimaginative assessment tasks. It is in the arena of assessment tasks and approaches to teaching that teachers are able to instigate fundamental change and transform mere information-gathering activities into meaningful activities for learning.

Students also feel strongly that unintentional plagiarism, at the far right side of the plagiarism continuum, is not deserving of punishment. They argue that where there is a lack of familiarity with citation conventions and confusion over what is valued in academic writing, that students who plagiarize unknowingly should be assisted, not penalized. Students argue that anything less than direct and explicit assistance is immoral because universities are taking their money but not providing the support they consider is promised and that they expect. This is particularly true for students who contend that they are accepted into courses as ESL/EFL students on the understanding that their entry-level scores in the English language are sufficient to allow them to study and pass units within their courses. These same students feel that they had been deceived by the university, as they were permitted entry into courses, but then abandoned by the university support networks to fend for themselves in the unknown mire of academic referencing conventions. At the "unintentional plagiarism" end of the spectrum, students say the policy is unfairly applied to students who act in ignorance and they are penalized.

Summary

Students' comments that plagiarism was a daunting convention to understand and avoid, confirmed their teachers' concerns that the resources and means for enacting university responsibilities in teaching students about plagiarism were not sufficient. Students were aware that the time needed to develop these skills was more than a 13-week preparatory course. They were also aware that they needed to employ specific techniques, such as patchwriting, in order to move beyond merely copying the words of others without their own voice becoming stronger. Students said this is where they needed the guidance of teachers. Teachers maintain that students need time and constant reinforcement of notions of textual attribution in all subjects to absorb these conventions, as well as access to professional assistance and further workshops or online modules to help them explore their developing academic writing skills. Clearly, students' inability to explain their understandings of plagiarism in a manner that is consistent with their teachers and university policy is of concern because conflict will inevitably arise where differing perceptions of plagiarism are held. The next chapter considers the ongoing issues for teachers and institutions and some processes that have been implemented to improve approaches to academic integrity.

CHAPTER 8

Plagiarism—Ongoing Issues

Looking to the underlying causes of plagiarism rather than just the symptoms provides the opportunity for fresh thinking about assessment and the roles and responsibilities of all the stakeholders in the learning enterprise—and thereby potentially reduces the complexity of the plagiarism issue.

(Ranald Macdonald and Jude Carroll,
2006, p.244)

It is clear that plagiarism continues to be of concern to universities, teachers, policy-makers and students. Although all acknowledge that it is an issue to be taken seriously at an institutional level, there does not appear to be a consistent manner across institutions of addressing plagiarism. In short, it is unclear in many cases how the responsibility for plagiarism is shared between the institution, teachers and students. In some institutions, it is uncertain who is responsible for dealing with allegations of plagiarism and the processes that should be followed. In institutions other than those where there is a zero tolerance policy, it is often imprecise as to who will decide whether plagiarism is "proven" or not. University policies often are silent on what happens to students where plagiarism allegations are proven and the student is permitted to continue their studies. What responsibilities lie with the student, staff and university to provide assistance so that plagiarism is avoided in the future? Of concern to teachers are the ongoing issues in dealing with plagiarism professionally, but without becoming "plagiarism police"[1] as Jude Carroll terms it. This chapter outlines some ongoing issues in plagiarism for teachers and institutions, as well as some responses. The chapter concludes with suggestions as to ways in which the plagiarism continuum can help reconceptualize learning and teaching practices with respect to plagiarism in academic writing.

Major Issues Raised by Teachers

The following are major ongoing issues for teachers:

- students are not adequately prepared for tertiary study—plagiarism appears a viable solution;
- different "interpretations" of plagiarism and knowledge by students—particularly ESL and EFL students;
- detection of plagiarism—time consuming and inconsistent across disciplines;
- responsibilities in reporting plagiarism are unclear—inconsistencies in outcomes, and teachers feel unsupported in the reporting process;
- curriculum guidelines that discourage assessment options that can deter plagiarism.

Students are Not Adequately Prepared for Tertiary Study

Teachers are concerned that students enter tertiary study without sufficient academic writing skills to succeed. This study and prior research indicates that many teachers assume when students win entry to a university place, on a competitive basis and within a competitive higher education market, that they possess requisite academic writing skills to cope. However, current research indicates that many students do not enter university courses with sufficient skills to successfully complete higher education degrees (Knight, 2001; Macdonald and Carroll, 2006). Commonly identified areas in which teachers consider students are not adequately prepared for university study include:

- poor time management skills—panic ensues and plagiarism seems a solution;
- difficulties in reading theoretically "dense" texts;
- difficulties in summarizing key ideas in more complex readings;
- an inability to incorporate their own voice into work;

- poor referencing and citation skills;
- a myriad of grammar, vocabulary and general language competence issues;
- an inability to write a sustained argument (more than 2,000 words); and
- problems using terminology in various disciplines correctly.

Some students are not adept at managing the workload expected at tertiary levels. They have poor time-management skills in juggling study, work, social and family lives. Many young students, even very bright students, have admitted to plagiarism because they simply ran out of time to complete set work. Where assessment items carry large mark weightings, a student with poor time management may be more likely to seek assistance at any cost to attain a pass grade. Students often complain that all major pieces of assessment are due on the same date—often the last day of the teaching semester. Assessment design and purpose is a key factor in reducing plagiarism. Teachers need to consider whether tasks set are "high stakes" assessment—which is where "those being assessed are likely to do all they can to conceal ignorance and suggest competence"—or "low stakes" assessment—which is "when learners are open about their limitations and don't try to conceal ignorance or bury mistakes" (Knight, 2001, p.3). The argument is that low stakes assessment is more conducive to overall learning taking place, as the students do not focus on the mark allocation for each task and therefore do not judge the value of their learning in that way. The purpose is that "low" stakes assessment tasks encourage students to do the work themselves, as failing one task will not mean an overall failure in the unit. Therefore the curriculum incorporates smaller tasks as part of the learning philosophy of an institution, rather than 100 percent examinations or one 80 percent essay. Students with less developed skills in writing are more likely to be identified by teachers, enabling additional opportunities for support to be provided. (It should be noted that although a range of smaller tasks are set, they are not all "graded" by the teacher, so there is no increase in marking load.)

Different Interpretations of Plagiarism and Knowledge

Teachers are concerned that students hold many different views about plagiarism and what is valued as knowledge. Many teachers are adamant that "cultural differences" exist in understanding plagiarism and some students are unaware of referencing requirements based on their prior learning experiences. This view is supported by earlier findings from Brimble and Stevenson-Clarke's (2005) study[2] where they said "staff identified problems arising out of cultural differences, where plagiarism may not be seen as a 'crime' in some cultures" (p.38). Teachers maintain that as different cultural perceptions of plagiarism exist, it is difficult to see how a "one size fits all" plagiarism policy is a workable solution. Some teachers feel that students may plagiarize inadvertently because they fear to fail and the loss of face for them at home would be worth the risk to plagiarize work in order to complete it on time or just pass. Some teachers are apprehensive that the university does not seem to understand the gravity of the issue of loss of face for many students, which, in their opinion, is not to be under-estimated as a reason that some students might plagiarize. These notions are tied to concepts of knowledge. CheeLing said:

> Face saving is very important because to be named in the class as the person who hasn't achieved something and lose face is far more important than something else that I can hide, that I don't need to reveal in the public. Losing face is about credibility and little bit of looking inferior and just look not as good as others and losing face is not just for yourself but for your family. It's not just my own problem, I lose my parents' face, because maybe they were so proud of me being in Australia and I didn't pass—that will probably be something they are very ashamed of and far worse than if I just copy a paragraph from you. My parents would feel so sorry that I haven't reached their expectations.

CheeLing's explanation supports Penelope Brown and Stephen Levinson's (1988) early research on issues of politeness and face where they proposed that the concept of face "is emotionally invested, and can be lost, maintained or enhanced and must be constantly attended to in interaction" (p.61). Similarly, researchers in cross-cultural studies also consider issues of face-saving as an important factor influencing students' learning strategies and techniques. Face-saving is not just a personal goal, but is a wider family and social concern, as pointed out by Watkins and Biggs (2001, p.7). The relationship between face-saving and academic writing was described quite comprehensively by CheeLing:

> In China, it is not a good idea to present ideas of your own. Whereas here, we say "What's your idea, what's your statement, what's your study?." So we always try to come to this individual argument. If I have no idea then I look bad in comparison with other people and I have very low marks and that make me lose more face. I mean, I can't be so different from everyone of my classmate. So I ask you, how are you going to be famous

calligrapher or famous painter or famous artist? Because you have read thousands of others poems and articles, and paintings and you become good, only after you have copied so many other people's work or repeat other people's work. Then that is your learning process and on top of that, then you can create something of your own. Never, never try to be your own from the very beginning—you look as if you don't respect the ancestors and the people who has been established in their reputations at the early days. Only from years of learning from others, then you feel it's time to have something of your own.

Our university and tertiary traditions, dating back to Socrates, assume that questioning provides ways of building knowledge. Ron and Suzie Scollon (1991, 1995, 1999) in their research on the influence of culture on the conceptualization of knowledge show that differences may arise from culturally based perspectives of knowledge. It is therefore important for teachers and the university as an institution to be very clear about what is valued as knowledge. If students are able to understand what is valued and why the academic community esteems individuals making their own meanings from intellectual inquiry, fostering a culture of shared academic integrity can begin. Clearly, open discussion between students, staff and administration about perceptions of plagiarism and the importance of understanding in knowledge development is the first step.

Plagiarism Detection

Most teachers say they rely on technology and search engines, such as Google, as well as general common sense to detect plagiarism. For example, where teachers read passages that are fluent and disarmingly worded, that are followed by passages that appear stilted and dramatically different in style and flow, suspicions are aroused. Some teachers also use commercial products, such as Turnitin, where the department or faculty has paid for a license (see the discussion in Chapter 5). The ongoing issues for teachers in plagiarism detection generally relate to their roles and responsibilities. Some are disturbed that they are becoming more "plagiarism police" than teachers, others are uneasy that the plagiarism administration takes the focus away from the teaching and learning relationship. Yet others are concerned about ways in which the issue of plagiarism in the universities is progressing—more towards a punitive and over-regulated outlook of education rather than a truly educative perspective. Some fear that the widespread use of electronic detection for plagiarism sends the wrong message to students and encourages them to seek "alternative" technologies to subvert this process (see the discussion in Chapter 5). Teachers do not appear to be as highly concerned about whether they can detect plagiarism in students' work as much now as they were three to five years ago. The focus has shifted to anxiety about balancing their roles as teachers with bureaucratic requirements to detect plagiarism in the current education climate.

Plagiarism: Whose Responsibility is it?

At times, it is unclear in policy and practice who is responsible for handling plagiarism. Furthermore, if plagiarism is detected, who is responsible for helping the student understand what to do to avoid it in the future? Naturally, it is often up to the teacher marking the work to identify suspected instances of plagiarism and take appropriate action under the university policy. However, as demonstrated in this book, teachers identify plagiarism in varied ways, depending on their own perspectives. Definitions and explanations as to what constitutes plagiarism are as diverse as the individuals engaged in the profession of teaching. However, is plagiarism just a matter for teachers? How transparent are plagiarism management procedures at an institutional level? Have institutions been diligent in providing information and support for their staff about plagiarism procedures and processes?

In some instances, once plagiarism has been detected, the issue then passes from the teacher to the institution, as it is dealt with through managerial processes such as course co-ordinators or committees, rather than between an individual student and the teacher. In other cases, individual teachers seek meetings with students to discuss the issue and the teacher decides whether to pursue the matter through the official university channels or not. Once invoked, it is difficult to halt the formal machinery of academic misconduct. Many teachers in this study were confused about what their precise responsibilities were in reporting suspected cases of plagiarism. Some teachers said that their job started and finished with plagiarism detection. Once detected, it immediately became an official university matter and was taken out of their hands. Others said that before plagiarism could be determined, each teacher had to get to the bottom of the incident. Many of these teachers preferred to call the student into a private meeting with them to discuss the issue, as well as the allegation of plagiarism, before invoking any formal process. At this point, some teachers negotiated an alternative outcome, such as the student repeating the task, providing evidence of drafting the piece and, if satisfactory, awarding a maximum grade of a "pass" only. At other times, teachers failed the piece of work and warned the student not to repeat the offense, suggesting the student seek help with academic writing issues. Outcomes differed depending upon the individual teacher and how each teacher interpreted the plagiarism policy. As can be seen, the issue of responsibility for the post-plagiarism detection process is problematic, unless there are clearly denoted personnel responsible for overseeing and providing assistance in the whole plagiarism management process.

Although it is expected that permanent or tenured members of staff identify plagiarism and adhere to institutional policy and processes, it is not often clear what responsibility lies on external markers or casual/sessional[3] teachers. Standard practice in many higher education institutions is that these teachers are paid per paper graded or per hour of marking with a set number of papers to be marked per hour. If casual teachers are on short-term marking contracts, there is usually nothing in the contract that specifies the casual teacher's responsibility for plagiarism detection and reporting. If the casual teacher is expected to check each paper for plagiarism, does the institution provide specific guidance as to what the expectations will be? Is formal training in plagiarism detection provided for casual staff? If anti-plagiarism software is used, are casual markers given access to the software and supported in learning how to use it? Who is responsible for any follow-up action if plagiarism is alleged by a casual marker? Where this sort of detail is unclear, or worse, not mentioned, then it is appropriate to question how seriously the institution takes the issue of addressing plagiarism in all facets of marking and providing feedback on students' work. In addition, issues of equity and fairness in assessing students' work are raised where some markers may not be as well versed in plagiarism detection and reporting as others. Where plagiarism procedures are not clearly laid out or accessible to staff, particularly new or casual teachers, there is abrogation of responsibility on the university's part to students and staff in plagiarism management.

The Role of Academic Writing Support Staff

One of the issues teachers identify as problematic in dealing with plagiarism is the lack of clarity over their roles and the roles of academic support staff, such as language support specialists and information literacy specialists. Language support staff are often well-versed in linguistics and TESOL/TEFL (Teaching English as a Second or Other Language and Teaching English as a Foreign Language) and are able to assist students struggling with all manner of academic writing woes. Sometimes language support teachers are located in a distinct arm of the university, which specializes in providing academic writing assistance and advice to students. Sometimes language support staff are dedicated faculty specialists and provide language support within one faculty or department. In either case, language support staff commonly have specialist knowledge of the issues that face ESL and EFL students as well as mature-aged students returning to study, often after considerable absence. These teachers can, and do, advise students in ways to approach tertiary study that can help students avoid plagiarism. Often lecturers and tutors will advise particular students to seek specific assistance from language support staff either on academic aspects of plagiarism or more technical aspects of plagiarism and/or academic writing. By academic aspects of plagiarism, I mean academic engagement with the literature and the intellectual work required to weave the literature into the body of the assessment task. The technical aspects of plagiarism are the mechanics of referencing and citing sourced materials as well as general academic writing issues such as structure, approach and style. However, language support teachers are thinly spread across a spectrum of student needs and are often booked out for individual appointments as, with much academic writing support, demand exceeds supply.

In most institutions, librarians are considered to be, among other things, information literacy specialists. They have considerable knowledge and experience in locating and sourcing information. They often deal with copyright issues for unit materials that teachers wish to use in class and have detailed knowledge about referencing and citation. Librarians, sometimes called information literacy specialists, are often happy to assist students with queries about accessing credible sources electronically or referencing queries, but they are not involved in plagiarism cases in their area of expertise—sourcing and appropriately referencing information. In some institutions, the library is given a specific brief to promote and provide information literacy education for all students. This involves providing information literacy services such as referencing workshops for subject-specific disciplines, using and referencing sources from catalogues and online databases and printing free student materials such as "how to" pamphlets and "guides to citation and referencing" in discipline-specific areas. In addition, individual assistance by librarians for students seeking one-on-one assistance in referencing is also provided. However, due to demand, the face-to-face contact is necessarily a limited service.

In response to the student demand for access to academic writing assistance, many institutions make available a series of self-help generic online tutorial programs that students can access. Part of the online series of tutorials covers plagiarism and also broader issues of academic integrity. The argument is that students can access the online help packages at any time and from anywhere in the world, so they are more cost-effective and reach potentially greater numbers of students than is possible through individual face-to-face consultation. Although these tutorials are often useful in a general overarching sense, they cannot provide direct assistance for specific subject-related student queries. In a recent study of university students at an Australian institution, Sylvia Cher (2007) found that ESL and EFL students overwhelmingly valued and needed the direct face-to-face assistance provided through contact with language support professionals. However, in many Australian institutions, budget cuts have forced reductions or amalgamations in academic writing support staff services.

The issue for teachers is that there is uncertainty about the shared responsibility in terms of academic writing support. In other words, teachers do not know who is really responsible for providing additional information and practical help where plagiarism appears to be misunderstood by students. It is not a case of simply allocating blame to individuals or institutions nor is it an issue of trying to shirk professional obligations of duty of care over plagiarism—the reasons are often embedded at the institutional operation level, discussed later in this chapter. Many teachers argue that they are employed by a particular faculty to teach in certain fields in which they are regarded as expert—usually linked to research interests. That is the draw-card for students—staff discipline-specific expertise. They contend that teaching students about referencing conventions and strategies needed in academic writing is not in their portfolio of responsibilities. Many also insist that they are not experts in the area of academic writing skills, but language support staff are skilled professionals in this field and it is they who should be employed to advise students about academic writing matters. Deciding who is responsible for giving students advice and practical help about plagiarism is not the only area presenting ongoing challenges for staff. Reporting plagiarism also appears to be an area of ongoing disquiet.

Reporting Plagiarism

Teachers are apprehensive about the ways in which incidents of plagiarism are reported. A number of teachers believe that the university reporting mechanisms are time consuming, burdensome for teachers and administrators, and place an inappropriate "burden of proof" on the teacher. One teacher, who spoke about preparing documentation for the University Disciplinary Committee, said "I felt like I was the one who was 'guilty' in this process, not the student!." Some teachers, particularly new members of staff, are unsure about the hierarchy of reporting and, due to staff turnover and changes of personnel in roles such as Associate Deans of Teaching, they are not sure who to contact for advice. One instance sums up a number of attitudes to the formal reporting mechanisms. In this case, Kate sought the advice of colleagues about a case of plagiarism because she was sure the student would "get off as he had done in the past." Kate eventually decided that she would not pursue due process, even though she had detected significant portions of unattributed text in the student's work. She explained the incident and also the reasons for her decision:

> I was absolutely shocked that a student could produce work copied directly out of a Supreme Court judgment. He must really think that I'm so stupid I haven't read the judgment. Do students really underestimate their teachers so much? This person is a student that we're sending into the community and we're saying that he's a fit and proper person to work in the Law. And this is a problem, because many of us don't believe he is. We should only be sending students out into the community that we consider to be fit and proper to work ethically and responsibly. Secondly, those of us involved in teaching students, we're actually teaching them about ethical standards. For the disciplinary system to let our students off charges of dishonestly appropriating the work of others is beyond my understanding. These students will deal with trust fund money, they are dealing with clients' property, and they are putting their shingle up and saying "I'm fit to practice." But we *know* that their own personal ethical standards are rock-bottom. And that doesn't get thought about by the Disciplinary Committee. I took the advice of my colleagues not to bother and I was convinced this person beyond a doubt was a cheat. If I'd done all the paperwork and gone through the whole process and gone before the committee if necessary—I would have been absolutely devastated in terms of my personal standards and morals if he was let off, as happened last time with another student. I didn't want to face that as a possible outcome so I didn't pursue it.

Kate's views are supported by Edward Saunders (1993), who argues that educators are "gatekeepers to the profession at admission" and therefore should ensure "scrupulous adherence by students to ethical codes of conduct" in matters such as academic honesty because "an unethical student is likely to be an unethical practitioner" (p.228). Similarly, Nonis and Swift's (2001) case study illustrates that dishonesty in university studies are likely to lead to dishonesty in the workplace. However, Kate did not believe that the Disciplinary Committee would consider the broader ethical consequences of what she believed to be a clear case of plagiarism, so she did not make any formal allegation of plagiarism. In fact, teachers in this study were in uproar when plagiarism allegations made by staff were dismissed by the

Disciplinary Committee. Staff regarded such decisions as professionally insulting and demonstrated a lack of support by the university for its staff. As Georgiou said:

> What the committee fails to realize is that the cases that it sees are only the tip of the iceberg, if that. If they think we take every little instance of plagiarism to them, they're gravely mistaken. We only take the really, really obvious ones—ones that are so blatantly cheating and undeserving of a pass grade that to let people like that through is undermining the integrity of study at tertiary level. When the committee lets these people off, it's little wonder that staff are reluctant to go for the small fry.

Similar sentiments were expressed by Athena, who said she had little faith in the formal university procedures when students are cleared of plagiarism allegations. She said that the "emotional wear and tear" of going through the committee process was not worth her time, particularly if the student gained a lenient penalty. She maintained that the Disciplinary Committee's failure to uphold staff allegations of plagiarism "undermines" their authority in trying to uphold professional standards of ethical behavior. Athena intimated that such decisions by the committee did little to halt plagiarism and, in fact, gave students the confidence to engage in plagiaristic acts with little fear of being penalized if detected. She says:

> You can't just have a strong policy and say if you breach it, maybe we'll whack you with a small penalty. I mean, where's the deterrence in that? It makes you think that it's just words written for university marketing about academic integrity.

The depth of antagonism felt by teachers and administrative officers involved in preparing plagiarism and cheating allegations for Disciplinary Committee hearings should not be underestimated. Teachers expressed frustration and disappointment that students were gaining an impression that plagiarism was not a serious academic offense, as the committee did not adequately punish students. Teachers appear reluctant, on the whole, to utilize the formal processes for the reasons and fears outlined above. In fact, Thivanka was quite emotive when responding to the issue of reporting plagiarism:

> This year was my first year here and I thought I was doing the right thing by reporting eight cases of plagiarism to the committee.

What happened was so unfair. The committee decided the students should be given a chance to resubmit their work and I had to grade all those essays again! How unfair is that? I do the right thing and get punished by getting to regrade a whole new set of essays for my trouble! I won't be doing that again!

Thivanka is not alone. Most staff wanted the committee to vindicate their decisions to report plagiarism officially. These attitudes are supported by previous research findings. As Howard (1999, p.26) says, "Teachers are often hesitant to prosecute plagiarism for fear of themselves becoming victims in the judicial process." Previous research also shows that detecting plagiarism, from a teacher's point of view, is only the beginning. The difficulty is following due process as prescribed by the university. In some cases, institutions have terminated the employment of staff who refuse to withdraw claims of plagiarism.[4] In other situations, teachers say they feel victimized by their peers because there are allegations that students plagiarize only where teaching is of poor quality or instructions given by teachers are ambiguous. Thivanka's feelings of betrayal, which are supported in some of the literature, tend to confirm one of the complexities of dealing with reporting of plagiarism—the level of emotional subjectivity involved in detecting and reporting plagiarism. It is unlikely that such subjectivity can be represented in any university policy. This becomes a serious issue where university policies mandate staff to formally report allegations of plagiarism to the relevant university personnel. The message in all this is clear—conflict occurs where there is dissonance between ways in which individual teachers interpret their roles under policy and what plays out in plagiarism practices. Individual teachers have discussed their approaches to dealing with cases of plagiarism but educational institutions have also responded to the issue of plagiarism management.

Plagiarism—Institutional Responses

The complexity of plagiarism management is an issue that is faced not only by teachers and students but also by universities and institutions of learning. There have been suggestions that institutions respond only when there is a plagiarism scandal or as a reaction to negative press for the quality of learning in higher education institutions (Clegg and Flint, 2006; Sutherland-Smith, 2005a). However, the fact is that universities and institutions involved in provision of educational services must acknowledge and respond to issues of plagiarism. These institutional responses can be grouped into three broad categories and some institutions adopt more than one approach:

- technological response
- procedural response
- holistic response.

Technological Response

Many universities respond to the issue of plagiarism by implementing technological solutions. Many individual teachers, both in this study and in other reported studies, use free software to check "suspect" phrases. Commonly used search engines or meta-search tools spoken about by staff in this study were Google, Alta Vista, Dogpile, HotBot and Mamma. Most teachers appear to be at ease using free software or search engines and many are also comfortable using commercial packages, such as Turnitin (see the discussion in Chapter 5). However, technological responses alone are insufficient. Where universities implement anti-plagiarism software and incorporate technological checking into policy and practice, deterrence can certainly result, as has been shown in prior research (McCabe, 2003; Macdonald and Carroll, 2006; O'Connor, 2002; Park, 2003). The issue of what educative value this serves still remains. By this I mean that although a student may have been deterred from plagiarism knowing that Turnitin is used to check the work for plagiarism, what has the student learned about why plagiarism is unacceptable, or how to avoid plagiarism? This is not to suggest that Turnitin cannot be used for educative purposes—it can certainly be used by students to check their work before submission for grading. However, if the software is not used in a way that can educate students about plagiarism, then the lingering concerns that technology can be used as a punitive measure instead of an educative tool remain.

Procedural Response

Many universities adopt procedural responses to plagiarism and examine their plagiarism management processes and procedures. Usually, various committees or working parties are set up to conduct an investigation into the formal channels of reporting plagiarism or the various measures by which outcomes are handled. Universities pour a great deal of time and money into such processes and often the project is overseen by senior executive management of the institution. Often the result is changes in policy and process. Some universities have made wide-sweeping changes to their policies as a result of such an inquiry.[5] Often, consideration needs to be given to the practical implications of introducing changes, such as an increase in cases being reported to Disciplinary Committees requiring more personnel and committee meeting dates. Other changes include broader options for committee decisions—including recommending additional workshops be undertaken by students and evidence of attendance at specialist writing workshop seminars. Naturally, resources in terms of money and staff must be made available to permit these outcomes to be of use. Other universities make minor amendments to policy and processes but do not appear to consider the ramifications of realizing these changes. For example, if a university decides to broaden the scope of "penalties" for plagiarism, but does not resource them, or fails to consider the consequences of students appealing decisions of the committee, the system can become unworkable. Although universities may allocate large sums of money and dedicate human resources to undertaking procedural reviews, unless the changes are supported by staff then there may be little progress made in reality. The examples of teachers' frustrations with the system, detailed earlier in this chapter, illustrate that no change will be implemented at teacher/student levels where staff do not consider processes effective or founded on a values-based teaching and learning relationship. As Clegg and Flint advocate, "While rule-based procedures and practices may act as a guide, a fundamentally virtues-based approach is required if we are to make good judgements in this area that will ultimately benefit us and our students" (2006, p.385). It is important, therefore, for universities and institutions to be clear that where Honor Codes, detailed plagiarism policies or other procedural approaches are taken the support of staff is crucial to successful implementation. Procedures must also be set in a culture of integrity that is overtly stated, modeled by staff and transparent to students, if it is to be successfully integrated into the learning and teaching environment. Otherwise, individual teachers will continue to operate outside official processes in a sort of underground culture of plagiarism management that can only mean inconsistent, individual handling of plagiarism, which is insupportable and inequitable for all parties.

Holistic Approach

Under a holistic approach, institutions examine their current definitions, processes and procedures in order to revisit the way in which the institution as a whole deals with plagiarism. Institutional recognition that plagiarism is a complex phenomenon and solutions need to be long-ranging and match the complexity of the issue is vital for change.

What a "holistic" model does is to share the responsibility for academic integrity between staff, students and the university or college. However, due process does not favor punishment above all else. The whole institution is involved as faculties and departments can no longer "do their own thing" and interpret university policy to suit their own departmental preferences. The university takes (and funds) procedures to ensure parity of response across departments and faculties to student issues of plagiarism. Such extensive scrutiny of fundamental practices means that a critical examination of broader questions relating to tertiary study must be the first step. Questions such as:

- Does the university itself profess and promote academic integrity as a major value of the university? If so, in what ways is that demonstrated and evidenced in provision of services to staff and students?
- What is the rhetoric and what is the reality of academic integrity in the university or college? The university Mission or Vision statements may claim integrity, excellence and international understandings in provision of learning opportunities, but what is the reality for students?
- What processes are actually funded to ensure that students have sufficient skills to undertake their tertiary studies? Are there sufficient language support and information literacy staff who are adequately qualified and experienced to meet the student demand?
- What professional development workshops exist for staff who wish to find out more about altering assessment tasks to reduce the likelihood of plagiarism?
- What assumptions are teachers making about the skill levels of their postgraduate students? Are these assumptions based on skills they assume English as first language undergraduates have mastered? If their assumptions are incorrect, what assistance can teachers call upon to help postgraduate students meet the demands of academic writing in universities?
- What support (if any) is available to staff who may have large numbers of students in their subjects without requisite undergraduate skills in writing at postgraduate level?
- What advice/mentoring is available for new staff who may not be experienced in dealing with plagiarism allegations?

These questions form the cornerstone of inquiry from which change is driven, as there is no point in undertaking complete review of plagiarism on an institutional basis unless such fundamental questions propel the examination. Universities in the United Kingdom have undergone intense review because in the late 1990s, government and external auditors, through the UK Quality Assurance Agency (QAA), developed a code of practice for the "Assurance of Academic Quality and Standards in Higher Education." This code of practice, which was issued in May 2000, mandated that institutions effectively deal with students breaching academic assessment regulations. It also required universities to examine how students were provided with information and guidance on their responsibilities in the academic integrity relationship. Specifically, the QAA required that definitions of plagiarism and forms of academic misconduct in assessment be clear and auditable.[6] The government set up the Joint Information Systems Committee (JISC) and currently funds the Plagiarism Advisory Service Board (PAS), which has responsibility to oversee quality assurance of issues of academic integrity for all higher education providers in the United Kingdom. What this means is that the government in the United Kingdom has taken a firm interest in ensuring that individual institutions address the quality and accountability of their academic integrity measures. Some universities have taken this opportunity to completely revise their approaches to plagiarism and cheating, adopting a holistic view.[7]

Oxford Brookes University, United Kingdom has adopted a process of collegial review by specialist academics called Academic Conduct Officers (ACOs). The impetus for this decision was the concern the Academic Registrar felt at the inconsistency of individual staff members making decisions about plagiarism management. ACOs, usually senior academics, are appointed in each faculty to manage plagiarism in their faculties. They report to the Dean of Teaching and Learning in each faculty, who has the portfolio for quality assurance in such matters for the faculty. The system works in the following way: individual academics still mark student work, but if they suspect plagiarism, the case is passed to the ACO to handle. It is the ACO's task to determine whether plagiarism is demonstrated or not—and this can be done in consultation with the academic or not. If the ACO decides plagiarism is detected, there is a limited range of actions each ACO can take.[8] One of the advantages of this system is that as ACOs handle all cases, there is a degree of consistency across the university in handling cases. ACOs from all different faculties and departments meet regularly to discuss their work, and also a central database of ACO action is kept to ensure that students are monitored as to their progress. Having the database as a central university system, rather than a faculty or department-based system, means that students who are enrolled in double degrees, such as Arts/Law, are able to be monitored cross-faculty. Oxford Brookes University argues that this system ensures consistency and fairness of outcomes for students and also support for staff, particularly ACOs, through regular exchanges of ideas and discussion of issues. As there is no "Disciplinary Committee" in this model, staff do not feel that they have been undermined in the process of plagiarism management.

Similar approaches to university-wide examination of plagiarism and cheating was carried out by the University of Newcastle in Australia. This university overhauled its approach to plagiarism and academic misconduct processes and procedures following intense, negative media scrutiny of serious allegations of plagiarism and corruption by a member of academic staff. The university commissioned an independent external inquiry that was conducted by the St James Ethics Centre in Sydney. The Commissioner, a Supreme Court judge, spearheaded the investigation into the university's practices and recommended 33 specific actions be undertaken by the University of Newcastle to review and revise in its management of plagiarism and issues of academic integrity.[9] Many of the support mechanisms for students, discussed earlier in this chapter, have been introduced into the culture of the university. The Ethics Centre adopted clear measures to oversee implementation of change by the university and this process is continuing. Initial feedback from staff and students indicates that the processes are much more transparent and easier to implement than previous procedures and policies, although it is too early to tell if there is any major reduction in plagiarism.

Teachers' Strategies to Reduce Plagiarism

A great deal of success in the classroom in overcoming issues of plagiarism has been the result of careful examination of the aims and purposes of assessment tasks. Assessment tasks should neither enable nor reward plagiarism by students. Overall, where the focus is on formative rather than summative assessment tasks, students do not fear failing the "ultimate test" and appear less inclined to resort to unethical means to achieve pass grades (Carroll, 2002; Carroll and Ryan, 2005; Hunt, 2002; Knight, 2001; Macdonald and Carroll, 2006; Park, 2003, 2004). Teachers in this study and in previous research have made some suggestions about how they reduce plagiarism in the tertiary classroom. They are:

- Regularly changing both form and type of assessment task (e.g. changing from essays to portfolio or performance tasks).
- Designing tasks that require students to draw on their own experiences—whether in laboratories, on placements or in the field—can also enable students to relate theory to their own practical experiences and reduce the risk of plagiarism or cheating.
- Exercising a variety of smaller assessment tasks that build skill levels. For example, setting a review task where students critically read two different journal articles on a topic and compare key points that are then shared in a class seminar. This sort of task enables the teacher to see whether students are grasping key ideas and are able to articulate (or rearticulate them) in their own words.
- Ensuring the teacher's own values of engagement with ethical practices are openly discussed and modeled (do you cite all references in your PowerPoint lecture, tutorial slides, or handouts?).

,sing the use of technology for detection of plagiarism and
students what you are prepared to do if you suspect plagiarism.
ar about your processes and procedures and discuss why you
)rt them.
1ssing plagiarism with the students and asking them what they
< it means or how they go about avoiding it. Some teachers start
. semester with a recent journal article and work through it with
lents. They observe and discuss how the students decide which
)rmation is important and which is not, as well as articulating
as in discussion and on paper. Naturally, citing and referencing
: a focus of discussion.
.suring students understand that they need to adopt a critical stance
1en using Web information and discuss criteria for evaluating Web
:sources.

ldition to these ideas, teachers should also examine their practices
t of the plagiarism continuum, as some teaching approaches may
te copying cultures. Are teachers adopting transmissive approaches
:hing that foster expectations of teachers talking (the font-of-all-
.edge model) and students listening and copying down what is said
;mitting information)? If this is the teaching approach modeled, is it
vonder that students approach learning with expectations that their
is to regurgitate information uncritically in an effort to provide the
1t" answer? Transmissive teaching practices are alive and well in our
.er education institutions. If teachers and universities are serious
ut promoting a culture of intellectual evolution in classrooms, then
1sformative teaching practices are an essential part of that growth.
.nsformative teachers uphold principles of a democratic teaching and
.rning relationship, where teachers guide and facilitate students' journeys
rough the subject-specific discipline. The focus is on students con-
ructing their own understandings and meanings from the literature and
rawing on their own experiences to make broader connections outside
1e classroom. Teacher-talk is limited and student engagement with ideas,
:ach other and the literature is high in transformative teaching spaces.
Open-ended inquiry and curiosity to share and develop deeper and wider
understandings drive the curriculum and also the classroom ethos.

Summary

This chapter highlights the complexity of plagiarism in its many layers.
Plagiarism is often intertwined with emotional responses from students and
staff linked to individual notions of ethical practices. The chapter details

ongoing issues for staff in terms of readiness of students for tertiary study, and their roles and responsibilities in detecting and reporting plagiarism. Some solutions are also offered both from the perspective of teachers and also institutional approaches to dealing with plagiarism. Finally, the plagiarism continuum is offered as a means by which teachers and institutions can reflect on teaching and learning practices modeled in higher education. Such practices can foster plagiarism or actively discourage it through the very implementation of challenging the status quo within teaching and learning relationships.

Epilogue

In the Board Room, the six teachers, the policy-maker and myself ponder the issues raised in these pages by teachers, students, policy-makers and university management. Although we all agree that plagiarism will be ever-present, as will cheating and other forms of academic misconduct, we know we can move forward to promote ideals of academic integrity and intellectual quality. We acknowledge that we probably cannot effect change in students who are determined to subvert the system for their own pragmatic reasons. What we can do, however, is to deter students from plagiarizing by weaving a tapestry of approaches that are bound in threads of academic integrity. At this point, the plagiarism continuum model I have devised is described, based on the results of this and other studies I have done over many years on plagiarism (see the model in Chapter 1).

The plagiarism continuum model is designed to spark discussion and reflection about perceptions of plagiarism and also related teaching approaches. The model is grounded in theory—critical legal theory, cross-cultural studies theory and literary theory. The range of teachers' and students' perceptions of plagiarism are represented along the axis of "intention." The axis is stretched between alternative theoretical stances. At the far left are legal notions of authorship which inform many plagiarism policies and at the far right are the literary theorists' challenges to such ideas. It is important that theories from different disciplinary areas inform the discussion, because, as we have seen, plagiarism is a complex and changing phenomenon that cannot be understood through just one theoretical lens. It is essential to grasp the idea that these theories permeate our understandings as well as our responses to plagiarism. Legal theory provides us with the known concept of authorship, ownership of text and authorial rights. The "Romantic" notion of authorship, where an author is an individual who creates an original work over which she exerts control, is embodied in plagiarism policies around the world. Most policies are saturated with the language of the law—offenses, misconduct, misdemeanor, penalties, sanctions, theft, misappropriation and stealing. It is imperative that teachers, students and policy-makers understand that it is no accident that intention is an integral part of so many plagiarism policies: it is an integral part of criminal law and the pivotal point around which penalties are decided. To illustrate this, I draw on Georgiou, Greg and Sanji's original comments that students must intend to plagiarize because the policy is clear. If this were accepted, then all cases of plagiarism would be regarded as intentional actions by students to gain an unfair advantage over their peers by misappropriating the work of another. The penalties prescribed in the policy would then be applied by the Disciplinary Committee. It is clear from both the wording in the policy and the ways in which at least three people in the Board Room interpreted the policy, that legal notions of plagiarism form one end of the spectrum of understanding plagiarism.

At the opposite end of the spectrum of understanding plagiarism are groups of literary theorists. They argue that looking at concepts of authorship is inappropriate (particularly in the age of the Internet) and that looking at the concept of "textuality" makes more sense. By this they mean that they consider texts are alive with meaning and are socially constructed by readers and writers. In short, students make sense of texts only when they understand them in context and when they have inhabited the discourse of the fields in which they study. In terms of plagiarism, literary theorists argue that readers determine meaning more than the writers, so that teachers need to reflect on their own responses to plagiarism before any steps are taken. When the experiences of teachers and theorists working in cross-cultural studies are added, a richer and more diverse set of understandings emerges about students' writing practices. We need to explore the diversity of expectations about learning and knowledge that our students bring to our institutions. We also need to appreciate that with such mixed perceptions of what is entailed in academic writing, as CheeLing points out, many students do not intend to deceive anyone. They are just struggling because of poor skills in academic writing, limited vocabulary, large workloads, limited (or no) understanding of the mechanics of referencing and a general lack of awareness of our expectations in academic writing. To punish these students by adopting a legal stance of "all plagiarism is intentional" and penalize them is inappropriate and miseducative. However, the axis of intention alone is not enough. Although teachers need to reflect on their own experiences and responses to plagiarism in relation to the axis of intention to see where, if anywhere, they stand, the issue of plagiarism is multi-layered and requires deeper excavation into other issues.

One of the issues is the increasing use of the Internet and Internet technologies in our teaching and learning spaces. The Internet is placed as a dotted, non-boundaried line around the model (Figure 1.1). This shows that the Internet will continue to provide new challenges and opportunities to expand learning as well as new forms of plagiarism in the next decades. Currently, the law is trying to regulate the Internet as though it were a tangible entity by applying traditional concepts of property rights to Web texts and Web spaces. The law always seems to play "catch-up" with the World Wide Web, as technologies present unlimited opportunities to inhabit uncharted places that the law cannot foresee, and therefore cannot regulate. The most obvious gauntlet the Internet throws down to us, as teachers and policy-makers, is to scrutinize our concepts of "authorship" and "text" in hyperspace. How do we view our concepts of authorship, ownership and plagiarism where unstable, evolving, non-linear and non-hierarchical texts exist? As clearly indicated by students and staff in this study, the Internet is a widely used resource for tertiary study. We must not be complacent in deeming that our print-based values will apply to Web texts. The Internet remains a fluid borderless feature of the model and it also encompasses ways in which teachers approach teaching and students approach learning in tertiary classrooms.

At this point, it is important to stress that the model I have devised represents the real-world experiences of teachers and students with respect to plagiarism. It reflects living policies representing international trends in the formulation of plagiarism, and current research and thinking around the world about plagiarism. The shading in the model (from darker gray on the far left to lighter gray on the far right) represents the reactions by teachers and students to issues of plagiarism as described in Chapters 6 and 7. In examining teaching approaches that were evident in this study, as well as reported research, case studies and analysis of teaching practices from Australia, Europe, the United Kingdom and United States, Henry Giroux's (1988, 1993, 1996) notions of teachers as transformative intellectuals, in combination with Stephen Sterling's (2001) concepts of sustainable education for the future, are significant. Two separate approaches to teaching are framed: transmissive and transformative teaching. *Transmissive* teaching is often used in content-driven, information-heavy sessions where teachers talk and students listen and write. A feature of this approach is that students copy down the teacher's words, notes, diagrams and whatever else is offered in the classroom. Little interaction is evident in terms of two-way discussion of ideas or key themes either with the teacher or between students. The question must be asked, where is the intellectual engagement for students? Is it surprising when modeling this kind of teaching that students' corresponding concepts of learning are based on copying rather than questioning texts? *Transformative* teaching offers an alternative approach. Transformative teaching is often observed where students are actively participating and leading learning sessions. Teachers adopting this approach have usually set the scene by outlining the necessity for students to make their own meanings from texts and discussion in the course. Intellectual engagement, active critique and sharing of understandings are stressed as the essence of these classrooms. Often, teachers operate as part of the group rather than a central focus for the class. Teachers' primary interest in transformative classrooms is to facilitate experiences of educative value. Here, students are stimulated to explore their own practices and experiences in class readings and discussions in a spirit of critical reflection. Interaction between peers is a key component of these sessions with questioning and critiquing of ideas forming the foundation of learning. Transformative teaching can operate in face-to-face classrooms as well as those taken by distance education or online. The point is that a balanced view of plagiarism cannot divorce the learning experiences that students have in our classrooms from their perceptions of academic rigor. The plagiarism continuum model is, by its very nature, a model steeped in the notion that concepts change. Our work lies in recognizing the need to reshape and rethink policies and practices to promote our goals of critical engagement with learning. The task is enormous, but so are our intellectual resources. Teachers and policy-makers have a crucial role to play in advancing values of academic integrity in our classrooms and educational institutions.

Notes

Prologue

1   Button, James (2006). Da Vinci author faces accusers who want his holy blood. *The Age.* Wednesday, March 1, 2006, p.13.
2   A term used by Colin Lankshear and Ilana Snyder in their book *Teachers and Technoliteracy: Managing literacy, technology and learning in schools* (2000). Allen & Unwin: St Leonards, NSW.
3   I am indebted to Diane Pecorari from Mälardalen University, Västerås, Sweden for sharing with me the insights on six elements from her doctoral thesis of 2002.
4   The term "patchwriting" was explained by Rebecca Moore Howard as "copying from a source text and then deleting some words, altering grammatical structures or plugging in one-for-one synonym-substitutes" (1995, p.788). The term has been widely adopted in subsequent publications around the globe to describe the ways in which copying forms an approach to learning—see Angelil-Carter, 2000; Buranen and Roy, 1999; Carroll, 2002; Cher, 2007; Hafernik *et al.*, 2003; Harris, 2001; Myers, 1998; Pecorari, 2002; Price, 2002; Ryan, 1998; Sutherland-Smith, 2003, 2005a, 2005b as some examples.

1 The Plagiarism Continuum

1   Sue Clegg and Abbi Flint talk about the way in which the debate about plagiarism has taken on the flavour of "moral panic"—particularly in press articles that fuel public and academic dismay. They advocate that rule-based approaches (such as definitive policies and penalties) may provide boundaries, but only a virtues-based approach (which they detail in the article) will benefit all involved in the teaching and learning relationship.
2   Augustus Kolich has been an Associate Professor in the Department of English and Foreign Languages at Saint Xavier University, Chicago, Illinois for over 20 years. His specialist areas of teaching and research are nineteenth- and twentieth-century American literature, literary theory and business communication.
3   Teachers advocating the necessity of examining the role of teacher-readers include: Ellen McCracken (1991), Rebecca Moore Howard (1995, 1999, 2007) in the USA; Galloway and

Sevier (2003) and Russell Hunt (2004) in Canada; Kate Cadman (2005), Cadman and Cargill (2004), Penny McKay (2001), Alastair Pennycook (1996) in Australia; Diane Belcher and George Braine (2005) in Hong Kong; Diane Pecorari (2002) in Sweden; Jude Carroll (2002), Ranald Macdonald and Jude Carroll (2006) in the UK.

4 Prynne (1633) K.B.764. The Star Chamber Court was originally created in 1487 to hear appeals for redress of wrongs. In the reign of King Charles I, it became a tool to suppress opposition to royal policies. Sessions were held in secret and its decisions were often more politically than judicially motivated. The court was abolished in 1641.

5 The Star Chamber judges in Prynne's case said: "Itt is said, hee had noe ill intencion, noe ill harte, but hee maye bee ill interpreted. That must not be allowed him in excuse, for hee should not have written any thinge that would bear [that] construccion, for hee doth not accompanye his booke, to make his intencion knowne to all that reades it." (Prynne, 1633 K.B.765)

6 For example, see the University of West Virginia's plagiarism policy.

7 Joyce Carroll, 1982, pp.92–93.

8 For examples of teachers who regard plagiarism as cheating see: Deckert, 1993a, 1993b; Drum, 1986; Kolich, 1983; Laird, 2001; Loveless, 1994; Mallon, 1989; Mirsky, 2002; Sherman, 1992.

9 Glenn Deckert retired from the University of Michigan in 2004 and is currently the Senior English Language Fellow in Azerbaijan at the Azerbaijan Teachers Association. At the time of writing this piece on plagiarism, he was working in Hong Kong.

10 Jude Carroll is Deputy Director, ASKe at Oxford Brookes University, Oxford, UK. She conducts research, writes and lectures widely on matters of plagiarism and is a consultant to an FDTL5 project at Lancaster University and for the JISC-funded Plagiarism Advisory Service.

11 Danielle De Voss is an Associate Professor and Director of Professional Writing at the State University of Michigan, USA. Annette Rosati is teaching at the Clarion University of Pennsylvania, USA.

12 Notions of the transformative ways in which teachers can approach their work are drawn from: Giroux, H. (1993) Teaching and the role of the transformative intellectual. In S. Aronowitz and H. Giroux (eds) *Education Still Under Siege* (pp.33–54). Westport, CT: Bergin and Garvey; Giroux, H. (1996) *Counternarratives: cultural studies and critical pedagogies in postmodern spaces*. New York: Routledge.

The ideas that we need to think about ways in which we can have "sustainable" education— education that inspires and really engages with concepts of learning are drawn from Sterling, S. (2001) *Sustainable education: re-visioning learning and change*. Totnes: Green Books for The Schumacher Society.

13 For a lengthy discussion of "cyber-pseudepigraphy" see: Page, J. (2004) Cyber-pseudepigraphy: A new challenge for higher education policy and management. *Journal of Higher Education Policy and Management* 26(3): 429–433.

14 See Peter Jaszi, Andrea Lunsford, Lisa Ede and Martha Woodmansee's works, cited in this book.

2 The Birth of Plagiarism

1 The masculine form is used as, at the time, only males were legally recognised as authors.

2 Elizabeth Eisenstein is Professor of History at Michigan University and consultant to the Library of Congress in the USA. She has written extensively about the history of early printing and its role as an agent of cultural change in the Middle Ages. She has also written about print and digital culture.

3 John Feather is Professor of Library and Information Studies at the University of Loughborough, UK. He has written many works in the field of publishing and the information society.

4 Marlon B. Ross is a Professor in the Department of English and Carter G. Woodson Institute for African-American and African Studies at the University of Virginia, USA.

5 Peter Jaszi is Professor of Law in the Washington College of Law at the American University, Washington DC, USA.

6 Mark Rose is Professor of English at the University of California, Santa Barbara, USA. His book titled *Authors and Owners: The invention of copyright*, published in 1993, provides an

extensive explanation of the connections between economic considerations, individualism and the emergence of copyright law from eighteenth-century England.

7   *Burnet* v. *Chetwood* 35 E.R. 1008 [King's Bench 1720].
8   *Pope* v. *Curll* 26 E.R. 608 [King's Bench 1741].
9   John Feather, 1994, p.208.
10 *Millar* v. *Taylor* 98 E.R. 201 [Chancery 1769].
11 Justice Aston, *Millar* v. *Taylor*, 1769, 98 E.R. 201 [Chancery 1769:224, 225].
12 For further details of the ways in which the French *droit moralé* worked, see the works of Françon, 1999; Gendreau, 1999; Passa, 1999.
13 *Fersing* v. *Buffet* Cour d'Appel, Paris, D. 570 [1962].
14 (Cour d'Appel, 1962, Paris, D. 570.)
15 In Mark Rose, 1993, p.131.
16 I wish to acknowledge the legal expertise of Mr John Blasko, Attorney-at-Law for Fox, Rothschild, O'Brien and Frankel, New Jersey, USA, for his patience and expertise in discussing US copyright law provisions with me.
17 Copyright Act (1968) C'th, s.40 (1).
18 Copyright Amendment (Moral Rights) Act (2000) C'th.
19 McLuhan, M. (1969) *The medium is the message*. Harmondsworth: Penguin, contains a detailed account of his concept of the world as a "global village"—connected via technology.
20 The Agreement on Trade-Related Aspects of Intellectual Property Rights (TRIPs) set out in Annex 1C to the Marrakech Agreement establishing the WTO, in Marrakech on April 15, 1994.
21 *Computer Edge Pty Ltd* v. *Apple Computer Inc* [1986] 6 IPR 1.
22 Computer Programs Act (1999) C'th and Copyright Amendment (Digital Agenda) Act (2000) C'th.
23 Copyright Act (1976) US.
24 For example, the Copyright Amendment (Moral Rights) Act 2000, Australia.

3 The Six Elements of Plagiarism

1   Article L121–1 of the French Intellectual Property Code. MISE A JOUR LEGIFRANCE 15/09/03.
2   In Schedule 1, Part IX, Copyright Amendment (Moral Rights) Act 2000, Australia.
3   As defined under ss.193 and 194 of the Australian Copyright Amendment (Moral Rights) Act 2000.
4   Australia's Crimes Act (1958) s.63; Canada's Criminal Code (R.S., 1985, c. C-46) and New Zealand's Crimes Act (1961) ss.217–305 outline criminal offenses against property such as kidnapping, theft and misappropriation; The United States Copyright Code ss.501–513 stipulates the "criminal offenses" under copyright.
5   Independent Commission Against Corruption (ICAC) 2005. Report on investigation into the University of Newcastle's handling of plagiarism allegations. ICAC: Sydney.
6   Independent Commission Against Corruption (ICAC) 2005. This is an independent government report conducted by Justice Hall of the New South Wales Supreme Court, investigating the University of Newcastle's handling of plagiarism allegations. ICAC: Sydney, p.4.
7   This information was correct at the time of writing, but national prevention schemes in China may have been set up since this work was published.
8   South-Coast University is a large university in Melbourne, Australia. It has a student population in excess of 32,000 students over five campuses in rural and metropolitan areas in Australia, as well as campuses and partner institutions in Singapore, Malaysia, India and Hong Kong. It has five major faculties: Medicine, Nursing and Health Sciences; Education; Business and Law; Science and Technology; and Arts/Humanities. There are specialist small faculties also, such as Marine Biology and Koorie (indigenous) studies.

4 Plagiarism—A Global Issue

1   Capitalization of "Author" exists in the original text.
2   For an interesting construction of textual consumption by students in cases of plagiarism, see Saltmarsh (2004).

3   See the work of Jay Bolter (1991), Richard Lanham (1994) and Annette Patterson (1995) for
      more detailed explanation of this.
4   See Howard (2007); Hutcheon (1986); Selden *et al.* (1977); Sullivan and Porter (1997) as
      well as Bahktin (1986) and Barthes (1977).
5   Professor James Porter is Professor of Writing, Rhetoric and American Culture at Michigan
      State University, USA. Professor Patricia Sullivan is Professor of the Department of English
      at Purdue University, USA.
6   The following studies used surveys to ascertain students' attitudes or responses to plagiarism.
      Surveys ascertained students' understandings of plagiarism as a definition or to find out
      what their attitudes to plagiarism and cheating were. Some studies asked students to note
      whether they engaged in "cheating" behaviors or not. Doris Dant (1986) in the USA; Glenn
      Deckert (1993a, 1993b) in Hong Kong; Barry Kroll (1988) in the USA; Christopher Hawley
      (1984) in the UK; Carolyn Matalene (1985) in China; Jane Sherman (1992) in Italy.
7   Margaret Kantz (1990) in the USA; Rebecca Moore Howard (1995, 1999) in the USA; Brian
      Martin (1994) in Australia.
8   For empirical studies on Internet plagiarism see O'Connor (2002), Sutherland-Smith (2005b),
      Zobel and Hamilton (2002) in Australia; Culwin (2006), Evans (2006), Szabo and Underwood
      (2004) in the UK; Marshall and Garry (2005) in New Zealand; and McCabe (2003, 2004) in
      the USA.
9   See the works of Carroll (2002), Park (2003), Ryan (2000), Sutherland-Smith (2005a) and
      Howard (1999) who talk about the issue of assumptions of skills for students entering
      university.
10   See Ashworth *et al.* (2003), Clegg and Flint (2006) in the UK; Briggs (2003), Godfrey and
      Waugh (2002), Zobel and Hamilton (2002) in Australia; and Vojak (2006) in the USA for a
      discussion of "moral" concepts of plagiarism and differentiation between plagiarism and
      cheating.
11   Coffin (2001); Crystal (2001); Graddol (2001); Haywood (1995); Jones (2000); Kachru and
      Nelson (2001); Modiano (2001); Murray (2001); Nunan (2003); Pennycook (1994, 2001);
      Phillipson (1992); Phillipson and Skutnabb-Kangas (1996); Stromquist and Monkman
      (2000); Waters (2001); Widdowson (1994).
12   See the works of Canagarajah (1999, 2001); Kachru (2001); Phillipson (2003); Said (1978);
      Thumboo (2003) for a discussion of post-colonial writers' claims of the cultural monopoly
      of international relations through the domination of English as the international language
      of trade and business.
13   Edward Said's (1978) groundbreaking work *Orientalism* provides an important critical
      backdrop to the way in which the English language has gained a form of cultural monopoly
      in today's globalized world. He describes the ways in which the Orient has been perceived
      as "the Other" against the Western "Occident," which is assumed as the normative "self."
      He draws upon Foucault's (1972) work in discourse theory to claim that while often
      "literature and culture are presumed to be politically, even historically innocent, the historical
      and cultural relations between east and west have been characterized by cultural domination"
      (1978, p.27).
14   Similar sentiments are found in Chanock's (2004) work.
15   See the following studies: Angelil-Carter (2000), South Africa; Buranen and Roy (1999),
      Howard (1995, 1999, 2000, 2002), Lunsford and Ede (1994), USA; Flowerdew (2000),
      Larkham and Manns (2002), Pecorari (2002), the UK; Galloway and Sevier (2003), Canada;
      Pennycook (1996), Hong Kong; Marsden (2001), O'Connor (2002), Sutherland-Smith
      (2003), Australia.
16   Roz Ivanič (1998) talks about individuals taking on an identity in relation to the communities
      they come into contact with. The construction of identity is in relation to the values and
      practices of the discourse community they seek to enter. Janette Ryan (2000) argues that
      students need time to enter the discourse community so that their own senses of identity are
      not shattered in the process. She argues that the social and cultural origins of plagiarism
      need to be part of that discussion. Ron Scollon (1995) argues that plagiarism is one of the
      gate-keeping forces that prevent students entering academic discourse communities. He
      argues that these barriers are imposed because the basis on which they are built is that there
      is common ideological ground and takes no account of the fact that plagiarism is historically
      and culturally constructed.

17   Sylvia Cher's (2007) study also considered the links between plagiarism and voice and supported the idea that assessment can be "creatively" designed to reduce plagiarism.

18   The phrase "in its appearing" is used by Peter Ashworth, Madeleine Freewood and Ranald Macdonald in their 2003 article "The student lifeworld and the meanings of plagiarism." They use it as a phenomenological question as part of phenomenological methodology from psychology, so that the focus of the study is restricted to "the elucidation of what the student means plagiarism to be in the context of their lived and felt experience, without imposing external conceptual framework (e.g. a moral one) on the results" (p.263). The phrase is also used by Sue Clegg and Abbi Flint (2006), who adopt Ashworth *et al.*'s phenomenological stance.

5 Plagiarism and the Internet

1   "Foreign Students in Plagiarism Scandal" *Sydney Morning Herald* newspaper. Wednesday, August 22, 2007 details a plagiarism scandal at the University of New England, in New South Wales, where full fee-paying international students were alleged to have cheated by plagiarizing in their postgraduate theses. "Dirty marks" by Geoff Maslen (2003) alleges that "cheats do prosper—as thousands of school and university students know. Plagiarism on campus is rampant and the internet has made it that much easier" p.18. The article details how plagiarism and cheating are "endemic problems" (p.21) and claims that cheating notes written on the arms of students in exams "have been overtaken by plagiarizing via the Internet" (p.19). Similar headlines exist in other countries—see Clegg and Flint (2006) detailing the "moral panic" arising from such publicity in the UK, Russell Hunt's (2004) article about Canadian media portrayal of the Internet as a "moral sinkhole" and Rebecca Moore Howard's article "Internet plagiarism" (2007), which quotes similar headlines in the USA.

2   My study was conducted at South-Coast University (pseudonym) between 2004 and 2005. Specific information on Turnitin was gathered in late 2005. Details of the site and methodology is in Chapter 7.

3   Teachers are concerned that students rely on Internet information as "truth." They are concerned at the lack of critical evaluation of Web-based sources. Also see Bolter, 1991; Burbules, 1997, 2004; Kress, 1997, 2003; Sutherland-Smith, 2002.

4   There is an open philosophy for most wikis that allows anyone to post and edit content. Wiki sites admit that there can be no assurance that people who enter sites to "edit" content are necessarily well-intentioned. The claim is that many editors of wiki sites tend to have good intentions, although on larger wiki sites, such as those run by the *Wikimedia Foundation*, vandalism can go unnoticed for a period of time.

5   The research project had ethics clearance from the university, and teachers used student work after the close of semester so that it was not used on "live work" nor did the use of the software impact upon students' marks for the previous semester.

6   From the Greek words *pseudes* (false) and *epigraphe* (inscription). Page says that the term comes from Middle Eastern practices of writers ascribing a false name as the author of a particular work, usually to give a piece of writing greater authority or credibility.

7   Masterpapers.com: www.masterpapers.com/promise.php. Retrieved September 17, 2007.

8   www.essayfraud.org/forum/Masterpaperscom-Fraudulant-Cancel-Orders-Madeand33-t379. html. Retrieved September 17, 2007.

9   An overall relationship of no statistical significance was observed, $\chi^2_{(1)} = 0.765$, $p \geq 0.05$.

10   The overall trend showed that of the 186 students, 68 percent (n=127) of students cited at least 75 percent of the information they used from the Internet (categories: all, nearly all, and most). The remaining 32 percent (n=59) of students cited 60 percent or less of the Internet information they gathered (categories: some, half, under half, one third). An overall relationship of statistical significance was observed, $\chi^2_{(4)} = 0.00$, $p \leq 0.001$. The findings indicated that students who could not define plagiarism were less likely to cite Internet sources than students who could define plagiarism and cited Internet sources.

11   A Chi-square test indicated an overall relationship of statistical significance was observed, $\chi^2_{(1)} = 0.020$, $p \leq 0.05$.

12   See works by Bolter, 1991, 1998; Burbules and Bertram, 1995; Kress, 1997, 2003; Landow, 1993; Lunsford and Ede, 1994; Patterson, 2000; Scollon, 1995; Selfe and Hilligoss, 1994; Snyder, 1996, 1997.

6 Teachers' Perceptions of Plagiarism

1   At South-Coast University, like many universities in Australia, the English language proficiency requirements are set by individual faculties, using both the International English Language Testing System (IELTS) from Cambridge University and the Test of English as a Foreign Language (TOEFL) system. Typically, faculties will require either a minimum of 6.5 in IELTS, with no band less than 6.0 or a score of 550 in TOEFL and a TWE score of 3.5+.

2   See Joel Bloch's work in describing various approaches to citation by Chinese students where he states "Chinese rhetoric does not place the same taboo on plagiarism that Western rhetoric does" (Bloch and Chi, 1995, p.238). In addition, Bloch has also written about the uncritical way in which many ESL students use Internet information (2001). He suggests that teachers need to be aware of poor Internet reading strategies in terms of deciphering credible sources when considering allegations of plagiarism.

7 Students' Perceptions of Plagiarism

1   In order to make sense of the questionnaires, I coded them using a standard software package—SPSS. A Chi-square (χ^2) test was used to determine whether response rates differed. The Chi-square formulation means:

Chi-square	degree of freedom	equals	Asymp. Sig. (2 sided)	degree of statistical significance	is less than or equal to	0.05—the point of statistical significance
χ^2	(df)	=	0.000	p	≤	0.05

A representation of the overall relationship between two variables, such as "gender" and "student ability to define plagiarism" for example, where there is no statistical significance, would be calculated as follows: $\chi^2_{(40)} = 0.367$, $p \geq 0.05$. The Pearson's statistic is not statistically significant, which would also appear in the graph.

2   See Carroll, 2002; Carroll and Ryan, 2005; Cher, 2007; Howard, 1995, 1999; Ryan, 2000 for illustrations where students comment about confusion between collaboration and collusion.

3   For studies in which students admit to engaging in cheating approaches to study see Marsden, 2001; McCabe, 2004; Nonis and Swift, 2001.

4   An overall relationship between the variables was observed, $\chi^2_{(1)} = 0.056$, $p \geq 0.05$.

8 Plagiarism—Ongoing Issues

1   Jude Carroll in a personal communication on April 8, 2007 in Adelaide. She spoke about the turmoil teachers in the UK and Europe felt in balancing the roles of professionalism and ensuring academic integrity in their roles as academics, with increasing demands placed on them by institutions to become "plagiarism police" and make detection of plagiarism one of their highest priorities.

2   Brimble and Stevenson-Clarke's (2005) study revealed that students' real reasons for plagiarism (as distinct from the reasons they told their teachers) seem to be connected to either time-management problems, problems understanding the assignment task or just gambling that the teachers will not find out.

3   In Australia, casual teachers are called "sessional" staff and are employed by universities and colleges to teach classes and mark students' work for short-term contract periods. They are paid per hour at a rate dependent upon qualifications and experience. Some "sessional" staff have been teaching at the same institutions on a casual, short-term contract basis for many years but they have no recourse to tenure.

4   See Professor Wang Mingming's comments (Jiang, 2002).

5   For example South-Coast University made broad changes to its policy over 2004–2005.

6   The QAA requires: definitions of academic misconduct in respect of assessment, such as plagiarism, collusion, cheating, impersonation and the use of inadmissible material (including material downloaded from electronic sources such as the Internet); accepted and acceptable

forms of academic referencing and citation. Taken from the Precepts and Guidance, paragraph 3—Quality Assurance Agency (May 2000) Code of practice for the assurance of academic quality and standards in higher education, section 6; assessment of students. www.qaa.ac.uk. Accessed July 1, 2007.

7   See Ranald Macdonald and Jude Carroll's (2006) study for a detailed explanation of their examination of three institutions that have adopted holistic university-wide approaches to plagiarism.

8   For a detailed description of the ways in which scales of penalties are used by Academic Officers, in a similar system to Oxford Brookes University, see Chris Park's (2004) article on plagiarism management at Lancaster University, UK. Of particular interest are the tables on pp.296–297.

9   The St James Ethics Centre's report is provided by Longstaff, S., Ross, S. and Henderson, K. (2003) *Independent enquiry: Plagiarism policies procedures and management controls.* Available online at: www.Newcastle.edu.au/services/academic-integrity. Accessed September 17, 2007.

References

Angelil-Carter, Shelley. (2000). *Stolen Language? Plagiarism in writing*. London: Longman.

Ashworth, Peter, Bannister, Philip & Thorne, Pauline. (1997). Guilty in whose eyes? University students' perceptions of cheating and plagiarism in academic work and assessment. *Studies in Higher Education*, 22(2), 187–203.

Ashworth, Peter, Freewood, Madeleine & Macdonald, Ranald. (2003). The student lifeworld and the meanings of plagiarism. *Journal of Phenomenological Psychology*, 34(2), 257–278.

Atkins, Thomas & Nelson, Gene. (2001). Plagiarism and the Internet: Turning the tables. *English Journal*, 90(4), 101–104.

Attorney-General's Department. (1968). Copyright Act (1968) C'th. Canberra: AGPS.

Auer, Nicole & Krupar, Ellen. (2001). Mouse click plagiarism: The role of technology in plagiarism and the librarian's role in combating it. *Library Trends*, 49(3), 415–433.

Australian Concise Oxford Dictionary. (1997). 3rd edn. Sydney: Oxford University Press.

Bakhtin, Mikhail. (1986). *Speech genres and other late essays*. (V. W. McGee, trans.). Austin, TX: University of Texas Press.

Ballard, Brigid & Clanchy, John. (1988). *Studying in Australia*. Melbourne: Longman.

Barlow, John Perry. (1994). The economy of ideas: A framework for rethinking patents and copyrights in a digital age. *Wired*, 2, 126–129.

Barthes, Roland. (1977). *The death of the author*. Glasgow: Fontana Press.

Belcher, Diane. (1995). Writing critically across the curriculum. In D. Belcher & G. Braine (eds), *Academic writing in a second language: Essays on research and pedagogy* (pp. 135–154). Norwood, NJ: Ablex.

Bhatia, Vijay. (2001). Initiating into academic community. In D. Belcher & U. Connor (eds), *Reflections on multiliterate lives* (pp. 38–50). Clevedon: Multilingual Matters.

Bloch, Joel. (2001). Plagiarism and the ESL student: From printed to electronic texts. In D. Belcher & A. Hirvela (eds), *Linking literacies: Perspectives on L2 reading-writing connections* (pp.209–228). Ann Arbor, MI: University of Michigan Press.

Bloch, Joel & Chi, Lan. (1995). A comparison of the use of citations in Chinese and English academic discourse. In D. Belcher & G. Braine (eds), *Academic writing in a second language: Essays on research and pedagogy* (pp. 231–276). Norwood, NJ: Ablex Publishing.

Bolter, Jay. (1991). *Writing space: The computer, hypertext and the history of writing*. Mahwah, NJ: Erlbaum.

Bolter, Jay. (1998). Hypertext and the question of visual literacy. In R. Kieffer (ed.), *Handbook of literacy and technology: Transformations in a post-typographic world* (pp. 3–13). Mahwah, NJ: Erlbaum.

Briggs, Robert. (2003). Shameless! Reconceiving the problem of plagiarism. *Australian Universities Review*, 46(1), 19–23.

Brimble, Mark & Stevenson-Clarke, Peta. (2005). Perceptions of the prevalence and seriousness of academic dishonesty in Australian universities. *The Australian Educational Researcher*, 32(2), 19–44.

Brown, Penelope & Levinson, Stephen. (1988). *Politeness: Some universals in language usage.* Gateshead: Cambridge University Press.

Buranen, Lisa & Roy, Alice. (1999). *Perspectives on plagiarism and intellectual property in a postmodern world.* New York: State University of New York Press.

Burbules, Nicholas. (1997). Rhetorics of the Web: Hyperreading and critical literacy. In I. Snyder (ed.), *Page to screen: Taking literacy into the electronic era* (pp. 102–122). Sydney: Allen & Unwin.

Burbules, Nicholas. (2004). Rethinking the virtual. *E-Learning*, 1(2), 162–183.

Burbules, Nicholas & Bruce, Bertram. (1995). This is not a paper. *Educational Researcher*, 24(5), 12–18.

Cadman, Kate. (2005). Towards a "pedagogy of connection" in research education: A "REAL" story. *Journal of English for Academic Purposes*, 4, 353–367.

Cadman, Kate & Cargill, Margaret. (2004). Revisiting English language pedagogy for the global research education marketplace. Conference paper, International Association for the Study of Cooperation in Education conference, titled "Cooperation and Collaboration: Diversity of Practice, Cultural Contexts, and Creative Innovations" June 21–25, 2004, Singapore.

Campbell, Cherry. (1990). Writing with others' words. In B. Kroll (Ed.), *Second language writing: Research insights for the classroom* (pp. 211–230). Cambridge: Cambridge University Press.

Canagarajah, Suresh. (1993). Critical ethnography of a Sri Lankan classroom: Ambiguities in student opposition to reproduction through ESOL. *TESOL Quarterly*, 28(4), 601–626.

Canagarajah, Suresh. (1999). *Resisting linguistic imperialism in English teaching.* Oxford: Oxford University Press.

Canagarajah, Suresh. (2001). The fortunate traveller: Shuttling between communities and literacies by economy class. In D. Belcher & U. Connor (eds), *Reflections on multiliterate lives* (pp. 23–38). Clevedon: Multilingual Matters Ltd.

Carnie, Andrew. (2001). How to handle cyber-sloth in academe. *Chronicle of Higher Education*, January 5, 47(17), B14.

Carroll, Joyce. (1982). Plagiarism: The unfun game. *English Journal*, 71(5), 94–97.

Carroll, Jude (2002). *A handbook for deterring plagiarism in higher education.* Oxford: Oxford Centre for Staff and Learning Development.

Carroll, Jude & Ryan, Janette (2005). *Teaching international students: Improving learning for all.* London: Routledge.

Cavaleri, Nicola. (2006). *Preventing plagiarism.* Cambridge University LTS News Issue 7(12) 1–3. Retrieved September 26, 2007, from www.admin.cam.uk/offices/education/lts/news/lts/news/ltsn7.pdf.

Centre for Academic Integrity, Duke University. (2007). *The fundamental values of academic integrity.* Retrieved January 9, 2008, from www.academicintegrity.org/fundamental_values_project/index.ph.

Chanock, Kate. (2002). Problems and possibilities in evaluating one to one language and academic skills teaching. In P. McLean (ed.), *Academic skills advising* (pp. 22–35). Melbourne: VLLN.

Chanock, Kate. (2004). Before we hang that highwayman: The LAS advisors perspective on plagiarism. In H. Marsden, M. Hick & A. Bundy (eds) *Educational Integrity: Plagiarism and other perplexities* (pp.19–25). Proceedings of the Educational Integrity Conference, November 21–22, 2003, Adelaide.

Cher, Sylvia. (2007). *Local and international postgraduate students' perspective on the use of sources in academic writing.* Unpublished Masters of Education (TESOL International) thesis. Monash University, March 2007.

Clegg, Sue & Flint, Abbi. (2006). More heat than light: Plagiarism in its appearing. *British Journal of Sociology of Education*, 27(3), 373–387.

Coffin, Caroline. (2001). Theoretical approaches to written language: A TESOL perspective. In A. Burns & C. Coffin (eds), *Analysing English in a global context* (pp. 93–122). London: Routledge.

Collins Dictionary of the English Language. (1992). 2nd edn. London: Collins.

Colon, Aly. (2001). Avoid the pitfalls of plagiarism, *Writer,* 114(1), 8.

Concise Oxford Dictionary. (1999). (ed. Judy Pearsall). Oxford: OUP.

Counsell, Jan. (2004). Plagiarism and international students. In H. Marsden, M. Hick & A. Bundy (eds) *Educational Integrity: Plagiarism and other perplexities* (pp.97–104). Proceedings of the Educational Integrity Conference, November 21–22, 2003, Adelaide.

Crystal, David. (2001). The future of Englishes. In A. Burns & C. Coffin (eds), *Analysing English in a global context* (pp. 53–64). London: Routledge.

Cuban, Larry. (1993). *How teachers taught: Constancy and change in American classrooms, 1890–1990.* New York: Teachers College Press

Cuban, Larry. (2001). *Oversold and underused: Computers in the classroom.* Cambridge, MA: Harvard University Press.

Culwin, Fintan. (2006). An active introduction to academic misconduct and the measured demographics of misconduct. *Assessment & Evaluation in Higher Education,* 31(2), 167–182.

Dant, Doris. (1986). Plagiarism in high school: A survey. *English Journal,* 75(2), 81–84.

Davis, Graham. (2003a). Cash cow campuses [television broadcast]. *The Sunday Program.* Sydney: Channel 9.

Davis, Graham. (2003b). The plagiarism scandal [television broadcast]. *The Sunday Program.* Sydney: Channel 9.

de Certeau, Michel. (1984). *The practice of everyday life.* Berkeley, CA: University of California Press.

De Voss, Danielle & Rosati, Annette. (2002). "It wasn't me, was it?" Plagiarism and the web. *Computers and Composition,* 19(2), 191–203.

Deckert, Glenn. (1993a). Perspectives on plagiarism from ESL students in Hong Kong. *Journal of Second Language Writing,* 2(2), 131–148.

Deckert, Glenn. (1993b). A pedagogical responses to learned plagiarism among tertiary-level ESL students. *Guidelines,* 14(1), 94–104.

Drum, Alice. (1986). Responding to plagiarism. *College Composition and Communication,* 31(2), 241–243.

Eagleton, Terry. (1983). *Literary theory: An introduction.* Oxford: Basil Blackwell.

Eisenstein, Elizabeth. (1983). *The printing revolution in early modern Europe.* Cambridge: Cambridge University Press.

Evans, Robert. (2006). Evaluating an electronic plagiarism detection service. *Active Learning in Higher Education,* 7(10), 87–99.

Fang, Xu & Warschauer, Mark. (2004). Technology and curricular reform in China: A case study. *TESOL Quarterly,* 38(2), 301–318.

Feather, John. (1994). *From rights in copies to copyright: The recognition of authors' rights in English law and practice in the sixteenth and seventeenth centuries.* Durham, NC: Duke University Press.

Fitzgerald, Brian. (2000). Conceptualising the digital environment. In A. Fitzgerald, B. Fitzgerald, C. Cifuentes & P. Cook (eds), *Going digital 2000: Legal issues for e-commerce, software and the Internet* (pp. 1–17). St Leonards: Prospect Media.

Flowerdew, John. (2000). Discourse community: Legitimate peripheral participation and the non-native English speaking scholar. *TESOL Quarterly,* 34(1), 127–150.

Foucault, Michel. (1972). The discourse on language. In M. Foucault (ed.), *Archaeology of knowledge* (pp. 215–236). New York: Pantheon Books.

Foucault, Michel. (1979). *Discipline and punish: The birth of the prison.* (Trans. Alan Sheridan). Harmondsworth: Penguin.

Fowler, Alaistair. (1976). *Writing in the modern world.* London: John Benjamin.

Françon, André. (1999). Protection of artists' moral rights on the Internet. In F. Pollaud-Dulian (ed.), *Perspectives on intellectual property: The Internet and authors' rights* (pp. 73–86). London: University of London.

Frow, John. (2000). Public domain and the new world order in knowledge. *Social Semiotics,* 10(2), 173–185.

Galloway, Ishbel & Sevier, Marti. (2003). *Plagiarism and advanced L2 writing.* Paper presented at the TESOL 2003: Hearing every voice conference (March 23–27), Baltimore, MD, USA.

Gardiner, Steve. (2001). Cybercheating: A new twist on an old problem. *Phi Delta Kappan,* 83(2), 172–176.

Garnaut, Ross. (2003). Cash-cow campuses [television broadcast, August 3]. *Sunday Report:* Australian Broadcasting Commission.

Gee, James. (1990). *Social linguistics and literacies: Ideology in discourses.* New York: Falmer Press.

Gendreau, Ysolde. (1999). Intention and copyright law. In F. Pollaud-Dulian (ed.), *Perspectives on intellectual property: The Internet and authors' rights* (pp. 1–24). London: University of London.

Gergen, Kenneth. (1991). *The saturated self: Dilemmas of identity in contemporary life.* New York: Basic Books.

Giroux, Henry. (1988). *Teachers as intellectuals: Towards a critical pedagogy of learning.* Critical Studies in Education Series. Westport, CT: Bergin & Garvey.

Giroux, Henry. (1993). Teaching and the role of the transformative intellectual. In S. Aronowitz & H. Giroux (eds), *Education Still Under Siege* (pp. 33–54). Westport, CT: Bergin and Garvey.

Giroux, Henry. (1996). *Counternarratives: Cultural studies and critical pedagogies in postmodern spaces.* New York: Routledge.

Godfrey, John & Waugh, Russell. (2002). Students' perceptions of cheating in Australian independent schools. *Education Australia Online,* 1–3.

Graddol, David. (2001). English in the future. In A. Burns & C. Coffin (eds), *Analysing English in a global context* (pp. 26–37). London: Routledge.

Gray, Paul. (2002). Other people's words. *Smithsonian,* 32(12), 102–104.

Gurak, Laura. (2001). *Cyberliteracy: Navigating the Internet with awareness.* New Haven, CT: Yale University Press.

Hafernik, Johnnie, Messerschmitt, Dorothy & Vandrick, Stephanie. (2003). *Ethical issues for ESL faculty: Social justice in practice.* Mahwah, NJ: Lawrence Erlbaum.

Handa, Neera & Power, Clare. (2004). *Bridging the gap: Lack of integrity or lack of skills?* In H. Marsden, M. Hick & A. Bundy (eds) *Educational Integrity: Plagiarism and other perplexities* (pp. 154–164). Proceedings of the Educational Integrity Conference, November 21–22, 2003, Adelaide.

Harris, Robert. (2001). The plagiarism handbook: Strategies for preventing, detecting, and dealing with plagiarism. Los Angeles, CA: Pyrczak Publishing.

Hawley, Christopher. (1984). The thieves of academe: Plagiarism in the university system. *Improving College University Teaching,* 32, 35–39.

Haywood, Trevor. (1995). *Info-Rich info-poor: Access and exchange in the global information society.* East Grinstead, UK: Reed Elsevier.

Hirsch, Edward. (1976). Objective interpretation. In D. Newton-de Molina (ed.) *On literary intention* (pp. 26–54). Edinburgh: University of Edinburgh Press.

Howard, Rebecca Moore. (1995). Plagiarisms, authorships and the academic death penalty. *College English,* 57(7), 788–806.

Howard, Rebecca Moore. (1999). *Standing in the shadow of giants: Plagiarists, authors, collaborators.* Stamford, CT: Ablex.

Howard, Rebecca Moore. (2000). Sexuality, textuality: The cultural work of plagiarism. *College English,* 62(4), 473–491.

Howard, Rebecca Moore. (2002). Don't police plagiarism: Just teach! *The Education Digest,* 67(5), 46–49.

Howard, Rebecca Moore. (2004). *Culture and academic discourse: Cultivating authority in language and text.* Retrieved June 25, 2004, from http://wrt-howard.syr.edu/Papers?TexamA&M.

Howard, Rebecca Moore. (2007). Understanding "Internet plagiarism." *Computers and Composition,* 24, 3–15.

Hunt, Elissa. (2003). Uni cheat gets off. *Herald Sun,* Wednesday, August 4, pp. 1–2.

Hunt, Russell. (2002). *Four reasons to be happy about Internet plagiarism.* Retrieved August 22, 2007 from www.stu.ca/~hunt/plagiary.htm.

Hunt, Russell. (2004). *Whose silverware is this? Promoting plagiarism through pedagogy.* JISC Plagiarism Advisory Service Conference (June 24–28), Newcastle-upon-Tyne, UK.

Hutcheon, Linda. (1986). Literary borrowing . . . and stealing: Plagiarism, sources, influences and intertexts. *English Studies in Canada,* 12, 229–239.

iParadigms. (2007). *iParadigms: Digital solutions for a new era in information.* Retrieved September 29, 2007, from www.iparadigms.com.

Ivanič, Roz. (1998). *Writing and identity: The discoursal construction of identity in academic writing.* Amsterdam: John Benjamins.

James, Richard & McInnes, Craig. (2001). Standards oil tertiary debate. *The Australian*, Wednesday, August 15, p. 28.

Jaszi, Peter. (1994). On the author effect: Contemporary copyright and collective creativity. In M. Woodmansee & P. Jaszi (eds), *The construction of authorship: Textual appropriation in law and literature* (pp. 29–56). Durham, NC: Duke University Press.

Jiang, Xueqin. (2002). Chinese academics consider a "culture of copying." *Chronicle of Higher Education*, 48(36), 45–49.

Johnston, Kay. (1991). Plagiarism in the classroom: Every teacher's nightmare. *Chronicle of Higher Education*, 44(12), 23–26.

Jones, Phillip. (2000). Globalisation and internationalism: Democratic prospects for world education. In N. Stromquist & K. Monkman (eds), *Globalisation and education: Integration and contestation across cultures* (pp. 27–42). Oxford: Rowman and Littlefield.

Kachru, Braj & Nelson, Chris. (2001). World Englishes. In A. Burns & C. Coffin (eds), *Analysing English in a global context* (pp. 9–25). London: Routledge.

Kantz, Margaret. (1990). Helping students use textual sources persuasively. *College English*, 52(1), 74–91.

Kerkvliet, Joe and Sigmund, Charles. (1999). Can we control cheating in the classroom? *Journal of Economic Education*, 30(4), 331–343.

Kitalong, Karla. (1998). A web of symbolic violence. *Computers and Composition*, 15, 253–263.

Knight, Peter. (2001). *A briefing on key concepts: Formative and summative, criterion and norm-referenced assessment*. LTSN Generic Centre Assessment Series No. 7. London: Learning Teaching Support Network Generic Centre.

Kolich, Augustus. (1983). Plagiarism: The worm of reason. *College English*, 45(2), 141–148.

Kress, Gunther. (1997). Visual and verbal modes of representation in electronically mediated communication: The potentials of new forms of text. In I. Snyder (ed.), *Page to Screen: Taking literacy into the electronic era* (pp. 53–79). St Leonards, NSW: Allen & Unwin.

Kress, Gunther. (2003). *Literacy in the new media age*. London: Routledge.

Kroll, Barry. (1988). How college freshman view plagiarism. *Written Communication*, 5(2), 203–221.

Kubota, Ryoko. (2001). My experience of learning to read and write in Japanese as L1 and English as L2. In D. Belcher & U. Connor (eds), *Reflections on multiliterate lives* (pp. 96–109). Clevedon: Multilingual Matters.

Kutieleh, Salah & Egege, Sandra. (2004). *Critical thinking and international students: A marriage of necessity.* Paper presented at the 8th Pacific Rim conference: Dealing with diversity (July 14–16), Melbourne, Australia.

Laird, Ellen. (2001). We all pay for Internet plagiarism. *The Education Digest*, 67(3), 56–59.

Landow, George. (1993). *The Digital Word: Text-based computing in the humanities*. Cambridge, MA: MIT Press.

Lanham, Richard. (1994). *The electronic word: Democracy, technology and the arts*. Chicago, IL: University of Chicago Press.

Lankshear, Colin & Snyder, Ilana. (2000). *Teachers and techno-literacy: Managing literacy, technology and learning in schools*. St Leonards, NSW: Allen & Unwin.

Larkham, Peter & Manns, Susan. (2002). Plagiarism and its treatment in higher education. *Journal of Further and Higher Education*, 26(4), 339–349.

Larson, Joanne. (ed.). (2001). *Literacy as snake oil: Beyond the quick fix*. New York: Peter Lang.

Le Heron, Judy. (2001). Plagiarism, learning dishonesty or just plain cheating: The context and countermeasures in information systems teaching. *Australian Journal of Educational Technology*, 17(3), 244–264.

Leask, Betty. (2006). Plagiarism, cultural diversity and metaphor—implications for academic staff development. *Assessment & Evaluation in Higher Education*, 31(2), 183–199.

Leatherman, Courtney. (1999). At Texas A&M, conflicting chares of misconduct tear a program apart. *Chronicle of Higher Education*, November 5, 46(1), A18–21.

Leverenz, Carrie. (1998). Citing cybersources: A challenge to disciplinary values. *Computers and Composition*, 15, 185–200.

Levin, Peter. (2006). *Why the writing is on the wall for the plagiarism police*. Retrieved August 18, 2007, from www.student-friendly-guide.coml.

Lincoln, Margaret. (2002). Internet plagiarism. *Multimedia Schools*, 9(1), 46–49.

Lincoln, Yvonna & Denzin, Norman. (2003). *Turning points in qualitative research: Tying knots in a handkerchief.* Walnut Creek, CA: Rowman & Littlefield.

Litman, Jessica. (2001). *Digital Copyright.* New York: Prometheus Books.

Logie, John. (1998). Champing at the bits: Computers, copyright and the composition classroom. *Computers and Composition,* 15(1), 201–214.

Love, Harold. (2002). *Attributing authorship: An introduction.* Cambridge, UK: Cambridge University Press.

Loveless, Edna. (1994). A pedagogy to address plagiarism. *College Composition and Computers,* 44(4), 509–514.

Lunsford, Andrea & Ede, Lisa. (1990). *Singular texts/plural authors: Perspective on collaborative writing.* Carbondale, IL: Southern Illinois University Press.

Lunsford, Andrea & Ede, Lisa. (1994). Collaborative authorship and the teaching of writing. In M. Woodmansee & P. Jaszi (eds), *The construction of authorship: Textual appropriation in law and literature* (pp. 417–436). Durham, NC: Duke University Press.

Lunsford, Andrea & West, Susan. (1996). Intellectual property and composition studies. *CCC,* 47(3), 383–411.

McCabe, Don. (2004). *Promoting academic integrity—A US/Canadian perspective.* Paper presented at the Educational integrity: Plagiarism and other perplexities conference (November 21–22, 2003), Adelaide, Australia. In conference proceedings (pp. 3–12) H. Marsden, M. Hicks and A. Bundy (eds), *Educational integrity: Plagiarism and other perplexities.*

McCabe, Don & Bowers, William. (1994). Academic dishonesty among males in college: A thirty year perspective. *Journal of College Student Development,* 35, 5–10.

McCabe, Don & Trevino, Linda. (1996). What we know about cheating in college. *Change,* 28(1), 28–33.

McCabe, Don & Drinin, Patrick. (1999). Toward a culture of academic integrity. *Chronicle of Higher Education,* 46(8), 28+.

McCracken, Ellen. (1991). Metaplagiarism and the critic's role as detective: Ricardo Piglia's reinvention of Roberto Arlt. *PMLA,* 106(5), 1071–1082.

Macdonald, Ranald & Carroll, Jude. (2006). Plagiarism—a complex issue requiring a holistic institutional approach. *Assessment & Evaluation in Higher Education,* 31(3), 233–245.

McLafferty, Charles & Foust, Karen. (2004). Electronic plagiarism as a college instructor's nightmare—prevention and detection. *Journal of Education for Business,* 79(3), 186–189.

McLuhan, Marshall. (1969). *The medium is the message.* Harmondsworth: Penguin.

Madden, James. (2002a). Academic thievery won't wash. *The Australian,* Wednesday, July 10, pp. 6–7.

Madden, James. (2002b). Plagiarism returns to haunt Vice-Chancellor. *The Australian,* Thursday, June 26, p. 4.

Malatesta, Grace. (2001). Cheat case not put to rest. *The Australian,* Wednesday, May 23, p. 44.

Mallon, Thomas. (1989). *Stolen words.* San Diego, CA: Harcourt.

Marginson, Simon. (2003). *Markets on higher education: The next generation.* Paper presented at the educational research: Risks and dilemmas (November 29 to December 3), Auckland, New Zealand.

Marsden, Helen. (2001). Who cheats at university? Unpublished Honors paper in Applied Psychology, University of Canberra, Canberra.

Marsden, Helen, Carroll, Marie & Neill, James T. (2005). Who cheats at university? A self-report study of dishonest academic behaviours in a sample of Australian university students. *Australian Journal of Psychology,* 57(1), 1–10.

Marshall, Stephen & Garry, Maryanne. (2006). NESB and ESB students' attitudes and perceptions of plagiarism. *International Journal of Educational Integrity,* 2(1), 26–37.

Martin, Brian. (1992). *Plagiarism by university students: The problem and some proposals.* Wollongong: University of Wollongong.

Martin, Brian. (1994). Plagiarism: A misplaced emphasis. *Journal of Information Ethics,* 3(2), 36–47.

Maslen, Geoff. (2003). Dirty marks. *The Bulletin,* Tuesday, June 10, pp. 18–22.

Matalene, Carolyn. (1985). Contrastive rhetoric: An American writing teacher in China. *College English,* 47(8), 789–808.

Matsuda, Paul. (2003). Second language writing in the twentieth century: A situated historical perspective. In B. Kroll (ed.), *Exploring the dynamics of second language writing* (pp. 15–34). Cambridge: Cambridge University Press.

Mirsky, Steve. (2002). Technology is making it harder for word thieves to earn outrageous fortunes. *Scientific American*, 286(4), 98–99.

Modiano, Marko. (2001). Linguistic imperialism, cultural integrity, and EIL. *ELT Journal*, 55(4), 339–346.

Monash University. (2007). *Discipline statute 4.1—plagiarism.* Retrieved February 22, 2007 from www.adm.monash.edu.au/unisec/academicpolicies/policy/plagiarism.html.

Moore, Tim. (2004). The critical thinking debate: How general are general thinking skills? *HERD*, 23, 3–18.

Murray, Denise. (2001). New technology: New language at work? In A. Burns & C. Coffin (eds), *Analysing English in a global context* (pp. 38–52). London: Routledge.

Myers, Sharon. (1998). Questioning author(ity): ESL/EFL science and teaching about plagiarism. *TESL-EJ*, 3(2), 1–21.

Navarazov, Alexi. (1993). Cheating: Alive and flourishing. *Chronicle of Higher Education*, 43(8), 37–42.

Noi-Smith, Swee. (2001). Approaches to study of three Chinese national groups. *British Journal of Educational Psychology*, 71, 429–441.

Nonis, Sarah & Swift, Cathy. (2001). An examination of the relationship between academic dishonesty and workplace dishonesty: A multi-campus investigation. *Journal of Education for Business* (November/December), 60–77.

Nunan, David. (2003). The impact of English as a global language on educational policies and practices in the Asia-Pacific region. *TESOL Quarterly*, 37(4), 589–613.

O'Connor, Steve. (2002). *Electronic plagiarism and its impact on educational quality.* Paper presented at the CAVAL electronic plagiarism conference (October 6), Melbourne, Australia.

Page, James. (2004). Cyber-pseudepigraphy: A new challenge for higher education policy and management. *Journal of Higher Education Policy and Management*, 26(3), 429–433.

Park, Chris. (2003). In other (people's) words: Plagiarism by university students—literature and lessons. *Assessment & Evaluation in Higher Education*, 28(5), 471–488.

Park, Chris. (2004). Rebels without a clause: Towards an institutional framework for dealing with plagiarism by students. *Journal of Further and Higher Education*, 28(3), 291–306.

Passa, Jérôme. (1999). The protection of copyright on the Internet under French law. In F. Pollaud-Dulian (ed.), *Perspectives on intellectual property: The Internet and authors' rights* (pp. 23–72). London: Sweet and Maxwell.

Patterson, Annette. (1995). Intention. In T. McLaughlin (ed.), *Critical terms for literary study* (pp. 135–146). Chicago, IL: Chicago University Press.

Patterson, Neil. (2000). Hypertext and the changing roles of readers. *English Journal*, 90(2), 74–80.

Pecorari, Diane. (2001). Plagiarism and international students: How the English-speaking university responds. In D. Belcher & A. Hirvela (eds), *The reading/writing connection: Perspectives on second language literacies.* Ann Arbor, MI: University of Michigan Press.

Pecorari, Diane. (2002). Original reproductions: An investigation of the source use of postgraduate second language writers. Unpublished PhD thesis, University of Birmingham.

Pennycook, Alastair. (1994). *The cultural politics of English as an international language.* London: Longman.

Pennycook, Alastair. (1996). Borrowing others' words: Text, ownership, memory and plagiarism. *TESOL Quarterly*, 30(2), 201–230.

Pennycook, Alastair. (2001). English in the world, the world in English. In C. Coffin (ed.), *Analysing English in a global context* (pp. 78–92). London: Routledge.

Phan Le Ha. (2006). Plagiarism and overseas students: Stereotypes again? *ELT*, 60, 76–78.

Phillipson, Robert. (1992). *Linguistic imperialism.* Oxford: Oxford University Press.

Phillipson, Robert. (2003). *English for or against European diversity?* Paper presented at the Language, education and diversity conference (November 24–29), University of Waikato, Hamilton, New Zealand.

Phillipson, Robert & Skutnabb-Kangas, Tove. (1996). English only worldwide or language ecology? *TESOL Quarterly*, 30(3), 429–452.

Price, Margaret. (2002). Beyond "gotcha!": Situating plagiarism in policy and pedagogy. *College Composition and Communication*, 54(1), 88–101.

Pyvis, David. (2002). Plagiarism and managerialism. *Australian Universities Review*, 45(2), 31–36.

Ramanthan, Vai and Atkinson, Dwight. (1999). Individualism, academic writing and ESL writers. *Journal of Second Language Writing*, 8(1), 45–75.

Richardson, Paul. (2001). *Reading and writing from textbooks in higher education: The danger of other people's words.* Paper presented at the Australian Association for Research Education (AARE) conference (November 23–29), Fremantle, Western Australia.

Ricketson, Sam & Creswell, Megan. (2001). *Intellectual property: Cases, materials and commentary* (2nd edn). Sydney: Butterworths.

Rose, Mark. (1993). *Authors and owners: The invention of copyright.* Cambridge, MA: Harvard University Press.

Ross, Marlon. (1994). *Authority and authenticity: Scribbling authors and the genius of print in eighteenth-century England.* Durham, NC: Duke University Press.

Ryan, Jane. (1998). Tools to catch cybercheats. Retrieved August 28, 2001, from www.asee.org/prism/december/html/student_plagiarism_in_an_onlin.html.

Ryan, Janette. (2000). *A guide to teaching international students.* Oxford: Oxford Centre for Staff Development and Learning, Oxford Brookes University.

Said, Edward. (1978). *Orientalism.* London: Penguin.

Saltmarsh, Sue. (2004). Graduating tactics: Theorizing plagiarism as consumptive practice. *Journal of Further and Higher Education,* 28(4), 445–454.

Saunders, Edward. (1993). Confronting academic dishonesty. *Journal of Social Work Education,* 29(2), 224–232.

Scanlon, Patrick & Neumann, David. (2002). Internet plagiarism among college students. *Journal of College Student Development,* 43(3), 374–382.

Scollon, Ron. (1995). Plagiarism and ideology: Identity in intercultural discourse. *Language in Society,* 24(1), 1–28.

Scollon, Suzie. (1999). Not to waste words or students: Confucian and Socratic discourse in the tertiary classroom. In E. Hinkel (ed.), *Culture in second language teaching and learning* (pp. 13–28). Cambridge, MA: Cambridge University Press.

Scollon, Suzie & Scollon, Ron. (1991). Topic confusion in English-Asian discourse. *World Englishes,* 10(2), pp. 113–125.

Selden, Raman, Widdowson, Peter & Brooker, Peter. (1997). *A reader's guide to contemporary literary theory.* London: Prentice Hall.

Selfe, Cynthia & Hilligoss, Susan. (1994). *Literacy and computers: The complications of teaching and learning with technology.* New York: Modern Languages Association of America.

Shaw, Peter. (1982). Plagiary. *The American Scholar,* 51(summer), 325–337.

Sherman, Jane. (1992). Your own thoughts in your own words. *ELT Journal,* 46(3), 190–198.

Simon Fraser University. (2002). Teaching policies: Misconduct. Retrieved July 24, 2002, from www.sfu.ca/policies/teaching/110–02.htm.

Skutnabb-Kangas, Tove. (2003). *Language death.* Paper presented at the Language, Education and Diversity conference, University of Waikato (November 23–29), Hamilton, New Zealand.

Snyder, Ilana. (1996). *Hypertext: The electronic labyrinth.* Carlton South: Melbourne University Press.

Snyder, Ilana. (1997). Beyond the hype: Reassessing hypertext. In I. Snyder (ed.), *Page to screen: Taking literacy into the electronic era.* St Leonards, NSW: Allen & Unwin.

Sterling, Steven. (2001). *Sustainable education: Re-visioning learning and change.* Totnes: Green Books for the Schumacher Society.

Stoney, Susan & McMahon, Mark. (2004). Bulletproof assessment, war stories and tactics: Avoiding cybercheating. Paper presented at the ASCILITE International conference, University of Western Australia (December 3–9), Australia.

Straw, Deborah. (2002). The plagiarism of Generation "Why not?". *Community College Week,* July 8, 14(24), 4–6.

Stromquist, Nelly & Monkman, Karen. (2000). Defining globalization and assessing its implications on knowledge and education. In N. Stromquist & K. Monkman (eds), *Globalisation and education: Integration and contestation across culture* (pp. 3–26). Oxford: Rowman and Littlefield.

Sullivan, Patricia & Porter, James. (1997). *Opening spaces: Writing technologies and critical research practices.* Greenwich, CT: Ablex.

Sutherland-Smith, Wendy. (2002). Weaving the literacy web: Changes in reading from page to screen. *The Reading Teacher,* 55(7), 662–677.

Sutherland-Smith, Wendy. (2003). Hiding in the shadows: The risks and dilemmas of plagiarism in student academic writing. Australian Association of Research in Education international conference, *Educational research: The risks and dilemmas* (November 26–December 3, 2003), Auckland, New Zealand.

Sutherland-Smith, Wendy. (2005a). Pandora's box: Academic perceptions of student plagiarism in writing. *Journal of English for Academic Purposes,* 4(1), 83–95.

Sutherland-Smith, Wendy. (2005b). The tangled web: Internet plagiarism and international students' academic writing. *Journal of Asian Pacific Communication,* 15(1), 15–29.

Szabo, Attila & Underwood, Jean. (2004). Cybercheats. *Active learning in higher education.* 5(2), 180–199.

Thumboo, Edwin. (2003). Closed and open attitudes to globalised English: Notes on issues. *World Englishes* 22(3), 233–243.

Turnitin. (2004). *Turnitin anti-plagiarism software.* Retrieved December 31, 2004, from www.turnitin.com.

University of Auckland. (2002). *Academic misconduct—plagiarism.* Retrieved November 13, 2003, from www.auckland.ac.nz.

Vojak, Colleen. (2006). What market culture teaches students about ethical behavior. *Ethics and Education,* 1(2), 177–195.

Walsh, Sharon. (2002). SUNY-Albany classicist loses chairmanship after being accused of plagiarism. *The Chronicle of Higher Education,* 48(26), 26–28.

Warschauer, Mark. (2000). Does the Internet bring freedom? *Information, technology, education and society.* 1(2), 93–200. Retrieved June 9, 2004, from www.gse.uci.edu/markw/freedom. html.

Warschauer, Mark. (2004). Technology and Writing. In C. Davison & J. Cummins (eds), *Handbook, of English language teaching.* Dordrecht, Netherlands: Kluwer. Retrieved December 13, 2004, from www.gse.uci.edu/markw/technology.pdf.

Waters, Malcolm. (2001). *Globalisation* (2nd edn). London: Routledge.

Watkins, David & Biggs, John. (2001). The paradox of the Chinese learner and beyond. In J. Biggs (ed.), *Teaching the Chinese learner: Psychological and pedagogical perspectives* (pp. 3–26). Hong Kong: University of Hong Kong.

Webster's Online Dictionary. (2004). Retrieved November 6, 2004, from www.merriam-webster. com.

Wertsch, James. (1991). *Voices of the mind: A sociocultural approach to mediated action.* Cambridge MA: Harvard University Press.

Whiteman, Sherri & Gordon, Jay. (2001). The price of an A: An educator's responsibility to academic honesty. *English Journal,* 91(2), 25–30.

Widdowson, Henry. (1994). The ownership of English. *TESOL Quarterly,* 28(2), 377–389.

WIPO. (2002). *Berne convention treatises and the TRIPS agreement.* Retrieved May 27, 2003, from www.wipo.int/docs/treatises/TRIPS.

Woodmansee, Martha. (1994). *On the author effect: Recovering collectivity.* In M. Woodmansee & P. Jaszi (eds), *The construction of authorship: Textual appropriation in law and literature* (pp. 19–37). Durham, NC: Duke University Press.

Woodmansee, Martha & Jaszi, Peter. (1995). The law of texts: Copyright in the academy. *College English,* 57(7), 769–787.

Yaman, Ebru. (2003). No "dumbing down" under Labor plan. *The Australian.* Tuesday, July 16, p. 30.

Yen, Alfred. (1994). The interdisciplinary future of copyright theory. In M. Woodmansee & P. Jaszi (eds), *The construction of authorship: Textual appropriation in law and literature* (pp. 159–173). Durham, NC: Duke University Press.

Zamel, Vivian. (1997). Toward a model of transculturation. *TESOL Quarterly,* 31(2), 341–352.

Zobel, Justin & Hamilton, Margaret. (2002). Managing student plagiarism in large academic departments. *Australian Universities Review,* 45(2), 23–30.

Index